Moral Education

Character, Community, and Ideals

Moral Education

Character, Community, and Ideals

Betty A. Sichel

Temple University Press
Philadelphia

Temple University Press, Philadelphia 19122
Copyright © 1988 by Temple University. All rights reserved
Published 1988
Printed in the United States of America

Library of Congress Cataloging-in-Publication Data

Sichel, Betty A.
  Moral education.

  Bibliography: p.
  Includes index.
  1. Moral education. 2. Character. 3. Moral
education—United States. I. Title.
LC268.S467 1988   370.11'4   87-10009
ISBN 0-87722-508-7

The paper used in this publication meets the minimum
requirements of American National Standard for Information
Sciences—Permanence of Paper for Printed Library Materials,
ANSI Z39.48-1984

To Gilbert Sichel and Patricia Brown

Acknowledgments

From the beginning to the end, numerous scholars, computer specialists, librarians, school teachers, friends, and colleagues have been of great help not only in the generous support of my research and writing, but equally by providing personal encouragement. My formative scholarly and intellectual development is greatly due to Louise Antz under whom I completed my doctoral dissertation on a Whiteheadean ethical theory and its implications for education.

I am thankful to Abraham Edel for his confidence in the development of my moral education theory. His contribution through insightful conversation and correspondence has been of immense value. His critical reading of the entire manuscript and his suggestions and questions have significantly added to the book's growth.

I owe a debt of special gratitude to my teacher and friend, Patricia Brown, one of the two people this book is dedicated to. Her enthusiasm, support, scholarly insight, and discussions helped to unravel many wide ranging philosophical issues.

Without the help of technical and editorial experts, completion of this book would have been impossible. I thank the librarians of Long Island University, C. W. Post

Campus Library, especially Marilyn Rosenthal, for their assistance in my research. The personnel of the Computer Center of the University deserve many thanks. In particular, without the computer expertise and patience of Ruth Sullivan, my manuscript would not have seen the light of day.

I thank Jane Cullen of Temple University Press for her belief in this book when it was still in its early stages. Throughout the many trials of writing this book, she provided encouragement and wise suggestions. I also owe a debt to Doris Braendel, Ed Cone, and the Temple University Staff for the careful refining and editing of the manuscript.

Finally, I thank my husband, Gilbert Sichel, the other person this book is dedicated to, for his patience, support, and enthusiastic belief in this book.

Contents

Moral Education

Character, Community, and Ideals

1

Introduction: A Race Between Education and Catastrophe

To describe morality as a race between education and catastrophe seems captious and pessimistic. Instead of having a negative cast, this phrase recognizes that human morality and moral education are fragile enterprises. Human beings struggle to remain moral, but often against their better judgment and firmly held beliefs fall prey to uncontrollable internal forces and unexpected external conditions. Adults strive to transmit moral ideals to the younger generation in the hope their children will lead good, right, and just lives and have moral visions that other generations only dimly perceived. This moral race is not a competition between individuals to see which select few will reach some moral height and who will succumb to darker forces. The metaphor "race" connotes an unarticulated acknowledgment that morality and civilized life remain frail endeavors that can unexpectedly disintegrate.

The race between education and catastrophe during a time of radically changing morality is often an implicit theme in literature.[1] Set in an age when many did not recognize the dimensions of the race, Henry James's *The Europeans* depicts this race and thus this novel is an appropriate beginning for this theory of moral education. Through the prism of a narrative, James highlights Tönnies's notion of a radical transformation of life from the *gemeinschaft* of the intimate agrarian community to the *gesellschaft* of contractualism and individualism. James first looks back to a traditional foundation for moral education, to the extended family, communal values, and moral unity.[2] In *The Europeans,* the moral education of Charlotte, Gertrude, and Clifford Wentworth and their cousin Lizzie Acton is assured by an idyllic family and community life and the religious ministerings of the Reverend Mr. Brand.[3] What could have been more appropriate in this *gemeinschaft* than for Gertrude to marry her cousin Felix even though he was an artist and dilettante,[4] Clifford to marry his cousin Lizzie, and Charlotte to marry Brand. With such marriages, all the best elements of the extended, righteous family were maintained without any taint of outsiders and their negative values.

The Europeans is not a quaint, naïve picture of an idyllic *gemeinschaft.* James realizes that the communal life and unified values of the *gemeinschaft* were being eroded and replaced by a *gesellschaft,* a society of solitary individuals with personally chosen, pluralistic values, and relationships dependent on contractual agreements.[5] The opening sentence of *The Europeans* casts a shadow over the entire novel and over the idyllic life of the Wentworth family. The description "A narrow grave-yard in the heart of a bustling indifferent city" also tells us something of the moral life of urbanized American society. Instead of living in a small, friendly community in which all inhabitants are extended family members and where the surroundings themselves seem to care about the welfare of each human being, the city is an indifferent place, where people are known only by their specific roles, where no one owes personal allegiance to the anonymous masses, and where care and sympathy are rare commodities. The bustling, indifferent city is the graveyard of the *gemeinschaft.*[6]

Instead of merely depicting a negative view of the past and present, James implicitly understands that the best ideas and practices of past and present must be refashioned for future morality and moral education.[7] Similar to the transformation James's novels foreshadowed, present changes in all areas of society and culture presage a new philosophy of moral education that must remember the salient features of older theories. Rather than looking at this restructuring through suspicious and pessimistic glasses, a new theory of moral education can open the way to more humanistic, sensitive, and rational moral alternatives.

In the moral race between education and catastrophe, bystanders do not automatically assume education will be the winner. A much more pessimistic feeling is now pervasive. During recent years there has been considerable apprehension about the quality of moral education that children receive and about morality in all segments of society. From all directions, voices have arisen to blame different groups or conditions for the lack of adequate moral education. Teachers complain about children's negative values and antisocial behavior, students' disrespect for fellow students and adults, and pupils' lack of warmth, responsibility, and moral commitment. Instead of looking at broader cultural and social conditions, educators fault the child-rearing techniques and the moral education imparted by parents. Children do not receive an adequate foundation of acceptable social behavior and a basis for more mature moral life.

Parents, on the other hand, claim schools mistakenly foster subjective moral relativism[8] and are unsympathetic to cherished communal morality. Parents are critical of schools for not providing adequate moral training for students. The term "training" is appropriate here since parents often desire that the school instill specific moral content and inculcate social rules. Some scholars acknowledge the plight of these parents and argue that child-rearing and moral education are no longer solely the responsibility of the family. The family, according to these thinkers, is no longer an effective institution and cannot even serve its original, primary purposes.[9] At the same time that parents have become powerless and feel frustrated, other agencies and influences have preempted parental roles. Social scientists point to the influence of television and criticize the materialism, rampant individualism, and competitiveness of so many people in every segment of society. In such a climate of privativism and materialistic values, social scientists question whether schools or parents can transmit rational moral standards and present radically transformed forms of morality and moral education than exist in the larger society.

Instead of being seen through a darkly shaded prism that reveals only negative conditions, meager possibilities, and a dismal future,[10] the present moral period, morality, and moral education can be interpreted in a rather different manner. We are living through a rapidly changing period, a time of transition when traditional and conservative values and moral standards are questioned and new standards, new ways of living, and new forms of moral education are still being generated. Far-reaching technological and scientific discoveries have simultaneously created numerous, unexpected moral problems that require new solutions and revitalized forms of moral education.

Extensive writings continually tell us about the radical transformation of all segments of social and intellectual life. The widespread craving for greater justice and increased rights has added to an already crowded moral domain, spawning new and different moral conflicts and increasing pressure on those proposing moral education theories. The blurring and changing of boundaries between certain traditionally separate domains create confusion about what situations should be included within the moral or what aspects of education are moral education. Where is the boundary between the public and the private,[11] between the social and the moral, between the individual and the community, between communities and society, between the affective and the cognitive? For example, the wandering border between the public and the private domains has created unique problems for moral education. What happens when large numbers of people who governed their moral lives with a morality suitable for the private domain enter the public domain? Have computer data banks destroyed the private domain or does new technology merely require a new conceptualization of the private domain vis-à-vis the public domain? Should the school transmit different moral consciousness for each domain or are the same moral standards equally valid for each domain?

Some might wonder whether schools can change the moral order and usher in a new morality for both private and public life. These concerns are not new stories. We read these messages during every historical period. Can we understand the present scientific and social transformation in terms of earlier changes? While this present period may be compared with earlier ages, it also contains the seeds of a radical departure from earlier transformations.

Many now argue that traditional forms of moral education and the inculcation of morality are outmoded and unacceptable.[12] Yet the older generation worries whether members of the younger generation will become fully moral adults who fulfill their community's social and political obligations. The present concern with morality and moral education is not unusual. During times of extreme cultural, scientific, social, and political change, there is uncertainty about morality and a loss of confidence in customary aims and methods of moral education.[13] History is replete with instances of adult consternation about youth's morality and fear about whether education or catastrophe will win the race. For example, many issues of Plato's dialogues were motivated by the radical transformation of his society and culture. These dialogues question which moral standards and education are justifiable for the youth of Athenian society. At the beginning of one dialogue, the aristocrat Meno abruptly asks Socrates, "Is virtue something that can be taught? Or does it come by practice? Or is it neither teaching nor practice that gives it to a man but natural aptitude or something else?"[14] With these questions, Meno does not merely repeat a common sophistic puzzle, but focuses on a critical educational and social problem for classical Athens, how virtue is acquired.

Similarly, current questioning of moral education is a symptom of extensive changes in science and technology, in social and political life. Arguing that any overly optimistic interpretation of the present period is misplaced and naïve, a skeptic would say that late twentieth-century life and moral problems cannot possibly be seen in the light of past transformations, that the relative complexity, the quality and quantity of changes in present cultural, social, political, and moral life are different from those of any past age.[15] The answer to this pessimistic questioning can be found only in the examination of the theoretical and practical options for moral education included in this book.

Conceptual Change and the Need for a New Theory of Moral Education

Older theories of moral education no longer fully address the complex moral dilemmas that have accompanied diverse intellectual transformations and social, political, and scientific changes. A new theory of moral education must transcend current fragmented concerns, concepts, and practice. Though considerable writings on moral education are available,[16] no thinker has posited a comprehensive theory that fully addresses the moral complexity and needs of this age. The dominant concepts accepted by those presently writing about moral education and development pervaded earlier modern thought. As important, only a small portion of possible categories is housed in any one moral education theory.

Even though present and past theories can be criticized, wholesale dismissal of all contending theories of moral education would be unfair and unrealistic. To claim that these theories are useless and provide few informative ideas ignores how their diverse ideas can contribute to moral education theory. Lessons must be harvested from the past to recognize that human life and morality have been a complex narrative with half-forgotten secrets. When we speak of searching for answers, we must begin to unearth what is already known.

In this book, I do not join the hunt by criticizing a number of representative moral education theories and applying conceptual bandages to a limited domain, but instead construct a broader arena for examining and conceptualizing moral education. While arguing that we must restructure the ways we look at moral education by refurbishing certain fundamental categories, this refurbishing does not mean the sweeping aside of older concepts.

During any historic period, the dominant categories of morality and moral education are rarely challenged[17] even if minor corrective surgery is continually practiced. The categories seem immune to challenge. One instance of this phenomenon is the present heated discussion about extending the concept "rights" into vast uncharted territories: the inclusion of children's rights, the rights of the unborn and the newly born, people's right to education and the right to read, the right to live and the right to die, animal rights, and the rights of the elderly. By attaining a central position in theoretical and practical discussions,[18] the pervasiveness of rights and rights theories has sometimes had unfortunate and unexpected influence on formal education. Gerald Grant, for example, suggests that competing rights claims have created a school climate that cannot foster the goals of moral education. The high school, according to Grant,

> threatens to become a container for adolescents who receive the ministrations of a greatly enlarged core of specialists in a setting in which presumed equals argue about their rights, and individuals pursue their moral preferences in whatever direction they please, so long as they do not break the law. . . . We no longer seem to recall Aristotle's language of intellectual and moral virtues; we speak only of a reductionist version of intellectual virtue, as reflected in standardized test scores.[19]

With all the analyses of how to extend the domain of certain moral categories such as rights and how to sharpen their conceptualizations, questions about the adequacy of the dominant categories rarely surface. Can all the problems of morality and moral education be resolved with the dominant categories? Or have the dominant moral categories pushed some situations into the sidelines and thus, are they never designated legitimate philosophic concerns?

Many thinkers assume that given the correct intellectual refurbishing, older categories can solve all educational and moral dilemmas and will supply theoretical foundations for moral education.[20] With this view, the underlying assumptions about morality and human life remain elusive. At times, those who highlight the inner features of fundamental concepts and criticize dominant categories are banished and shunned, as were a host of earlier thinkers from Socrates to Spinoza. At present, we might not put such critics or heretics to death. We might not banish them. But we have just as powerful means of silencing their thoughts; we publish their writings and ignore them.

The unchallenged acceptance of certain key categories for morality and moral education may continue unabated during a few periods of hegemony, of general social and political agreement. When there is considerable disagreement about life-styles and extensive, accelerating changes in all segments of societal and cultural life, a rather different picture emerges. Older or even present conceptualizations of categories no longer serve the changing needs of moral education. When Richard Rorty announces the death of Philosophy with a capital "P" and the need to do philosophy with a small "p," he implies that the categories and ways of thinking that dominated modern and twentieth-century philosophy are no longer capable of doing their jobs. What is required now, according to this way of thinking, is a new set of categories, a new way of tackling and resolving theoretical problems. With a theory of moral education as with any other theoretical and practical educational endeavor, we cannot just sweep the room clean and begin with no furnishings whatsoever.[21] Instead of building a wholly different home and employing an interior decorator to design a new way of life, we must remember that human beings live in societies with cultural, social, and political furnishings. Our forms of moral education cannot begin afresh. It is not just that the psychological and social costs are prohibitive. With human thought and moral life, clean slates are not just wasteful but impossible. Any radical shift of categories exists within a historic context and this context continues to inform our views of

moral education. Thus, this present theory of moral education faces a difficult situation: at the same time that new
categories and concepts are needed, old categories and
concepts cannot be abandoned. What is the way out of this
dilemma? As Martin Buber realized, we must walk a narrow ridge to allow older and newer ideas to interact
reflexively.

Rejected Methodologies

Rather than choosing a single beginning to tell this
moral education story, this book has a number of begin-
nings that reveal the multidimensionality of moral education theory and practice. A historical perspective, for example, provides various insights into moral life and moral
education, that is, about the unique and the relational, the
subjective and objective, and the personal and univer-
salistic.

Jung refers to the tragedy of forgetting our past and
the illusion of living only for the future:

> Once the past has been breached, it is usually annihi-
> lated, and there is no stopping the forward motion.
> But it is precisely the loss of connection with the past,
> our uprootedness, which has given rise to the "dis-
> contents" of civilization and to such a flurry and haste
> that we live more in the future and its chimerical
> promise of a golden age than in the present within
> which our whole evolutionary background has not yet
> caught up. We rush impetuously into novelty, driven
> by a mounting sense of insufficiency, dissatisfaction,
> and restlessness. We no longer live on what we have,
> but on promises, no longer in the light of the present
> day, but in the darkness of the future. . . . The less we
> understand of what (past generations) . . . sought, the
> less we understand ourselves.[22]

The less we look to the past for messages, the less we find
the tools and resources to provide adequate moral educa-

tion. Though seeming to forget the roots of moral life and moral education, people live and relive these histories every day of their individual and communal lives, in every decision made, in every emotion felt, with every interpersonal relationship, and with every instance of benevolence and compassion. Instead of consciously or realistically informing moral life and moral education, the past too often remains an unconscious force that haunts all our educational efforts.

Besides rejecting an ahistorical view of moral education, this book also excludes a recent renewed effort to revive false idols in the form of conceptual dichotomies. Earlier in the twentieth century, John Dewey criticized and rejected unwarranted dichotomies, those between mind and body, theory and practice, abstract and concrete, fact and value, general and particular, and between formal and informal education. Even if Dewey himself never wholly bridged these dichotomies and at times overlooked some of the complex conceptual problems that needed to be solved to forge a new unity, he at least painted a philosophic and educational agenda in broad strokes. Surprisingly, moral education theorists quickly veered from the course Dewey charted and were sidetracked by the paths of narrow conceptual and linguistic issues. Though Lawrence Kohlberg, for example, cites Dewey as a progenitor of his moral development theory,[23] such is hardly the case. Kohlberg's claim to adhere to a Deweyan heritage must be rejected since Kohlberg resurrects the very dichotomies Dewey rejected. For example, in direct opposition to Dewey's call for an elimination of dichotomies, Kohlberg only posits cognitive stages and denies the affective domain any viable role in morality.

The narrow, fragmented concerns of moral education writings include many topics. Some thinkers emphasize methods of thinking and making judgments, the cognitive processes underlying moral decisions, and the principle justifying these judgments. Many pour accolades on personal autonomy with such autonomy then the primary aim of moral education. Others criticize indoctrination and wonder how the hidden curriculum can become more transparent.[24] One group concentrates on behavior, another accepts an amalgamation of behavior, judgment based on anticipatory control, and modeling,[25] still others speak of the function of the personality in society.[26] Simultaneously, many writers examine what the aims of moral education should be and criticize public schools for not articulating and implementing valid moral education purposes. Many theoreticians remain generally uninterested in practice. Some writers advocate practice that is little more than shallow panacea.

Dewey's advocacy of the dynamic interrelationship and continuity of moral education categories was forgotten, and in its place we are left with many disconnected concepts and interests. At first, these conceptual fortresses did not appreciate the intellectual advances made by thinkers in opposing camps and different disciplines. These separate fortresses are now fashioning windows to examine other intellectual work.[27] It is now realized that each respective view can contribute to the improvement of moral education.

Methodological Commitments and Conceptual Revision: Summary of the Proposed Theory

Methodology

The fashioning of a philosophy of moral education requires appropriate methodological tools. While writing with a philosophic pen, my words are derived from many disciplines, from literature and sociology, psychology and educational theory and practice, and in general the rich letters of human thought.[28] If "by the early twentieth century," as Richard Rorty noted, "poets and novelists had taken the place of both preachers and philosophers as the moral teachers of youths,"[29] then a philosophy of moral education may find key ideas by digging through some of these sources. The same theme noted by Rorty has been expanded in a different direction by Lawrence Cremin[30] and John Goodlad[31] in their assertions that education in general and thus moral education take place in diverse educational networks. These networks not only include the works of poets and novelists, but also movies and their recent offspring, video cassettes, as well as popular music, television, sports, organizations for youth, religious institutions, and numerous other social organizations and experiences. All these educational networks influence the moral education of youth. Thus, when I turn to some of these diverse influences, I do so in the belief that they have subtle and important functions in moral education. The school, according to this view, is not a wholly disconnected institution that can ignore the constraints and opportunities of other educational networks.

Moral education thus is not a distinct, wholly separate discipline and cannot be understood through the tools and resources of any one discipline. Rather, it exists at the intersection of many disciplines. An adequate philosophy of moral education must not only be cognizant of this interstitial status, but of the various disciplines that touch on that intersection.[32] The major themes of moral education cannot be discerned by following one single strand, but must be based on an intricate, coherent tapestry woven from many diverse threads.

Proposed Theory

This philosophy of moral education has a number of goals. First, there is attention to questions about the territory of a theory of moral education. In recent years, other disciplines like psychology and sociology have posited moral development theories and gathered empirical data. These other disciplines often used philosophic concepts without sufficient analytical sophistication and made practical moral education recommendations with little relation to their theories. The problem posed here is which territory belongs to philosophy, what comprises a philosophy of moral education. The question, "what should be included in a philosophy of moral education?," also refers to territorial problems within philosophy itself and to the types of moral concepts that this theory should include. For example, troublesome problems are how to affix the boundaries of the moral domain and the relationship between a theory of moral education and educational practice.

Instead of searching for a few favored concepts, I argue that moral education like morality includes many diverse elements.[33] Character and rational judgments, emotions and feelings, rules and principles, ideals and good, will and intention all have their place in morality and moral education. This theory of moral education examines these notions in greater or lesser detail and then questions how they relate to each other. The following are main threads of this theory of moral education:

1. Character and virtues in the form of moral excellences are not quaint vestiges of a bygone age, but should again be a vital dimension of moral education.[34] The advocacy of a theory of moral education that includes character and virtues does not mean that these concepts can be the sole basis of morality or that moral education should foster only character and virtue development.

Chapter 2 includes justification of why character and virtue should be fundamental notions in moral education, examination of the parameters of the moral domain, and discussion of why earlier theories of character are no longer appropriate for moral education. Chapter 3 is an interlude between the two main chapters on character. This interlude chapter includes an examination of one particular moral excellence in the belief that such an examination can indicate aspects of moral life that other ethical theories cannot address. Chapter 4 examines the ideas and categories that must be included to understand character and character education. Throughout these three chapters, there is some discussion of moral education. After investigating the various elements of the notion "character," Chapter 5 presents a more systematic account of the implications of character for moral education practice.

2. The next group of chapters move in a different yet interrelated direction to take into account other elements of moral life, such as equipping agents with the reasoning tools, means, and standards by which to evaluate character and assess the position of personally accepted moral char-

acter vis-à-vis the moral expectations of public roles. An issue here is how intellectual and moral virtues interact in resolving a moral dilemma. Chapter 6 addresses these issues by examining the battle between very different ways of looking at how moral judgments are made, these being ethical principle theories and theories of altruistic emotions. Both utilitarian consequentialism and neo-Kantian deontology are examined as examples of ethical principle theories. Though it has had a poor press and has not found many advocates among those developing moral education policy, utilitarianism implicitly still underlies some educational policy. Thus, a section of this chapter analyzes the possibility of utilitarian principles underlying various aspects of moral education. Then, neo-Kantian deontology is examined by investigating Lawrence Kohlberg's moral development theory and moral education recommendations.

The hegemony of neo-Kantian ethics is now challenged by ethical theories that stress altruistic emotions, care, compassion, and networks of communication. Some of the writers advocating these theories argue that men and women speak two different moral languages. The moral language of care, response, and compassion is spoken by women, the moral language of rights, abstract reasoning, and justice by men. The final part of Chapter 6 looks at these newer views of morality and asks what they might contribute to moral education.

Chapter 7 concentrates on what teachers can contribute to moral education. The problem raised in this chapter is how teacher morality and the moral character of teachers can influence the moral education that students receive.

Chapter 8, the last chapter, responds to a number of unanswered questions. In Chapter 6, it was argued that neither ethical principles nor altruistic emotions alone or together can furnish the basis of moral education. These aspects of moral life may be necessary conditions for certain moral judgments, but cannot provide the sufficient conditions for a theory of moral education. At the same time, in earlier sections of the book, it was recognized that character alone cannot be the whole territory of moral education and morality. Thus, in this final chapter we must answer another set of questions, what form of morality, what moral standards, what ways of solving moral dilemmas can complete our picture of moral education? Another question must be answered. If moral excellences are fundamental to moral character, then against what standards are moral excellences evaluated? For these standards, we turn to moral ideals and question how these moral criteria relate to ethical theories of principles and of altruistic emotions.

2

Moral Education: Character and Virtue

In this chapter, I investigate various notions, indicate where my theory stands on a number of theoretical issues, and note what sorts of assumptions are made and which are rejected. Since character and virtue form the first part of this theory of moral education, these ideas must be examined from different perspectives. First, I investigate why these concepts should be given a central role in a theory of moral education. The second part of the chapter examines why the intellectual climate of the recent past was not particularly hospitable to theories of character education; finally I analyze a few conceptualizations of character that weathered this arid climate. Included in this last section are reasons why in themselves older conceptualizations of character cannot serve this present theory of moral education.

Just as castor oil is rarely prescribed for children's health, character and virtue are still not advocated for moral health or moral education.[1] Through silence, many theoreticians summarily dismiss attempts to give character and virtue a salient place in moral education.[2] Those criticizing character's role in morality and moral education might examine the circumstances and societies in which a morality of character and virtue would be nourished and

19

thrive. In comparison with earlier ages, critics would say that the present period has advanced beyond the constraints of character morality. The argument would be that late twentieth-century society has moved beyond the social order and constraints necessary to foster character and virtue education. A brief elucidation of the character or virtue (*arete*)[3] morality of an ancient society highlights features of an earlier character morality and its recommended form of moral education. We can then answer the question of whether the constraints and parameters of a character morality are far narrower than what is required by the present generation.

The Homeric Age was dominated by a unified group of virtues that imbued the character of heroes and aristocrats. Moral education for Homer was the modeling of youth's character after the qualities and virtues possessed and personified by great heroes and respected aristocrats.[4] Not only did the cult of gods and goddesses, the manly virtues and heroic actions of warriors present the character acceptable in Homeric society; but another factor guaranteed the maintenance of a set of recognizable virtues as the basis of character education. Homeric society's structural and ideological base was dependent on a limited number of coherent, unified virtues, which were known by all and were easily translated into character and moral action.[5] Everyone could not aspire to follow in the footsteps of Odysseus or Penelope, but all members of that society *admired* these ideal types. Through epic tales, children recognized their social rank in the world and how their place determined what moral behavior was acceptable. If there were heroes and aristocrats as glorious as Odysseus and Achilles, then there had to be serfs, warriors, artisans, and servants who accepted the status and rule of heroic, aristocratic leaders. The moral character of these followers would not be that of heroic aristocrats, but was molded according to the features of the Homeric world, and that world elevated agreed upon virtues to the highest rank. In any hierarchical society such as that portrayed in the Homeric epics, the maintenance of the moral and value system depends on the lower levels of the hierarchy as well as the higher. The masses must continue to accept their subservient rank and simultaneously extole the higher, unattainable moral standards.[6] Late twentieth-century critics of character and virtue education may look at Homeric society and other traditional views of character and ask whether any similar or recognizable form of character and virtue education can exist in a pluralistic society in which there is little agreement about morality, moral action, and moral judgments, and in which change causes a continual flood of practical, increasingly complex moral problems. The answer to this problem is yes and no. Unquestionably, the earlier content of character morality and character education together with their theoretical and social underpinnings cannot be repeated within this present age.[7] A new conceptualization of character and a different set of interlocking concepts are necessary. But at the same time, we can learn certain lessons from the Homeric Age.

Thus, before leaving Homer, we add other thoughts not so much to clarify this older view of character education, but to introduce notions that should be vital concerns for late twentieth-century moral education theory. Heroic aristocrats did not rule complex nation states, but controlled and safeguarded individual *oikos*. The Greek term "*oikos*" refers to a home, a shelter for a family. *Oikos* denotes a large extended family or what we might now term a community.[8] Though twentieth-century thinkers would note the deleterious conditions of a serf's or servant's life in an *oikos*, another feature of this life can be recognized. Even though there was no room for individualism or self-fulfillment, for freedom or personal aspirations, the *oikos* included characteristics that enrich moral life. By belonging to a given *oikos*, a person was also rooted within a moral world, belonged to a moral community, and cherished the virtues and character that ensured harmony within that moral world and community. A moral world was not just dependent on the particular *oikos*, but on the *oikos* having a place in a larger universe, a historical and religious setting,[9] a location in time and space, and a theme within an ongoing narrative. To suggest the replication of the early Greek *oikos* in late twentieth-century life would be whimsical. Yet certain features of that *oikos* persist as ideals that moral agents crave: belongingness, rootedness, and cherished communal ties. The question we must ask is how moral education can include communal features like rootedness and belonging, and simultaneously surmount the negative elements of traditional societies.

At the same time moral life within the *oikos* had a considerable measure of rootedness and belongingness with accompanying moral order and tranquility, moral life was fraught with uncertainty. Who can read the *Iliad* or *Odyssey* and not wonder about fate and luck, uncertainty and *hubris*, regret and absurdity, sadness and tragedy? The rootedness and unpredictability, the belonging and absurdity, the grandeur and tragedy are integral parts of the Homeric world and moral life. Until very recent years, it has been popular to ascribe the negative and unpredictable qualities to the gods and goddesses or to a hero's tragic flaw. The causes of unpredictable events are not the issue here, but instead that the ancient Greeks understood these crucial and unfortunate aspects of actual moral life: that no matter an agent's cleverness, foresight, rank, intelligence, or reasoning ability; the quality of moral life cannot be guaranteed. Events may conspire against societies and agents; the winds of fortune may blow one's moral ship into unexpected straits; the most perfect hero at one moment may forget the consequences of his actions and cause the death of a beloved friend; a leader may have to make an impossible choice between the life of a daughter and the lives of his followers. Mid-twentieth–century ethical theory for the most part has worshipped the rational moral agent who wholly overcomes inner and outer forces. At times, however, inner and outer forces sometimes contribute to tragedy.[10] The issue we must now assess is how a theory of moral education can simultaneously balance a number of concerns, community life and its moral world, the potential tragedy and sadness of actual moral life, and the moral ideals and standards necessary to search for moral greatness.

One final point about the Homeric Age and the subsequent Classical period sets the stage for the remainder of this chapter. Those who have compared Homeric and Classical ages have usually posited a disjunction between these two periods. For example, the competitive values of the Homeric period are distinguished from the cooperative and quiet values of the Socratic age.[11] The customs and honor of the Homeric Age are contrasted with the law and justice of the Socratic age.[12] What we find, however, when studying the Socratic dialogues, for example, is not that the competition, manly virtues, shame, and honor have disappeared. They have been refashioned and broadened to have different meanings for this later period. In this book, we face a similar problem. Instead of wholly rejecting all earlier ideas, we need to ask what aspects of previous moral education theories can contribute to this theory. In what ways do earlier notions need to be restructured to be serviceable for this theory?

Why Character and Virtue Education? A Justification

Moral character and virtue are not outdated moral vestiges, but should be integral parts of morality and moral education. Character and virtue form necessary components of early prerational moral education, are foundational to moral agency, and continue to be viable forces throughout adult moral life. Character, however, rarely remains the sole basis of all moral judgments and actions.

At the same time that advocacy of moral character does not constrain moral education to a rigidly conservative stance, character education does at times seem to emphasize traditional values. Character does not necessarily refer to an unexamined morality or code of conduct. Instead, certain moral ideals, certain ways of treating other human beings and animals, certain attitudes toward nature and oneself have remained a part of morality and have continually been revitalized, reconceptualized, and restructured with changing historical periods. New thinkers and distant cultures, social and political revolutions contribute to a refurbishing of basic moral ideals. An ideal's initial impetus does not die, but remains a "unit idea," possessing "focal meanings"[13] to guide the course of individual and communal moral development.

Instead of older moral ideas vanishing, they make way for newer posibilities. As Whitehead noted, "There are perfections beyond perfections. All realization is finite and there is no perfection which is the infinitude of all perfections."[14] Older moral ideals and views of perfection do not always keep pace with the call for a new perfection. During some ages, a shadow falls over people's moral eyes and their moral being withers to include only a small portion of what moral ideals could be. With each new intellectual, social, or political crisis, some older moral ideal is criticized, and then it appears in newly reconceptualized garb. Sometimes, there is silence and some ideals seem banished from the moral domain, no longer examined or having a vigorous part in moral education. At a later time these ideals again make their entrance and inform morality and moral education.

To reintroduce character as a fundamental concept is to say that this discarded notion should again enrich moral education. Some might interpret this inclusion as a reversion to an outdated traditional concept, a cherished antique with little serviceability for actual moral life. To meet such criticism, I begin with a justification for the inclusion of character by considering six points: questions about the boundaries of the moral domain and how the concepts a theory includes determine these boundaries; problems about the relationship between commonsense morality and moral education; an examination of why certain types of moral dilemmas require the concept "character"; an investigation of how common educational practices assume moral ideals and moral character; questions about whether moral reasoning and rational thought processes require some foundational moral baggage.

How Changes in Boundaries of the Moral Domain Also Require the Inclusion of the Concept "Character"

Which concepts are included in a theory of moral education is partly dependent on how the moral domain is viewed, on what sorts of situations are included in the moral. Yet how the boundaries of the moral domain are constructed and which dilemmas and situations fall within it simultaneously depend on what ethical theory and theory of moral education is accepted. The moral domain has in recent years been defined primarily by the conflicting claims, rights, and interests of different individuals and groups. When faced with a moral conflict of competing claims, interests, or rights, an agent must decide what ought to be done, what judgment is right or wrong, and which claims, interests, or rights should be upheld. Thus, any situation that does not include conflicting claims, rights, or interests is hardly considered a moral dilemma,[15] but has to be classified in a different way. Some conduct and values are called matters of taste or are not discussed at all since they elude the current classificatory schema. In the main, contemporary moral theories have sustained this view of the moral domain by almost exclusively concentrating on moral dilemmas for which there can be conflicting judgments about conflicting rights, interests, and claims. In addition, moral problems are not seen as particular or unique concrete dilemmas within a larger situational structure that includes historical roots and networks of people and communities, and that will have numerous consequences for the life of those people and communities. Moral dilemmas, according to many contemporary theories, are abstract problems in which all actors are placemarks. The solutions to these dilemmas can be extrapolated to all similar situations. There is the assumption that identical solutions to moral dilemmas can be applied to different situations with different people, at different times and in different places.

Moral education suffered from this delimitation of

the sorts of situations that are included within the moral domain. Moral education concentrated on the development of particular thought processes to resolve moral dilemmas of conflicting claims, rights, and interests.[16] The goals of moral education have not related to what sorts of moral persons students become or the condition of their inner moral being or what moral ideals they eventually cherish. Rather, a narrowed conception of the moral domain dictated what moral education should be.[17] This narrowed view of the moral domain, morality, and moral education is untenable. Other directions must be explored to discover different explanatory phenomena and concepts. Some might question not merely why character and virtue should again be given a role in morality and moral education, but why the moral domain needs expansion. The task at hand is to examine one way of enlarging the moral domain and why this particular way requires the addition of character to moral theory.

Moral life is not merely punctuated by a series of discordant moral dilemmas requiring extensive thought and the examination of alternative moral judgments and their respective consequences.[18] Morality also must be judged by the quality of ordinary relationships, the intimate relationships between friends and casual meetings with acquaintances, unexpected encounters with strangers, ordinary business dealings, and working with colleagues. These seemingly trivial interchanges are rarely analyzed or questioned. Morality in these cases comes upon one unheralded and requires an instantaneous, intuitive response. Numerous actions in a simple, uneventful day have moral import. These instantaneous actions most often are not even remembered, but they contribute to the moral climate of our lives and communities. Such intuitive, instantaneous action can be traced to the character of the moral agent and thus in part to the early educational lessons that are forgotten remnants of the moral agent's dreamworld.

During earlier periods, these ordinary instances of social interaction were ignored, probably because the quality of relationships was taken for granted. There was minimal unpleasantry or disagreement in daily meetings.[19] This picture has changed in that the quality of common social interactions has deteriorated, and simultaneously people are more conscious of unacceptable, paternalistic, or abusive conduct. This deterioration of common interactions takes many forms. On one side, there are numerous instances of explicitly offensive behavior and on the other side, numerous examples of bland behavior by which an actor unfeelingly follows role prescriptions. The spectator in this latter interaction is never recognized as a unique presence. The actor does not act from an abiding notion of how others should be treated. Rather, the perfunctory behavior is the hollow, role-directed behavior of a robot.

The moral dimensions of ordinary social interactions can be sought in two scenarios. (a) In a minor business or social encounter, an agent is considerate, caring, and fair. None of the parties in the interaction is offended, critical or disturbed. No one attaches moral import to this brief meeting. (b) In a slightly changed situation, an agent is curt and uncaring. Even if the declared purpose of the interaction is successfully completed and fairly executed, spectators would criticize the agent. The first minor situation not only was transformed into something unpleasant, but in the second case took on moral dimensions. Why this difference between the morally neutral first example and the second morally charged situation? Why might a few words or change of tone transform what was not moral or morally neutral into a moral situation?

Only by stepping away from these ordinary, daily moral occurrences and comparing them with a moral dilemma of conflicting claims can we respond to these and other questions. An agent is faced with a moral dilemma involving conflicting claims and after adequate reasoning makes a moral judgment based on an abstract principle. In this case of conflicting claims, the conflict itself signals the existence of a moral dilemma and only then are moral tools applied to the dilemma. The moral agent's ensuing action is judged approbative or disapprobative depending on the intentions, reasoning, and moral principles of the agent. With a trivial social interaction, a spectator's evaluation is quite different. Only when the actor in this interaction is judged disapprobatively does the interaction have moral dimensions. Actors are not judged approbatively if the taken-for-granted atmosphere is acceptable. Instead of conferring approbation on an agent, spectators think nothing of common, trivial interaction. Why should approbation be withheld if disapprobation is possible? We cannot say that the agent in the situation judged disapprobatively did not give adequate thought to the moral dilemma or did not use suitable moral principles. We cannot say that the agent in the approbatively judged situation used more adequate formal reasoning and possessed more appropriate, abstract moral principles. These two ways of examining the situation do not succeed.

At this point, a critic may question concern with the taken for granted and argue that it was in the forgotten and concealed fissures of the taken for granted that inequities and injustice existed. Lunchroom counters, railroad station waiting rooms, buses, and lavatories were unseen moral places. At times, it has been true, the taken for granted harbored numerous "invisible" men and silenced women whose claims and interests were never heard. Since ordinary interaction seemed satisfactory to the dominant group, these forgotten, hidden people were never seen or heard. Someone may thus claim that any advocacy of a moral climate that includes morally acceptable taken-for-granted interactions is a reversion to this rejected submersion of the interests, claims, and desires of the previously silent masses. In answer to this charge, two points are made. On one side, the taken-for-granted moral world continually requires investigation and questioning so that never again will silent moral inequities exist in ordinary social life. In fact, this ongoing investigation is necessary because the moral climate of the taken-for-granted world may be the first gauge for revealing the morality of society. On the other side, we can take our hints from ideas presented by both Trilling and Hall. Similar to how Trilling likened culture to a prison, the morality of the taken-for-granted world can be likened to a minimum security prison. For the morality of the taken-for-granted world binds and restrains interactants. But then to extend an idea Hall made about culture, the moral climate of the taken-for-granted world does not smother as a prison would, but provides "a medium in which to move, live, breathe, and develop."[20] The moral medium of common, ordinary social interactions does not merely contribute to comfort and well-being, but also allows human beings to concentrate on more difficult, complex, and challenging moral dilemmas.

Thus, we are left with two very different relationships that agents and spectators have with the moral dimensions of the taken-for-granted world. In the first case, agents investigate the moral dimensions of ordinary life, and in the second case, they interact within the taken-for-granted world without considering its moral dimensions. This two-fold relationship with the moral aspects of the taken-for-granted world should create no consternation. In a sense, Buber's distinction between analyzing a relationship and having one is appropriate here. If a human being must constantly investigate the moral dimensions of ordinary interactions, that person is in Trilling's prison. The interaction itself has little meaning and the investigation comes to the fore. At the same time, if an agent never examines the moral quality of ordinary life, then moral deterioration can softly enter into the most ordinary relationships. The position taken here is that at this time the moral dimensions of the taken-for-granted world cannot be ignored.

With a moral dilemma of conflicting claims, the moral import of the situation seems obvious. The moral conflict is barefaced. The daily commonplace situation, however, reveals nothing out of the ordinary; agents often carry out daily social interactions without raising the specter of morality. Their actions are taken for granted, part of the unexamined background of a moral community. The expression "taken for granted" itself indicates that events so described are not noticed. When the taken for granted is no longer in the background but enters the foreground and thus when some unacceptable behavior occurs, there might be moral disapproval. Evaluations are likely to be disapprobative if the *negative* quality of the interaction causes interactants to notice the moral dimensions of the situation.[21] Taken-for-granted interactions without being excessively negative usually are not examined by philosophers[22] for two reasons. First, since they are part of the taken-for-granted world and often occupy the unexplored recesses of a community's moral world, philosophers are more concerned about the prominent, central moral dilemmas of a society. Why be concerned with the passing moral offence when there are major moral problems involving equal opportunity and justice, when life begins and ends? Second, present trends in ethical theory highlight conflicting claims and do not possess the conceptual tools to examine the moral quality of the taken-for-granted world. Since at times these ordinary social occurrences can be the heart of daily moral matters, we need a moral theory and theory of moral education that makes room for these trivial, commonsense situations. Character can serve this purpose; a person's moral character surfaces when these common interactions occur. This inclusion of ordinary social interaction within the moral domain has implications for moral education in schools. If ordinary social interactions and the taken-for-granted world of the school have moral dimensions, then the ethos of a school cannot just be stated as the school's philosophy, but must relate to the actual life of everyone in that school.

A detractor may still argue that so many complex moral dilemmas confront human beings that it is a waste of time to worry about taken-for-granted morality. The argument against this criticism includes at least three points. First, the overall quality of morality and personal interrelationships cannot be measured only according to their complexity but must also be measured in light of the everyday interactions and situations commonly lived by every human being. Second, the moral cannot be seen as a disjointed, exceptional event, detached from the experiential stream of a person's life. The moral must be seen as intruding on all of life. At times, the moral remains in the background and is hardly noticed. At times, it comes to the forefront and insists on being seen. Third, stressing the taken for granted does not negate other sorts of more complex moral situations, but emphasizes that taken-for-granted morality is a necessary underpinning of other more complex moral situations.

Classifying everyday, commonsensical occurrences or personal interrelationships as possibly falling within the moral domain raises another problem. We greet a casual acquaintance, shake hands with her, ask after her family, show sympathy about the illness of her father, share her joy and happiness over success in her chosen work, speak about the health and achievements of her children, are genuinely interested in her personal concerns, demonstrate sincerity when sending regards to her loved ones, and warmly bid the acquaintance good-bye. There are also certain restraints on each party in this interaction, such as not prying too deeply into the other's private life.[23] Why should any aspects of this interaction be described as possessing moral dimensions? Some would insist this interaction exemplifies good manners, not morality.

The problem posed here is where the boundaries should be affixed between the moral and etiquette. The boundaries between morality and etiquette, character and manners cannot be drawn accurately;[24] these domains at times overlap. How a table is set for lunch or whether someone eats with a fork, spoon, or chopsticks is a matter of etiquette, usually without impact on the moral domain. But how an agent greets another person and whether personal interest and concern are expressed could be matters of both etiquette and morality. Instead of being purely artificial forms of behavior, etiquette can concern respect for others, sensitivity to their interests and feelings, and care for their general well-being. Though different forms of etiquette may exist in disparate societies or communities, these forms most often serve similar purposes. On one level manners are outward daily manifestations of interpersonal concerns, caring for the personhood and integrity of other individuals. Manners may reveal an agent's inner self and are representative of a moral self. Some forms of etiquette are necessary, even vital, parts of ordinary moral relations. One may even wonder whether a viable morality can exist without etiquette and acceptable moral dimensions in the taken-for-granted world. Yet etiquette cannot be the whole of morality. Just as a considerable portion of etiquette is nonmoral, morality similarly extends well beyond etiquette and ordinary interpersonal relationships.

In closing this section, three other points need to be noted. First, it was previously stated that emphasizing the moral dimensions of the taken-for-granted world recognizes the necessary, silent moral underpinnings that make the good life possible and free human beings to consider more complex moral dilemmas. Only the relationship between the moral underpinnings of ordinary social interactions and the good life are mentioned here. Though the good life is inextricably intertwined with the moral life, it includes other dimensions beside the moral. It may include planting and caring for flowers, playing the piano, perfecting a new pastry, puzzling over the meaning of a novel, enjoying the pleasures of family and friends, watching a sunset, appreciating banter, playing chess, and watching a sleeping infant. None of these activities or events need include the moral. Yet one must wonder whether any of them would survive without a moral background. What would the good life be if human beings perpetually had to attend to moral dilemmas? Thus, the issue here is not just the relationship between etiquette and morality, but the larger problem of the moral underpinning of ordinary social life.

Second, even if the relation between etiquette and morality were smaller problems within the larger agenda sketched here, the question of how to affix the borders between these two domains still remains. When does a situation have moral dimensions and when is it wholly a matter of etiquette? Again, this problem can be highlighted by looking at instances where etiquette is problematic. A "rough," seemingly unmannered person at times can do the supererogatory, while the exceptionally polite, well-mannered individual may be insensitive and unfeeling to more complex moral dilemmas. Superficial manners do not necessarily indicate an agent's moral commitment, and simultaneously, "rough" manners may be based on the agent's primary communal affiliation. In these situations the superficial, outward manners obviously do not relate to these actors' moral character, intentions, and moral actions. Whether a person's etiquette is connected with morality can in part be judged on whether these manners relate to *genuine* concern for another human being or whether they are perfunctory regulators of conduct.

Finally, why should character be the phenomenon cited as a reason for someone's behaving in a way that both describes the moral and etiquette? In particular, why should character be cited as explaining why agents maintain the moral climate of the taken-for-granted world? Whether social situations and interactions are on the border of the moral and etiquette or whether they are part of the taken for granted is not the issue. Agents in these cases need to interact and behave without considerable thought. These actions are dependent on the type of moral person the agent is and thus the character of the moral agent. Principles are of no use here. Only character rightly describes conduct that may conform with some expected manners, but also involves consideration, respect, and compassion for others in ordinary, taken-for-granted encounters. In these ordinary, taken-for-granted situations, the moral agent does not have time to think What should I do? What moral principle should govern my actions? Rather, character as an intrinsic part of the person's moral agency governs the moral action in these everyday interactions and situations.

Commonsense Morality and Character

Commonsense comments and literary descriptions about moral actions and moral agents continually refer to character. What should be said about the use by average people and writers of the term "character?" Should we say that these individuals should not use this term, that they do not realize its obsolescence? How can we explain its ongoing acceptance? Even in scholarly works, the term is sometimes used in a general way without providing it with any depth or connecting link with the matter being discussed. Are these literary and scholarly uses of the term residual references to commonsense morality?

Should a moral theory pertain to commonsense morality? What then of moral education? Should a theory of moral education include components like character because they are in popular linguistic usage? Should other educational networks and forms of moral narrative contribute to our understanding of morality and moral education, even if their morality is commonsensical and has little relation to theoretical concerns? Since moral education is a multi-institutional responsibility, can schools be expected to escape a society's implicit, commonsense moral commitments and instead, embrace some philosophically sophisticated moral theory? Unlike the formal teaching of Latin, physics, geometry, and other school subjects, morality and moral education envelopes children throughout their lives. Thus, can schools base moral education on a theory that has little relationship to societal views, other educational networks, and commonsense morality?

Moral philosophers and social scientists in their search for universal, objective moral standards are often seen as an elite that knows how a community's children *should* be educated and what form of moral education is best. This role has created an ongoing struggle without any easy resolution. One way out of this difficulty may be to recognize that a number of forces simultaneously vie for primacy: the moral concerns of communities and the moral standards and values they transmit to children; the larger society's need to foster a public, more highly articulated morality; and intellectual and scholarly proposals of even more abstract, clearly conceptualized moral theories. Instead of moral education remaining a struggle among these forces, we need to ask whether there are methods of fostering greater dialogue and understanding among these three ways of looking at morality and moral education. We need to examine what each area has to contribute to moral education. Rather than each group asking, "How do I impose my moral education proposals in all areas?," the questions should be, "How do we begin dialogue?" "In what areas can there be agreement?" The reorientation here is in line with the belief that we must find ways to move beyond a conflict model for interpreting social institutions and communities' or groups' relationships to these institutions and to each other. Instead of beginning with differences and conflicts, it seems advisable to begin with the places where there is agreement about moral education. At what level is there agreement? Understandably, there may be little agreement about the more abstract aims of moral education, but there may be some agreement about specific practices and short-term goals. How can each group contribute to the furthering of moral educational goals and share the concerns and tools each possesses? Rather than a moral education theory being derived solely from philosophy, from moral development theory, or from commonsense morality, moral education theory is a meeting point connecting a number of different interpretive frameworks: the commonsensical, philosophical, sociological, historical, and psychological. All these perspectives contribute to the fashioning of a theory of moral education.

Even if this way of looking at the relationship between commonsense moral education and moral education theory is accepted, another problem remains: Does the interstitial status of moral education theory justify the inclusion of character in a theory of moral education? Does commonsense morality's references to a moral agent's character require that character be included in a theory of moral education? Character is not made a centerpiece of moral education theory because of its ongoing linguistic function in common speech and literature. Rather, this continuing usage relates to the need to have some term to describe and appraise the personhood of moral agents. The term *character* is not a shorthand or placemark for more complex reasoning processes. Character represents the unified, enduring ways by which moral agents handle simple and perhaps trivial moral interactions. Character includes a set of moral excellences or virtues that represent for a moral agent principles and means of justifying moral actions. In addition, character provides agreed upon ways of describing the ongoing, persistent moral being of an agent. Novelists take advantage of these qualities to create "ideal types" to highlight specific character virtues or vices. By ignoring character, scholars have focused on ways of resolving complex moral dilemmas, but have not considered the unified moral being of the person who governs daily, ordinary morally charged interactions.

Character and the Temporal Constraints on Moral Dilemmas

Character and virtue involve settled, holistic, internalized ways of feeling and motivations for moral action.[25] The temporal constraints on certain difficult moral dilemmas imply that there must be instantaneous action without the complicated reasoning of an ethics of principle. For example, John Hersey alludes to such temporal constraints when describing how someone rescues a drowning person: the "action, which could not have been mulled over in his mind, showed a deep, instinctive love of life, a compassion, an optimism."[26] Similarly, a stranger's instantaneous action helps someone fleeing from the Nazis. Ruth, a Jewish woman, did not know where to hide.

> As she [Ruth] walked slowly from the building a taxicab stopped at the entrance. Out stepped a young woman, a few years older than Ruth, but so strikingly similar in looks that she might have passed for her sister. . . .
> Many times thereafter Ruth would wonder what had gone through Hilde's mind in that first moment of recognition. Was she, with her frank and admiring appraisal, offering that acknowledgement one attractive woman gives to another? Whatever Hilde was thinking, Ruth felt herself swept up by her own wave of intuition.[27]

Not thinking of her own husband, an S.S. officer and commander of a "work" camp, Hilde immediately offered to hide Ruth.

In these examples, the moral agents' behavior is not foolhardy or accidental. Their intuitive awareness of the total situation is actually based on settled character excellences and virtues that allow each moral action to be carried out with sympathy and compassion, elegance and precision, style and speed. Since character is a settled dispositional structure, an agent can act without cognitive thought. However, this does not imply that an agent acts without reason. In retrospect, the mature moral agent could cite reasons for the particular action. But these reasons are not in the form of some abstract analysis of the problem and moral principles for making a moral judgment.

Someone may seem to explain moral action naïvely—"I am just that sort of person"—and not be able to articulate the virtues that underly his or her moral character. Even more self-conscious, thoughtful moral agents may have difficulty giving satisfactory reasons for actions. They might refer to their own character, the moral ideals and virtues that are personally important and make them the sort of moral persons they are. They might refer to the ideals of their community, to ideals they have sought and dreamed about, and the moral self they have struggled to create. Though some of these descriptions might not be the substance of a philosopher's analysis of the virtue or ideal accepted by the moral agent, still enough credence can be given to these personal accounts for them to be springboards for a further study of moral character, virtues, and ideals.

Educational Practice, Moral Ideals, and Character

The inclusion of character in a theory of moral education can also be justified through a brief examination of educational practice. Educational theorists and policy makers relegate character to the shadows and ignore its role in moral education and morality. But this does not seem equally true of teachers and their practices. The rules developed by elementary school teachers designate how students should behave in classroom interpersonal relationships. Teachers often want students to be thoughtful of other students, to share with others, and to be sensitive about another's feelings. These characteristics are not just necessary for maintaining a positive teaching-learning environment, but are embryonic dimensions found in adult moral life. By developing structures to govern classroom life, teachers do not just guarantee congenial teaching-learning situations. They also seek to influence the type of moral persons students become. The enforcement of rules by a teacher does not imply autocratic techniques, but creates conditions and experiences, appropriate interpersonal relationships between teacher and student, student and student, curriculum design and material, and methods to foster the development of moral virtues. With the acquisition of humane and sensitive ways of treating other human beings, children also become imbued with a sense of moral ideals. A child who helps a peer and sees the admiration and gratitude in the other's eyes dimly glimpses a moral ideal that remains a beckoning light. A child who treats a classroom pet with kindness and seeks to understand the animal's needs begins to listen with a "third ear" and understands the silent language of morality.

The mention of moral ideals requires brief comments about a few dimensions of such ideals in the context of educational practice. First, moral ideals do not imply the negation of pluralistic moral views or values. At times, different communities accept the same ideals, but seem to interpret them quite differently. At other times, communities may agree about certain fundamental ideals. Schools need to ask themselves at what points is there such agreement among communities for constructive moral education in schools. Second, all children when entering school may not possess an adequate glimmer of these ideals or satisfactory moral character as the bases for mature morality. Children may not have been members of communities that transmitted moral excellences, or they may not have been nurtured within caring homes with sympathetic, compassionate human relationships. The school may thus provide the first community and moral ideals known to the child. Third, the moral ideals and excellences transmitted in communities and schools are not the final or sole measure of fully mature moral development or morality. Moral ideals instead suggest that the child should first become part of an ongoing but evolving moral universe with its moral vision. The case for moral ideals and visions must be argued at a later point. For now, it is sufficient to note that unchanging ideals have not been accepted universally in identical form throughout the ages. Certain ideals have continued to thread their way through human history. At different times, various ideals are seen from a new perspective and their light shines on a larger population. At other times, some unusual person becomes an "ideal type," the living, breathing personification of the ideal. Ideals like love, justice, equality, respect for other human beings and living creatures, integrity, and courage are only a few of the ideals that have continued to have a place in morality.

The question of whether certain ideals have continued to wend their way through human history may seem an empirical question that can be settled by examining extant writings and positing a history of ideas to validate this claim. But moral ideals are never that simple; philosophers would question whether any single ideal was substantially the same or whether very different ideals informed different ages and societies. As ideals wander through history and intrude into different social territories, they change and become enriched and enlarged.[28] Yet even with such changes in moral ideals, a morality that puts moral ideals and moral excellences at its center will have rather different implications for education than one that concentrates on thought processes and moral principles. In later sections of this book, questions are raised about how formal education would be modified if schools took moral ideals seriously.

Questions About Philosophy's Present Concentration on the Age of Rationality[29]

Neo-Kantian ethical theories analyze the formal attributes of moral reasoning and how a moral judgment should be based on abstract principles. Any judgments or actions that fall outside this favored circle are unacceptable and discreditable. The only aim moral education can have according to neo-Kantian ethical theory is for students to

attain the acceptable formal criterion of abstract, principled moral reasoning. Reasoning and rational processes
became the hallmark of moral education. Moral development theories recommended techniques to introduce moral dilemmas and the making of reasoned moral judgments
to younger children[30] These techniques aim to encourage
higher-level, more complex thought processes. If moral
education theory begins with a rational bias, then it also
seems obvious to concentrate on the cognitive domain and
how to improve a moral agent's reasoning processes for resolving moral dilemmas. These comments are not meant to
reject practical reasoning or rational methods. Instead, two
other aspects of moral education implicit in neo-Kantian
theory are rejected.

First, recent moral education recommendations include a narrowed view of moral reasoning. These narrow
attributes of moral reasoning overlook other broader approaches to moral reasoning. One of these broader approaches is problem solving as advocated, for example, by
John Dewey. Included in such a broader method of solving
moral problems would be stating the moral dilemma and
assessing which data should be sought and included; which
knowledge and moral standards are pertinent; how the
context influences every aspect of the problem; how emotions, impulses, interests, and desires contribute to the
moral problem; how to assess whether the valued is valuable and the desired desirable; what judgments and actions
are possible; and imaginatively rehearsing the outcome of
alternative judgments and actions. This interweaving of
the dimensions of problem solving does not do justice to
Dewey's conceptualization of intelligence and reflective
thinking. Without moral action, reflective thinking has not
been completed. Reflective thinking terminating in action
is not actually the end but part of a continuing process of
changing, clarifying, and enriching the moral self and moral life. At the present time, some might argue that Dewey's
scientific method and reflective thinking do not include
other dimensions and ways of resolving moral dilemmas.
For example, feminists might question Dewey's notion of
science and the scientific method.[31] Dewey, however, did

not posit the necessary and sufficient conditions or eternally valid characteristics of science. Science as a basis for understanding morality, resolving moral dilemmas, and improving individual and society life is a dynamic category. In a sense, Dewey's notion of science is akin to Plato's and Hegel's view of science as philosophy rather than some sort of narrow specialization. Dewey posits one set of ideas about problem solving. Enlarged conceptualizations of practical reasoning and problem solving explode well beyond the narrow boundaries of the abstract, formal reasoning of neo-Kantian ethics. However, these enlarged views of practical reasoning rarely comprise moral education programs.

Second, the rational bias of neo-Kantian education programs is unfounded for another reason. No one begins moral reasoning without already being a certain type of person, without having unarticulated moral views, attitudes, abilities, feelings, emotions, desires, interests, and without having already lived in a moral world. If rational processes are a part of mature morality, then a young person should enter this thought arena with certain appropriate moral equipment acquired by being a member of a moral community.

By saying that certain moral equipment, certain moral character, is a prerequisite for optimum rational morality, a number of claims are made. First, though there may be various forms of optimum moral character, many children may have acquired few necessary components at some character type. For some human beings, it may be possible at a later time to restructure incomplete character and incorporate moral excellences by various means, such as through rational judgments about the adequacy of present character or because of the influence of some event or by being impressed by the moral lessons of some novel. The school can be one institution that fosters the development of this moral character. Second, what may be optimum moral qualities for a child would probably be immature moral character for an adult. Moral character can develop to more adequate levels and more complex forms. Character and thought should maintain parallel growth, each dependent on and interrelating with the other. Third, even if a child seems blessed with intuitive moral sense and meritorious, admirable moral character, there is no guarantee of the quality of this child's adult moral life.[32] The promise of childhood may flounder on the pressures of adolescence and adulthood and on uncontrollable internal and external conditions. Moral education is not accomplished at one time, but must be the continual effort of a lifetime.

A criticism of the rational bias of one form of moral education raises questions about the status of Piagetean moral cognitive development theories. Piageteans claim that certain psychological phenomena such as character cannot explain or predict[33] moral judgments and actions. Rather than character and emotions, early childhood development is a form of intelligence; early childhood experiences involve cognitive processes. While more recent criticism casts a shadow on the validity of Piagetean theory,[34] anyone positing a theory of moral education cannot avoid the seminal theories of this field, and Piagetean theory is one of these theories. Yet it can no longer expect unquestioning allegiance. Piaget must be seen in a wider light.

Character, Moral Philosophy, and Moral Education: The First Half of the Twentieth Century

The literal sense of the term *character* is derived from the Greek term *karacter,* which refers to "that which is cut in or marked, the impress or stamp on coins, seals, etc."[35] According to the *Oxford English Dictionary,* character is "a distinctive mark impressed" or engraved, a symbol, and "a distinctive significant mark of any kind." Only in its figurative sense does the term acquire moral features, meaning "the sum of the moral and mental qualities which distinguish an individual" and also, the "moral qualities strongly developed and strikingly displayed." This figurative definition still reflects commonsense descriptions of a person's character.

Through the first third of the twentieth century, the concept "character" seemed to retain a foothold in moral theory and writings on moral education. However, no matter the quantity of these writings, character had already become an outmoded means of explaining moral action. In the Hasting's *Encyclopedia of Religion and Ethics,* for example, even the article on charms is longer than the article on character, the one on charms being sixty pages while the one on character fewer than two pages. Though Eucken, the author of the essay on character, deplored "the dearth of character" during his age and pictured character education as "one of the most serious and urgent [problems] of the present day,"[36] he did not discuss what attributes were sought or included when educators aimed to achieve character development. Eucken's cry about the need for character education seems outdated, and only a few years after Hastings, the recent *Encyclopedia of Philosophy* does not even contain a citation "character."[37] This recent omission of a reference to character is not a mystery, as even the most cursory look at the history of twentieth-century philosophy, psychology, and education demonstrates.

During the first third of this century, philosophers despaired of finding a rational or objective basis for understanding character and connecting it with moral action. The problem was not a dearth of empirical evidence to sustain a character morality, but the changing nature of philosophy. Up to this period, metaphysical positions dominated ethical and moral education theory. Both ethical theory and moral education theory and practice, it was argued, had to have some grounding in a metaphysical view.[38] In some way, these earlier metaphysical theories assume that moral character would be the "stamping" of moral reality into the person. The more clearly moral agents would have metaphysical ideals impressed within their character, the more their character should be approved. This confabulation, however, is wholly unfair to metaphysical positions in a number of ways. But this is not the issue here. The only issue is why the demise of character and character excellences as basic phenomena to be nourished by moral education? First, some thinkers realized that neither character nor its moral excellences could be understood outside a specific context: some society at a particular time, diverse roles, and communities. Second, the great thinkers of the nineteenth century—Marx, Freud, and Darwin—posited views of humanity and human nature that revolutionized how we saw morality and moral education.[39] The universe and human nature became open-ended, without the teleological end that marked previous theories. The moral could not be spelled out in absolute terms. These comments about the transformation of philosophy and the withering of metaphysical systems could continue to include the different political and social structures of this period, economic and industrial forces, changing demographic patterns, and so on. However, the concern here is not with this earlier period but with why ethical theories of the last four or so decades could not sustain the concept "character." Thus, we turn to two of those theories.

Emotivism became the ascendant moral philosophy of an earlier period. With emotivism, philosophers denied the possibility of finding any objective, rational means to adjudicate conflicting moral beliefs or decide the validity of different moral emotions or judgments.[40] Moral utterances, according to emotivism, were merely expressions of emotions. Both in its theoretical configuration and its practical implications for moral education, emotivism was flawed. Emotivism, we have been told, evolved out of epistemological theory and thus divulged something about the status of various classes of propositions. One set of propositions could be overtly or covertly proven. Their knowledge and truth status was assured by comparing their contents with that of the actual world. On the other hand, among other experiences and utterances, moral beliefs had no currency in the physical or scientific world. Even though one could assess that a moral agent believed x or that a society followed y or that a tribe accepted z norms, there could be no proof about the adequacy or truth of these various moral beliefs. These beliefs were not propositions that could be given true-false values but were akin to taste, neither provably true nor false. They had no objective warrant.

Though human beings possess the cognitive abilities to judge the empirical truth or falsity of scientific and logical propositions, they possess no tools for judging the relative merits of respective moral beliefs or emotions. Someone could correct faulty logical, factual, or empirical errors; such propositions were corrigible. If a moral belief contained some logical, factual, or empirical error, it could be corrected. Unlike logical and factual propositions that could be evaluated according to the canons of logic and science, moral beliefs had no external, objective yardstick. All value beliefs, whether religious, aesthetic, or moral, were equally tenable. Since a yardsitck for measuring the truth of a moral belief did not exist, cognitive abilities, thought, or reasoning were useless tools for judging the worth of a moral belief. The epistemological difference between two types of statements—logical or factual propositions and moral beliefs—meant that each was consigned to a different domain. Logical and factual propositions were the province of the cognitive domain and could be tested by the canons of logic and science. Moral beliefs on the other hand were consigned to the affective domain and were emotionally upheld.

Though emotivism was fundamentally an epistemologically rooted moral theory, it also tacitly subscribed to a theory of human nature and a form of psychology. Human nature was divided, with the rational and cognitive abilities on one side of the schism and the affective on the other. The cognitive could not judge the merit of emotions or value beliefs. At the same time, the emotive had no passport to enter into cognitive territory. Actually, a proposition would be held suspect if it were tainted with emotive elements. This schism between the factual or scientific and the moral had unfortunate implications for both science and morality. The factual or scientific could not be assessed in a morally objective manner. If there was any moral comment about scientific issues, it was a totally different type of expression than scientific discourse. Simultaneously factual material or scientific findings could not have any real impact on fundamental moral beliefs. A "two-culture" knife not only cut into the heart of human intellectual endeavors, but into human nature itself. This exaggerated separation between the cognitive and affective, the rational and emotive had serious implications for the practice of moral education.

Emotivism also served to describe much of moral education during more than a single decade.[41] Moral education seemed to be a form of cheerleading, with different sides vying for a crowd's allegiance to opposing moral beliefs. Parents and teachers used various emotional appeals to inculcate moral beliefs in children. If emotional appeals were ineffective, other nonrational or irrational devices could be used. These might include the superior power of adults in dispensing favors and inflicting punishment, the use of manipulative techniques and shaming.[42] Other cheerleaders besides parents and teachers sought to convert children to their moral beliefs (e.g., movies championed particular ways of life[43]). Youth organizations such as Girl Scouts and Boy Scouts also transmitted moral beliefs.[44] Instead of being concerned with students' moral character, the only aim of moral education was for students to behave in appropriate ways and unthinkingly accept dominant moral beliefs.[45]

Emotivism was not just a moral theory but an accurate interpretation of certain aspects of social and political life. Converts to a moral belief did not acquire character but just temporary emotional allegiance to that moral belief. The emotional condition of the moral agent is the basis of moral belief. With the heightened political emotionalism of the thirties, the masses in some European countries unthinkingly and emotionally followed the whims and accepted outrageous moral beliefs of charismatic leaders. With such emotional adulation and thoughtless acceptance of moral beliefs, with such unthinking allegiance of transfixed masses, it was no wonder that moral education at this period can be described as the implanting of feelings about moral beliefs and not rational character education.

Some might argue that in the United States, instead of emotivism being the basis of moral education, character was at the heart of moral education programs. The means used might be emotive, but the end would be character formation. Through moralizing, exhortation, and propagandizing,[46] adults could mold children's character. In retrospect, the moral education of this earlier period was purchased at an exhorbitant price. Those who seemed to personify acceptable character were rarely given the tools to question or modify dominant character traits or moral beliefs. For some groups, moral education *qua* character formation was a means of social control, one reason they did not question their lives or limited aspirations. Other people lived their lives submerged far from the dominant moral beliefs.[47]

When the reign of emotivism officially ended, the crown was given to linguistic or ordinary language analysis. According to linguistic analysis, the clarification and analysis of moral concepts would also resolve moral problems. Moral dilemmas were effectively whitewashed as mistakes or confusion about moral language. Criticism of linguistic analysis is now readily available.[48] For moral education, linguistic analysis had unfortunate consequences. At a time when human life was constrained by mass media, necessary social and economic interdependency, and overt and covert government control, linguistic analysts proposed a very narrow form of moral education. Moral education, it was assumed, should be a quest for individually chosen moral principles based on neo-Kantian formalism. Formalism, it was argued, would not champion particular moral content, but just the "correct," logical form of making moral judgments. Fully mature morality required the development of autonomous moral agents. This philosophic agenda ignored the context within which personally chosen principles and autonomy existed. There was no consideration of what actual conditions might constrain personal autonomy and how evidence would modify moral judgments. Fact was effectively divorced from value.[49]

Moral education was affected by linguistic analysis in a number of ways. First, though philosophers argued that linguistic analyses of moral concepts were neutral and had no normative import, this was hardly the case. The unstated assumptions, the concepts chosen for analyses, and the ahistoricity of the enterprise all supported certain forms of moral education. Second, linguistic analysis tacitly assumed that analysis of moral concepts would improve morality, and thus an examination of moral concepts should have a role in moral education. Third, linguistic analysts found neo-Kantian formalism and principles congenial to their mode of "doing" moral philosophy. Since neither formalism nor abstract principles included content, linguistic analysts argued they were not making substantive moral recommendations. Linguistic analysis only recommended a method for making judgments, the form such judgments should take, and the abstract principles for making them. With moral judgments justified by neo-Kantian principles and moral reasoning based on neo-Kantian formalism, form and content were separated.

At the same time as linguistic analysis became the dominant moral philosophy, the moral ground Americans stood on experienced an earthquake that revealed numerous alternative moral positions. Anthropological writings, television programs and other mass media, widespread travel to radically different societies, the emergence of Third World nations, and the vocal aspirations of previously disenfrancised groups all told a similar story: Different people and groups accepted somewhat different moral standards and conduct. The actual content of human life was fraught with moral diversity. At that time, many thinkers argued that the acceptance of pluralistic moral beliefs should not just be tolerated, but applauded as the very essence of a democratic credo. There seemed to be a tolerably happy marriage between linguistic analysis and moral pluralism. Though it championed certain formal criteria and advocated analysis of moral concepts, linguistic analysis did not recommend any single moral way of life. It ostensibly remained neutral regarding all pluralistic moral beliefs.[50]

One might ask how the linguistic analysis of moral concepts could possibly relate to a theory of human nature. Though this is a much longer story than can be told here, a few themes indicate that linguistic analysis possesses an underlying view of human nature that excludes moral character. During the heyday of linguistic analysis, the dominant psychology in the United States was behaviorism.

According to behaviorism and its major proponent of the time, B. F. Skinner, only behavior in all its many forms could provide the evidence and explanations of psychology. What was within the skin was unpredictable and unreliable. Linguistic analysis was not concerned with all forms of human behavior, but only with linguistic behavior. There was no attention to the inner world, to the person within the skin who uttered certain linguistic expressions, made judgments, and had feelings. The inner person had become unimportant since the use of language could be traced to forms of life, to social affiliation, to societies and culture, and could be assessed with logical criteria. The single human being seemed to have no part in the formation of linguistic communities or larger social structures or to forms of life. All human beings possessed the potential for using logical canons and abstract formal principles to assess alternative moral claims and judgments. The reasoning and results of these deliberations were expressed in readily available, logical linguistic form. One no longer had to look for the inner person or for character, but just analyze the form of the person's moral language. Thus, in a manner akin to behaviorism, linguistic analysis had no need of the person within the skin. Only the person's linguistic utterances counted as evidence.

Moral education had to motivate children to become members of linguistic communities and to employ analytical techniques to correct their use of language. Formal and logical standards replaced moral standards. In the two primary institutions of a child's life, moral education was influenced in the following manner.

Parental Uncertainty and Teacher Neutrality

The acceptance of moral pluralism and diversity by society created many problems for educators trying to transmit moral standards and engender in their students the good, humane, and moral life. Which moral ideals and standards should a teacher transmit when confronted with pluralistic moral views? The moral pluralism of society and the linguistic analysis of theoreticians could not provide substantive moral standards for teachers to transmit to students. Teachers often took refuge in moral neutrality and claimed that instead of transmitting specific values or moral beliefs, they respected students' diverse moral beliefs. Yet these assertions did not ring true. Teachers did not actually accept all forms of student conduct. Teachers personified and unconsciously accepted certain moral beliefs and forms of behavior, and these were revealed in every aspect of their personal and teaching lives. Even the way they dressed and presented themselves revealed their values and moral beliefs. Teachers' moral beliefs influenced their teaching techniques, methods of controlling classes, ways of treating students, and how they spoke to and about students. In other words, the hidden curriculum was normative and moral.[51]

Educators' uncertainty about which moral standards were valid proved unfortunate in another way. Education is not morally neutral. Educational policy cannot be generated from empirical studies alone. Educational policy and practice have always required moral decisions and standards. In their confusion about which substantive moral standards and principles should be used, educators took two courses. First, they floundered, accepting educational practices because of propaganda, exhortation, popularity, or political pressure. Though this is not the place to discuss and argue about how political pressure still influences and dominates formal moral education or how moral education has been politicized, still a few comments must be made about this situation. Reasons have been given for the demise of educational consensus and the excessive politicalization of schools. With these changes, questions about moral education have actually become political issues. This problem can be seen in another way, this direction in part related to the missions and goals of formal education. One might argue that a philosophical and intellectual vacuum created conditions by which it was much easier for the excessive politicalization of moral education to occur. Earlier visions of education's purposes and the moral ideals schools should transmit had vanished and were not replaced by a new view. Those who might have been able to address this problem were more concerned with formal criteria, analysis, behavior, and neutrality. This vacuum was filled not with ideals and visions, but with political strategy and pressure.

Educational policy and practice became the newest fashion-conscious industry to parade its latest styles each year. Educators accepted the policy and practice recommendations of social scientists without questioning what hidden moral agenda or standards were embedded in these policies. Most often, social scientists did not recognize their own moral assumptions. Statistical findings and analyses were followed by recommendations that had little relationship to the statistics and evidence; the analyses contained hidden moral assumptions. In their desire to accept moral pluralism and remain neutral, teachers tacitly assumed that social science recommendations were value-neutral, objective findings and would thus resolve the moral diversity dilemma.

Parents did not find any easier way to decide about which moral standards should be enforced or transmitted to their children. Parents often remained uncertain about which moral beliefs or moral behavior should be conveyed to children.[52] Both teacher neutrality and parent uncertainty were consistent with linguistic analysis. At the same time, philosophers argued that linguistic analysis was neutral and thus did not dictate substantive, normative moral prescriptions. Schools and families ostensibly seemed to be neutral forums where various moral languages were spoken. Was there no moral yardstick to apply to these diverse languages?

School and Family Discussions of Moral Dilemmas and Moral Concepts

There was another way of dealing with diverse, pluralistic moral beliefs and simultaneously promote neo-Kantian moral education goals. Teachers who claimed moral neutrality motivated classes to discuss moral issues, clarify moral preferences, and analyze the validity of alternative moral judgments. In these instances, teachers did not promote a moral point of view, but acted as facilitators of discussions of moral beliefs and problems. All too often these discussions and analyses amounted to little more than sophisticated wordplay.[53] Changes in students' moral judgments or beliefs were not always based on rational decision-making processes and objective moral standards, but tacitly on the personal appeal and charisma of the author of the moral belief or judgment.

Since parents were uncertain about which moral standards to transmit, they discussed moral problems with children and thereby attempted to foster rational, analytic moral thought. Both families and schools paid little attention to the possibility of achieving consistency between analysis of moral issues and moral action. In both cases, there was little purposeful attempt to structure an environment in which children could acquire some reasonably harmonious moral foundation. Moral education in the sense of encountering realistic moral dilemmas remained the product of haphazard experiences.[54] All too often, parents sheltered children from moral responsibility and thus unwittingly deprived their children of realistic moral experiences. Since parents and schools concentrated only on moral reasoning and accepted moral pluralism, reasoning did not imply that specific moral content or ideals were necessary. An agent had only to know how to reason and analyze language. Reasoning about moral problems and analyzing moral language in no way related to an individual's moral being. It is no wonder that character education was deemed outmoded.

Psychological studies also contributed to the elimination of character as a viable contender for explaining and predicting moral behavior. After 1928–1930, most writers noted the demise of the concept "character" and dated its death to the publication of the Hartshorne and May studies. Hartshorne and May investigated whether children's character and thus their character traits were generalizable to diverse moral dilemmas (i.e., whether traits would be generally exemplified in a variety of different moral situations). Ostensibly, these researchers failed to find evidence for the generality of such character traits as honesty. Though it has been argued that Hartshorne and May effectively destroyed the notion that human beings possess moral character and distinct character traits, in recent years not only have a few thinkers timorously resurrected the concept "character," but also some investigators now assert

> A full reading of Hartshorne and May's report reveals . . . that it would be wrong to cite them as having demonstrated that there was no generality or individual consistency of moral conduct, that acts of resisting temptation were completely situationally determined with nothing attributable to individual differences in the subjects.[55]

Instead of silencing philosophical and educational writings about character, the Hartshorne and May studies in retrospect seemed a convenient excuse for terminating philosophical and psychological investigations of character. Other conditions and events contributed to the questioning of the efficacy of character as an explanation of moral judgments and conduct, for example, the emergence of emotivism and then linguistic analysis as dominant philosophical schools, and in American psychology, the popularity of stimulus-response associationism and behaviorism.[56] In both philosophy and psychology, human nature and thus the moral agent were viewed in ways that could not admit the concept "character." Character refers to internal qualities and the nature of the person within the skin. The dominant psychological and philosophical theories of this earlier time looked only at outward behavioral attributes and thus had to dismiss character as a concept that could inform their concerns.

Earlier Views of Character

At the same time that philosophy and psychology were generally inhospitable to the concept "character," a few thinkers continued to speak about it. As a first step in the search for a new view of character, I briefly note some of these earlier ideas about it. Through this study, it will be possible to assess which aspects of these earlier theories can no longer inform moral life and which aspects can be integrated within a newer conceptualization.

John Stuart Mill's notion of character parallels how many nineteenth-century thinkers viewed character. According to Mill,

> A person whose desires and impulses are his own— are the expression of his nature, as it has been developed and modified by his own culture—is said to have a character. One whose desires and impulses are not his own has no character, no more than a steam engine has character.[57]

An individual's character should not be a mass of fragmented, uncontrollable emotions, wishes, or impulses that are continually buffeted by external stimuli and manipulated by others. If a moral agent's desires and impulses are her own and not controlled by others, then that agent must self-consciously realize that she possesses a certain character that requires a given set of desires and impulses. However, recognition of one's character and its connected desires and impulses is not sufficient for Mill. Adherence to one's character implies that the moral agent can evaluate that character and its allied desires and impulses. Is the character one's own or is the agent controlled by other forces? Are the desires and impulses the agent follows consistent with assumed character or are they indicative of rather different character traits? Since desires and impulses may be inconsistent with accepted character, the agent must have the means of assessing each of these and the ability to decide whether present character should be accepted or rejected. If rejected, the person must then have the means and ability to modify what is unacceptable. Offensive or unacceptable desires and impulses can be transformed into ones that are self-consciously judged worthwhile. What are these desires and impulses? Are they housed within some basic structure? What is the system of interlocking habits or settled dispositions that make the person have particular desires and impulses?

Mill does not consider the possibility of deeply unconscious, unknowable desires and impulses controlling character, moral beliefs, and action. Is Freud rather than Mill correct in arguing that during infancy and childhood certain desires and impulses become unconscious determinants of later adult character? According to a Freudian interpretation, a person with a miserly character like that of Scrooge is a *victim,* fixated at an early, unresolved developmental stage. As unconscious drives, these desires and character traits would be most difficult to change. Instead of cognitive processes, objective criteria, and rational judgments being the primary means of altering desires and impulses, Freud would advocate some form of psychoanalysis to tap the unconscious to obtain knowledge of which forces control the person.

Though it may be argued as Mill does that the culture provides the constraints within which character is etched, this view cannot do justice to late twentieth-century pluralistic society's complex influence on character development. Mill's view seems adequate for certain bygone ages, the manly virtues of Homeric society or Bradley's world of human beings accepting the imprint of their stations and its duties. But how would today's educators implement a Millsean view and transmit the character excellences of this contemporary culture? Which cultural and societal moral excellences should be accepted? Which of the diverse moral views bombarding children should parents and teachers transmit and reinforce?[58]

What sort of stable or integrated character could be formed by anyone continually being assaulted by contradictory, discordant moral beliefs? At present, for example, television has such considerable influence on children's moral beliefs that some writers claim television has replaced parents.[59] This focus on television does not suggest that it is the only factor affecting children's character; rather, it is one prominent influence among many. Can very young children make rational judgments about which diverse moral beliefs presented by television should be included in their character?[60] If these are not rational choices and Mill does not indicate that young children make such rational, self-conscious choices, how do young children watching television accept some moral beliefs and reject others? Is this merely a random process or are some television programs and stimuli more persuasive than others? Finally, does the child possess some internal propensity that influences selective acceptance and rejection of television stimuli? The issue here is not what effect television has on children or whether that effect is good or bad. The question is whether some recognizable, agreed upon *culture* presently molds everyone's character. The question is whether culture can be conceptualized to give us the hegemonic view that Mill assumes. Or at this particular time and place have exceptionally diverse societal values replaced the hegemony of an earlier culture?

While Mill knew what it meant to be a nineteenth-century Englishman or Englishwoman and what moral character and virtues were acceptable for each, we now might ask whether Mill referred to one class, the cultured or aristocratic English gentleman and gentlewoman. Leslie Stephen personified at its highest level the character of the English gentleman. As Stephen's daughter, Virginia Woolf quoted from a cardboard strip over the fireplace, "What is it to be a gentleman? It is to be tender to women, chivalrous to servants."[61] Even in the twentieth century, we can vicariously meet these gentlemen whose moral characters overflowed with suitable traits, including the standards quoted from Woolf's "chocolate coloured strip." In Trollope's novels we meet these gentlemen and recognize their sterling characters. Plantagenet Palliser, Phineas Finn, John Grey, and the old Duke of Omnium rekindle our belief in the moral character of nineteenth-century Englishmen. And we can easily distinguish them from their opposites, those whose character is unworthy, the deceitful George Vavasor and Mr. Bott. Lady Glencora Palliser personifies the best character of an aristocratic Englishwoman, while those like Mrs. Marsham must be condemned by us just as she was by Lady Glencora. It did not matter if only these few and perhaps also the Duke's secretary, physician, and curate also possessed the character traits of a gentleman. For even this was a very small portion of the total population. In one sense, the character and moral standards of the rest of the population were unimportant, unimportant in that they could in no way aspire to the character or station of a Plantagenet Pallisar. Yet the character of the masses assumed great importance. The masses had to accept "their stations and its duties" for the continuing strength of the morality and character of the nineteenth-century "proper" Englishman and Englishwoman.[62] One must thus wonder whom Mill was speaking about when he described character "developed and modified by his own culture." Was this character possessed by anyone other than certain members of the intellectual, educated, and aristocratic classes?

There is no such agreed upon standard or model of the ideal moral character for the late twentieth-century American, Englishman, or Englishwoman. Thus, if today's educators look for the central moral traits required by our culture, what they might discover is disagreement about the central, important features of our culture's moral traits.[63] Is it wholly valid to claim that no central character features can be agreed upon? Can character be the basis of moral education if there is no agreement concerning the central features of culture and the values and moral ideals that moral agents should accept?

During the early part of the twentieth century, Dewey defined character as "the interpenetration of habits," which "can be read through the medium of individual acts."[64] This definition interrelates with the remainder of Dewey's philosophy, ethical theory, and theory of human nature. According to Dewey, habits and thus character develop through an interaction or transaction between inner and outer, between passive and active, between subject and object, between duty and interest, and between impulse and habit. The individual's habits are what define that person's character, and that character can be recognized through the external acts performed by the person. If someone possesses character, she also acts in certain ways. It would be impossible to claim that someone possesses a certain character and yet be unable to cite any relevant instances of conduct or acts performed. Character and conduct, for Dewey, as well as motive and act, will and deed are inseparable.[65]

Dewey steers away from the "eulogistic cover" of the expression "judgments of principle" and is content to refer to judgments of tendency. Character is thus not only the interpenetration of habits, but also the *tendency* to act in certain foreseeable ways. With weak, underdeveloped, or fragmented habits, there will be less tendency to perform the acts correlative to those habits; while the person with a strong interpenetration of habits, but yet not rigid, dogmatic habits, will be much more likely to perform his or her corresponding acts. The strength of particular habits or interacting groups of habits are the defining mark, what has engraved itself to become the image of character. Rather than saying an agent lives according to certain moral principles or acts on moral principles, Dewey would claim that the person's habits are so structured as to create a greater tendency to act in a given manner. Only a saint or Kant's moral agent with a perfect will or "good will" would always perform the right act; in this case, we could not speak of "tendency," since in all situations the actions would be right, good, and correct. For "normal" human beings, according to Dewey, only the tendency to perform a moral act can be expected. In response to the Hartshorne and May studies questioning the generality of character traits, Dewey would say that these studies demonstrated the obvious, that children and even adults will not unswervingly act in accordance with certain character traits.

Using Dewey's notion of character, how would a person's character be evaluated? Are all forms of character equally valid? What type of character should educators aim to develop in their students? Though Dewey does not shun these difficult questions, his answers at times raise additional, equally difficult problems. Let's take the first two questions first and then look at the educational issues Dewey's views raise. Dewey distinguishes between different character structures and their habits. He rejects both fragmented, unconnected, weak habits and rigid, narrow habits and advocates habits that will foster growth and have positive qualities.[66] All character and habits are not equal; some are of far greater value. Speaking of the interpenetration of habits and habits that foster continuing growth does not resolve the problem of which habits and which quality habits should be sought. Logically, there could be a great variety of habits that would meet Dewey's criteria of being educative, growth producing, interpenetrating each other, and possessing other positive qualities. But as Dewey recognized, a great variety of habits is not the same as all habits. The problem we are left with is how to assess what quality habits and which character is the most advantageous.

If there is no single moral character or no group of moral characters that are recommended, how would educators know which habits and which character to foster? Dewey wrote during an era of transition, but that period had a rather different configuration from the present period of radical value change. The Protestant ethos and a civic hegemony still dominated children's lives. The diversity that educators now confront had not surfaced. Dewey did not have to be concerned with large segments of the public rejecting the cultural hegemony and questioning what the school's mission should be. When the Progressive movement accepted student-directed education, Dewey chafed. He expected that the society, the family, and the school would provide a settled environment of the best experiences as these had developed historically. With these agreed upon experiences, the child's moral character would form and serve as the basis for later moral education. Dewey's vision of a liberal democratic society and public education that used all the many tools science had developed has not survived unscathed. Dewey's position no longer seems to serve our moral education purposes. It is not just Dewey's educational agenda that needs reforming, but also some of his ideas about character and the moral person.

Dewey saw the need to change and clarify some of his concepts. But the way he modified or rather downgraded the concept "character" within his ethical theory must cause us to wonder about other aspects of his theory. Using Occam's razor, we could shave the concept "character" from Dewey's theory and a coherent view of human nature and morality would still remain; moral conduct could still be explained and understood. In other words, why use the term "character" as a synonym for the interpenetration of habits and tendency to act in a certain way? Why not just speak of the habits themselves, their interpenetration, coherency, continuity, flexibility, inflexibility, and/or fragmentation? Perhaps Dewey assumed that the concept "character" was an unnecessary residue from older theories. For example, a comparison of the two editions of Dewey and Tuft's *Ethics* reveals that character does not retain the same role and importance in both editions. It almost seems that Dewey gradually eliminates the notion "character" and wholly relies instead on habit, reflective thinking, and intelligence. But Dewey's view of character cannot be dismissed too quickly. For it is much more far-reaching than indicated here. Dewey posits both a process by which a child's character develops and the means to change this original character, and he extends morality and moral education to include intelligence as a broader notion than rational thought processes and problem solving.

During the last decade, R. S. Peters traveled against the philosophic tide and analyzed the concept "character." While admitting that character and character traits can include a wide host of both negative and positive qualities, Peters points to the ambiguous nature of the concept. Statements about character can be noncommittal, refer to types of character, or designate an agent having character.[67] According to Peters,

> Character-traits [and thus, one's character] are shown in the sort of things a man can *decide* to be, where it may be a matter of forcing himself to do something in the face of social pressures or persistent temptations. . . . His inclinations and desires, which are part of his 'nature', may suggest goals; but such inclinations and desires only enter into what we call a man's

'character' in so far as he chooses to satisfy them in a certain manner, in accordance with rules of efficiency like persistently, carefully, doggedly, painstakingly, or in accordance with rules of social appropriateness like honestly, fairly, considerately, and ruthlessly.[68]

A person's character is revealed "in what he does about . . . (desires, appetites, cravings, or lust), in the manner in which he regulates, or fails to regulate them."[69] Character, according to Peters, is not goal-directed, but refers to the style or manner in which some goal is reached or rule followed.[70]

In addition to linking "character and some sort of personal effort,"[71] Peters argues two other theses. First, character and character traits can be self-chosen and thus are rational "sorts of things." Second, since character indicates the style or manner in which some goal is pursued and not what goal is sought, there must be another means by which the agent chooses a goal. Moral education, according to this view, is "the development of an autonomous type of character who follows rules in a rational discriminating manner, and who also has character."[72] Rules are to be justified with higher-order principles. Only one problem with this account of character is noted here. Peters poses an unwarranted dichotomy between character and rules, with character being the style by which rules are carried out. If an agent possesses character traits like persistence, honesty, and fairness,[73] then not only will rules (desires and goals) be satisfied in certain ways. Just as important, the character traits will be factors in determining what goals and rules the agent accepts.

In another essay,[74] which does not refer to character, Peters attempts to bridge the gap between habits and rational thought. Akin to the views of Plato, Aristotle, and Dewey, Peters's argument is that early childhood habit formation is consistent with the later development of rational thought processes. This same position can be used to maintain that the early formation of character in no way negates a mature moral agent's rational thought processes, ability to use moral principles, or questioning of moral character.

Fundamental to the development of morality and character is the quality of education received during infancy and early childhood. Moral education does not begin at the age of reason and is not the sole purview of teachers and schools; rather, it is a continuing process. As Protagoras recognized, parents, teachers, and society in general "teach and admonish . . . from earliest childhood till the last day of their lives."[75] Rather than a narrowed view of education as formal schooling, I return to the earlier generalized use of education as it has been understood from Protagoras and Socrates, Plato and Aristotle to John Dewey. Dewey, for example, extends education by saying that "philosophy may even be defined *as the general theory of education*."[76]

With other subjects, whether algebra, geography, or chemistry, it seems perfectly sensible to refer to formal education and thus use the term "education" in some suitably narrowed sense.[77] At the same time that becoming moral and acquiring character may be similar in certain ways to acquiring the skills and knowledge of formal school subjects, there are still formidable differences. The disparity is based on formal school subjects and morality having domains of very different sizes and types. Moral education, as Ryle once noted, is not something apart from other subjects, but actually cuts across and occurs within these subjects. Someone does not become a good accountant or a good scientist in the sense of only acquiring certain skill and knowledge. The acquiring of the skills and knowledge of a subject, profession, or trade includes acquiring its moral dimensions.

Moral education is different from school subjects in another way. A considerable portion of moral education, for example, happens outside the school, in every corner and every aspect of a person's life. Yet even though moral education is different from formal school subjects and extends far beyond the school into all sorts of educational networks, the school has a special role in effective moral education. School is distinguished from the remainder of a child's environment and experiences. As Martin Buber recognized,

Character is formed by the interpenetration of all those multifarious, opposing influences. And yet, among this infinity of form-giving forces the educator [teacher] is the only one element among innumerable others, but distinct from them all by his *will* to take part in the stamping of character and by his *consciousness* that he represents in the eyes of the growing person a certain *selection* of what is, the selection of what is "right", of what *should* be.[78]

Though the theory of moral education developed in this book looks at some of the infinite form-giving forces and how they influence character, the main emphasis will be on those few forces that should have the greatest conscious impact on the development of moral character (e.g., primarily parents, schools, and teachers).

In the long journey of this chapter, we have seen why the notion "character" should again be included in a theory of moral education. A number of issues were included in the discussion of the role of character in morality and moral education: questions about the parameters of the moral domain and about what situations are inherently moral. The question of why character was eliminated from moral education theories was answered by turning to two Anglo-American philosophic positions that dominated long periods of the twentieth century. We discerned during that investigaton that these theories did not just relate to the moral but also included assumptions about the nature of the moral agent. Finally, we considered a few recent positions that included the notion "character" and thus seemed to take a different direction from mainstream moral philosophy.

Before positing a different view of character in a later chapter, we should note another criticism of these recent investigations of character. Just as mainstream twentieth-century moral philosophy tacitly accepted underlying assumptions about human nature and moral personhood, the few very recent theorists who wrote about character also made assumptions about human nature and accepted a psychological position. Even if this psychology was not a carbon copy of earlier faculty psychologies, it did inherit some of their weaknesses. For example, the development of character like other learning was additive, based on the sum of the parts. The moral agent, in this case, became the sum of desires, impulses, habits, emotions, and the like. Whereas some had the problem of not accepting the concept "character" as a viable notion underlying moral agency and moral personhood, the few moral philosophers positing the concept had a mistaken idea of human nature, and this psychological view of the moral person could not sustain a concept like character. At times, a theory of character does not include a concept of self. Without a self, it is difficult to understand how the concept "character" can be sustained.[79] Later chapters address this issue of how a moral theory and theory of moral education must include an adequate theory of human nature.

3

An Interlude: Character Excellence— Fidelity

One moral excellence, "fidelity," is examined in this chapter to provide another introduction to the conceptualization of character. Fidelity is chosen as an example of a character excellence for a number of reasons. First, friendship and fidelity do not require any extraordinary intellectual ability. Friendship has never been monopolized by one group of especially fortunate or superior individuals. All human being have been experts in this area. Second, like other character excellences, fidelity is not a singular excellence, but a structure of various excellences. These other necessary excellences are not always writ large on the face of fidelity, but exist below the surface and are tacitly assumed. An explanation of the complex structure of any one moral excellence indicates some of the difficulties confronting moral education.

Third, as concepts of intellectual interest, friendship and fidelity have had an unfortunate recent history. Why, some may wonder, has ethics relegated friendship and fidelity to the dustbin though these concepts should have basic meaning and importance in every human life.[1] Why have these concepts been ignored at a time when friendship and fidelity, like all other human interpersonal relationships, are undergoing considerable change? Finally, why has no philosopher of education been concerned with the problem of fidelity and friendship?[2] The demise of interest in these two concepts has gone hand in hand with the direction ethical theory has taken.

An investigation of the character excellence "fidelity" can thus serve a number of purposes. Fidelity can provide a wedge to question the shortcomings of neo-Kantian and utilitarian ethics as the sole bases of moral education. In addition, this concept suggests that moral education is not just some icing on an educational cake. It cannot be limited to a single course. Instead, moral education in the form advocated here would radically transform American education. Though the character trait fidelity applies primarily to friendship and marriage, in this section only fidelity's relationship to friendship is examined.

Fidelity, Utilitarianism, and Neo-Kantian Ethics

As a character excellence that includes loyalty, devotion, and faithfulness, the fidelity of friendship cannot be understood through a utilitarian consequentialist ethic or neo-Kantian deontological ethic. This investigation of why teleological and deontological theories cannot accommodate a moral excellence like fidelity begins with an example. In his youth J. Robert Oppenheimer had no interest in politics or issues of social welfare. Science was his whole life. But the world prior to World War II was full of social and political unrest. The severity of the Depression in the United States and emotional enthusiasm for the ideals of the Russian Revolution created conditions for many intellectuals to believe that perhaps the American experiment had run its course and that there had to be a more humane society and political system. As a young faculty member, Oppenheimer's social life included numerous people who were Communists or had Communist sympathies. During a brief time, Oppenheimer himself studied Marxist writings and listened to discussions about social issues and Communism. When Oppenheimer was to be named director of the Los Alamos project to develop the atomic bomb, security issues were raised. Government agents questioned whether he was loyal to the country or a security risk. Had he met with Russian agents? Who among Oppenheimer's friends or relatives might have suggested such a meeting? Oppenheimer's innocence or naïvité, his intent or motivation was not the issue. Loyalty to country could be demonstrated only by naming names. Should Oppenheimer have given the security agents the one name they wanted, that of his friend Haakon Chevalier? The answer to this question, some might say, can be found in utilitarianism. The issue for utilitarianism is the consequences of respective plans of action. A utilitarian might argue that Oppenheimer had to consider the greater good when he weighed loyalty to his friend against loyalty to his country. Loyalty to country outweighed friendship because the development of the atomic bomb would save thousands of lives and end the Second World War. In a calculus of goods, loyalty to country and saving thousands of lives would certainly calculate to a greater good for a greater number than maintaining personal loyalty to a single friend.

Actually, the moral dilemma noted here cannot be correctly understood if it is described through the language of utilitarianism. Critics of utilitarianism have noted difficulties with the calculative reasoning necessary to compare the consequences of alternative courses of action. With a moral excellence such as fidelity even more serious difficulties arise. The concept "fidelity" itself cannot even exist in this ethical theory's vocabulary. This assertion can be sustained by a closer examination of how a utilitarian would resolve a moral dilemma. When confronted by a moral dilemma with two or more incompatible, alternative courses of action, a moral agent should choose the one whose consequences maximize the good for the greatest number, the good often being human happiness. If one alternative involves infidelity of informing on a friend and the other fidelity, utilitarianism cannot come to grips with the heart of the problem. Utilitarianism looks only at the consequences of the act, not at what happens to the agent's moral self or character.[3] The problem here is twofold.

First, the concept "fidelity" does not refer to consequences of actions, but to the quality of the relationship between two (or more) human beings.

Second, utilitarianism is a behavioral form of ethics in that what happens inside the moral agent's skin—how the moral self changes—is relatively unimportant. The insignificance of the self and the lack of a credible theory of self means that moral excellences fundamentally grounded in a notion of self are eliminated.[4] Only the external consequences of some overt action measurable in happiness units can satisfy the tenets of utilitarianism. A utilitarian cannot cite a moral agent's fidelity to a friend since fidelity refers to the inner condition of the moral agent and thus is not measurable in the way prescribed by utilitarianism. The utilitarian would reword the dilemma and cite external matters of fact, referring to the actual behavioral acts (e.g., informing on a friend, gossiping about a friend, never seeing the friend again, or dating the friend's beloved). In each case, the moral excellence "fidelity" does not enter the scene; only particular behavioral events and their consequences are considered.

This utilitarian calculus has an even more difficult aspect. It cannot consider a friend as a more or less important category of human beings. Rather, a friend would be dissolved into the larger category "human beings"; the calculus of goods would not change whether the person were a friend or any unknown human being. The alternative would thus become "informing on another human being." In a sense, this is a dire problem. If a friend is nothing more than an abstract notion, "human being," and has no more or fewer claims and no more or fewer obligations than any other human being, then the category "friend" has no moral meaning. Every human being becomes a friend and a friend every human being. Though a utilitarian resolves the moral problem confronting Oppenheimer, the dilemma is moved into a different arena and changed so drastically that its original, concrete dimensions are unrecognizable. What was an intimate relationship between two caring friends has now become a moral equation that involves two abstract human beings in a situation with many other equally important human beings.

A deontological ethic of principles would also claim to resolve the Oppenheimer moral dilemma. Oppenheimer could devise a universalizable principle such as, "if a moral agent can save thousands of lives, he should reveal secrets about a friend." Yet this resolution ignores Kant's other categorical imperative and uses the friend as a means, though a means to save thousands of lives. Any decision to be true to one's friend and ignore the interests of unknown thousands would treat those human beings as means. These comments, however, do not make sense of the problem. As with utilitarianism, a neo-Kantian principled judgment has no place in its theoretic net for the moral concept "fidelity." Neo-Kantian ethics eliminates such person-qualities or person-virtues as fidelity and detaches a moral dilemma from the concrete life and personal characteristics of the moral agent and anyone else involved in the moral dilemma.[5] In place of the inner moral qualities of the moral agent, neo-Kantian ethics stresses the agent's ability to reason and judge in accordance with formal principles. The moral agent and friend become placemarks in an abstract analysis that uses universalizable formal principles.

Though the importance of neo-Kantian theory for public moral dilemmas between unknown individuals and groups can be understood, two caveats about its monopolization of moral theory are noted here. First, in the public domain neo-Kantian ethics must be tempered with other features of the moral life.[6] A judgment based on Kantian criteria according to this view cannot stand by itself. It needs to be moderated and compared with some other sorts of standards. In other words, the logical in itself cannot furnish wholly tolerable moral judgments and actions. Second, deontology's appropriateness for personal, intimate relationships must be questioned. If every moral dilemma involving a friend is resolved with formal principles, then does the moral agent refer to friendship or to the treatment of another person *qua* human being? Fidelity eludes the grasp of either utilitarianism or Kantian theory.

The criteria governing fidelity cannot be dependent on abstract, formal principles or even on whether a friend "behaves ill."[7] Since the moral theory and methods he advocates cannot catch fidelity in its net, Sidgwick understandably notes the "difficulties in determining the moral obligations of friendship."[8] Why not respond to Sidgwick by first agreeing that the moral obligations of friendship are indeed difficult to judge? The obligations of friendship may be even more difficult to assess when they conflict with other interests and obligations. Such theoretical difficulties, however, should not eliminate consideration of fidelity, since all types of moral obligations may also be exceptionally difficult to assess. If fidelity is taken out of the utilitarian or neo-Kantian theater, fidelity acquires different dimensions and can be based on a different rationale.[9] The point here is that if an ethical theory cannot make room for a fundamental human interpersonal relationship, then perhaps the problem lies with the ethical theory, not the relationship or virtue. Why say, as Sidgwick has, that it is difficult to assess the obligations of friendship? Why not say instead that we need an ethical theory that can include such qualities as fidelity?

Fidelity: Point-Counterpoint: Criticism and Response

A dissenter may contend that my change of venue does not resolve the actual problem posed at the beginning of the last section (e.g., the Oppenheimer-Chevalier dilemma), and cannot resolve other similar moral dilemmas involving fidelity and other moral excellences. In response to challenges, four sorts of issues are considered.

a. The first of the problems confronting a moral excellence like fidelity concerns mutuality and questions of whether there can be degrees of fidelity. What of the friend who "behaves ill" instead of maintaining fidelity? Does that friend possess the requisite character excellence "fidelity?" These questions contain a number of problems. To discuss them without tripping over designations in a two-friend dyad, I refer to friend A and friend B as the two parties of the friendship. There is the problem of whether the friend is actually a friend or a passing acquaintance. This is noted as an issue since the term "friend" often has multiple referents and is used in an ambiguous manner. If a passing acquaintance is boorish, insulting, or morally offensive in some manner, this would not justify an agent's behaving ill to that person. It might mean that the agent must make moral judgments depending on moral standards other than fidelity. If the person is a friend, unacceptable behavior could be explained in two ways: First, friend A may possess the character excellence "fidelity" in such a weakened form that infringements of fidelity frequently occur. Now the question arises whether friend B should accept the infringements of fidelity by friend A or whether there must be some mutuality of fidelity between friend A and friend B. Whether or not fidelity is wholly mutual does not negate fidelity as a moral excellence for one moral agent. The lack of mutuality does not excuse the infidelity of one friend, either friend A or friend B. With fidelity as with integrity, sincerity, and other moral excellences, whether friend A possesses the moral excellence should not influence friend B's struggle to maintain that excellence. Other matters that may influence a withholding of fidelity must be considered in another section.

An absence or inadequate form of fidelity must be extended to consider another idea. Friendship and fidelity are not two wholly separate notions since in order for friendship to exist, there must be some sort of fidelity as well. Even a friendship of use, according to Aristotle a lesser form of friendship, must include a degree of fidelity in the friendship as a use relationship. For without fidelity, there can be no loyalty, confidentiality, or trust between the two members of the friendship. In stronger terms, there can be no friendship, even of the lesser quality designated by Aristotle.

Even if both friends possess fidelity, shortcomings are possible. As Hume notes, "we know, in general, that the characters of men are, to a certain degree inconstant and irregular."[10] Fidelity is an ideal that human beings can seek

to achieve and yet occasionally fail to maintain in actual
interpersonal relationships. This failure in no way negates
the actuality of fidelity. As perhaps with Oppenheimer, one
may forever remember and regret the infidelity. In a person's life, it may be a tragic shadow whether excusable or
inexcusable. Moral life is exceptionally complex and no
theory can promise moral agents will always make the right
choice or that moral life will be without its errors and scars
or that there will be no remorse. A theory should address
all the complexities and diversity of moral life and include
the moral victories and failures, the tragedies and heroism.

   b. What happens if a friend is faced with a moral dilemma that goes beyond the borders of fidelity? For example, perhaps the Oppenheimer-Chevalier problem was not
merely a matter of fidelity. With this case, the moral agent
not only confronts a conflict between the loyalty felt toward
a friend and the responsibilities toward country, profession, scientific knowledge, and other unknown human
beings. In addition, there may be a conflict between one's
inner character (i.e., who the moral agent is) and the demands and interests of a public life. The moral agent per-
ceives himself or herself as being a particular type of person and as possessing a particular moral character. In the
present moral dilemma, the moral agent's character is
called into question. The demands of the moral dilemma
are not resolvable with the moral agent's character excellences. If the moral agent, in this case Oppenheimer, expects to remain an active participant in public and professional life, he cannot ignore the dilemma or just react
according to well-accepted modes of conduct.

   The final judgment Oppenheimer made or might
have made is not the issue here, but what sorts of questions
the moral agent might consider. First, questions may be
raised about whether the other person is really a friend or
just someone who has been manipulating the moral agent.
This problem of manipulation instead of friendship can be
seen by briefly turning to another example. In an altogether different case, the American Michael Straight,
while a Cambridge University student, was asked by his
university tutor to become a mole for a foreign power.

Straight was told that some friends had decided that this was the direction he should follow.[11] What Straight did or what he actually thought at that moment is relatively unimportant. What might have been the questions someone would have asked about Straight's relationship with these various "friends?" One might have wondered whether Burgess and others who wanted Straight to become a spy were bona fide friends. Were those requesting that Straight become a mole unfairly manipulating him for their own or a foreign power's advantage? However, even wondering about the relationship between Straight and his friends seems misplaced. The requests made of Straight go far beyond the borders of friendship and fidelity. Similar questions about the quality of a friendship may at times occur in far less disastrous situations than Straight's. Friend A may discover that friend B's conduct and intentions have been manipulative. The sadness that accompanies such questioning and negative discoveries may in one sense relate to the cessation of fidelity in that particular case. And yet even here, with the cessation of a friendship, friend A may do nothing to damage the moral excellence "fidelity." Even though friendship requires fidelity, fidelity is not friendship. Agents may not question their moral excellences and character, but they will question whether some action is required by the excellences or whether moral excellences are appropriate for certain situations.

Let's return to a moral dilemma where there is a question regarding whether friend A should remain loyal to friend B or should follow a rather different course and be disloyal. In this particular dilemma, the problem may not be whether the moral agent betrays a friend and displays infidelity. Whereas the agent interprets the problem as involving fidelity, the moral problem is incorrectly interpreted. To demonstrate his loyalty to his country and prove he was not a security risk, Oppenheimer had been told to reveal the names of Communist sympathizers. Had Oppenheimer steered the questioners in this direction as a means of insuring himself a much coveted position? Perhaps Oppenheimer did not have the dilemma stated above. In other words, he might have informed on his friend to further self-interest and attain greater power and prestige. He might have created a moral dilemma that could have been avoided. Whether or not this hypothetical interpretation of Oppenheimer's moral dilemma is valid is of little importance.[12] The only issue here is that at times the dilemma in question does not involve disloyalty to a friend as one price of resolution.

c. Must fidelity always be maintained? Must one always remain loyal to a friend? Certain reasons cannot be given to justify infidelity, disloyalty, and faithlessness. Reasons such as a greater hedonistic pleasure, personal aggrandisement, materialistic gains, or the quest for power hardly seem justification for the negation of a character excellence. Though friends should not continually make peevish or churlish demands, in another sense the marks of friendship and fidelity are often recognized just because they are maintained in extreme situations and no matter the agreeableness of the friend. In many extraordinary and difficult situations the moral agent does not cease being a friend or reject the responsibilities of fidelity. Unfortunate experiences or demands may enter any friendship and yet the friendship and its concomitant fidelity are maintained. Here as elsewhere, Aristotle's idea of the mean may apply. Fidelity accordingly would not be a positive quality that opposes some negative quality. Rather, fidelity is the mean between two negative extremes, in one case perhaps disloyalty and on the other side, henpecked meekness.

d. The comments made so far about the maintenance of fidelity seem unrealistic in certain ways. Fidelity is not just tested in daily interactions with a friend or because of petty personal demands. There are more serious moral dilemmas in which fidelity to a friend is only one dimension of the situation. In what sorts of cases and under what conditions can the intrusion of alternate moral considerations affect a character excellence such as fidelity? With some friendships (e.g., that of Achilles and Patrocles[13]) other issues could rarely intervene into the primary relationship.[14] If any character excellence like fidelity could easily be swept aside, it would be a rather weak and ineffective basis for certain interpersonal relationships. One would hardly expect fidelity, for example, to be questioned frequently, because friendship and thus some form of fidelity is a dominant characteristic in the average person's daily life. One tragedy of moral life is the tragedy Oppenheimer experienced, that his fidelity was tested by an exceptional situation and perhaps, with his solution, he could not measure up to the character standards he had set for himself.

However, this matter must be viewed in yet another way. Though character excellences can be foundational for a considerable portion of moral life, there is no guarantee that they can determine all aspects of a moral life. At times, moral excellences may conflict with each other. At other times, unusual events or moral dilemmas cause one to question moral priorities and even modify already formed moral character. Should friend A protect and be loyal to friend B no matter the situation and no matter friend B's actions? What if friend B had committed heinous crimes, had been blatantly cruel, or was selling drugs to children? What if friend B psychologically abused his family or his firmly held character changed in such a negative way that it became morally offensive to friend A? Before deciding what friend A should do, whether friend A should remain loyal to friend B, we turn to two metaphoric expressions to clarify the decision friend A must make and suggest what sort of standard can be used to make this judgment. To understand these metaphors, we must make a brief detour.

In Plato's Allegory of the Cave, prisoners are chained so they can see only reflections of objects and hear echoes of words. After a prisoner is freed, the first steps toward enlightenment are described in this way: The freed prisoner is "compelled to stand up suddenly and turn his head around and walk and to lift his eyes to the light."[15] The metaphor expressions of interest here are "turning around" and "lifting one's eyes." Neither of these ideas is foreign to the Platonic corpus. Cloaked in a considerable variety of linguistic forms, these metaphors continually symbolize the search for moral knowledge and moral bewilderment, learning and sophistry, awakening to one's ignorance and confusion, inner uncertainty and external moral standards. Turning one's head around represents the first search to understand what the actual situation is. This is a delicate process. Just as the freed prisoner would like to turn away when the light is too bright, one might "turn away" when not prepared to understand.

In other dialogues, the interlocutors of sophists are not turned around. At times, they are entertained and flattered and thus continue to look at what they had previously believed. A Sophist may also make interlocutors dizzy, twirling them around so swiftly that they become wholly confused and cannot focus on what they really believe and disbelieve. In the early dialogues, Socrates aims to jar or stun an interlocutor only to the extent that the interlocutor is turned in the correct direction and begins to question firmly held moral beliefs. But this examination of sincerely held moral beliefs eventually cannot just involve logical dimensions. Instead, as Plato recognized by using the idea of lifting one's eyes, there must be some external standard(s) by which to evaluate firmly held moral beliefs. The issue here is not whether lifting one's eyes refers to a different level of moral reality. Instead, the question is what sorts of objective standards can influence and even compel a moral agent to reconsider whether a moral excellence such fidelity or loyalty applies to a particularly difficult situation. Gazing in a different direction, turning around, and lifting one's eyes to the light all refer to the notion of seeing the moral situation in another manner and focusing on which external standards should be applied to it.[16]

How do these comments about turning around and lifting one's eyes apply to how friend A views or assesses the moral situation and relationship with friend B? The Oppenheimer-Chevalier incident is much more complicated than indicated thus far. The variety and complexity of the dimensions suggest that neither Oppenheimer nor Chevalier was faced with a simple problem or choice. The whole political, social, intellectual, and scientific climate together with the exceptionally complex personalities of the main protagonists might have to be considered to understand what was at stake when we ask whether Oppenheimer should have remained loyal to Chevalier, whether the question was loyalty to country or friend, and finally, whether Chevalier with his knowledge of Oppenheimer's betrayal should have remained loyal to Oppenheimer.

In terms of the metaphoric expressions of turning around and lifting one's eyes, we might speculate that Oppenheimer had turned around and lifted his eyes. But the standard(s) his eyes were focused on were those of physical science and the life of the scientist. His interest in social inequities, political movements, and the suffering of various people was comparatively casual. It did not involve the long, painful search and the examination of standards that science continually compelled. Science was the master and Oppenheimer the slave.[17] What would an alternative have been for Oppenheimer? What if he had sought a "higher" standard, one that referred to the moral dimensions of life? Might Oppenheimer have made a different choice? Might Oppenheimer have acted in a manner that would simultaneously have insured his loyalty to country and loyalty to friend? Unquestionably, one can depict a number of alternative scenarios in which Oppenheimer was a more skillful tightrope walker. We can think of how at many crucial junctures he might have overcome his own quest for self-aggrandisement. With this turning around and turning away from self to look in another direction for a higher moral standard, Oppenheimer might have done otherwise. But in these alternative scenarios, Oppenheimer would not have been Oppenheimer. Oppenheimer like all tragic heroes possessed a tragic flaw.

What about more common cases of fidelity versus infidelity, loyalty versus disloyalty? With many of these cases, this dichotomy between fidelity and infidelity or loyalty and disloyalty is not tenable. Friend A is loyal to friend B. Friend B acts in a way that friend A questions. Friend B is the psychologically abusive parent, completely thoughtless of other people's feelings, excessively selfish or greedy, or generally begins to display various forms of behavior and character structure friend A cannot accept. Friend A may continue to feel love, sympathy, and pity for B. But must friend A's character excellence "fidelity" still be maintained? With the metaphors thus far noted, we can en-

visage how friend A might approach this situation. If some
higher and external standards have exerted a force on
friend A, this person will simultaneously turn toward those
standards and keep an eye on the moral dilemma. This is
not the dogmatic and passive acceptance of an authoritarian credo. This is the reflexive struggle to understand what
is the right and true way. During this struggle, friend A
might not remain silent, but might discuss the situation
with friend B. Friend A may suffer and almost despair,
may search for additional evidence and seek to clarify the
situation. But yet the mind remains affixed on the moral
excellence, the higher moral standards, and the friend
within this moral situation. If friend A decides that loyalty
cannot be maintained, that the higher moral standards require another way, this does not imply that friend A no
longer possesses the moral excellence "fidelity." Instead,
this decision and ensuing action suggests that fidelity and
loyalty were not the appropriate moral excellences for this
situation.

Further comment is necessary. Friendship is one dimension of the good life. To say that friendship can be
questioned does not mean that there is a continual assessment of a friend or that such situations arise because of
small misunderstandings. Instead, there is recognition that
at times situations can arise when friendships are tested.
During these periods, most human beings search for ways
of maintaining the friendship and this means maintaining
the loyalty to a friend. There is the recognition of the ordinary failings of ordinary human beings, the moral excellence requirements of friendship, and the intuitive understanding of the value of such relationships. However, there
are rare times when even a friend must be prepared to
turn toward higher moral standards. Subsequent decisions
may then be accompanied by sorrow and tragedy. For the
friend was not some transient external good, but an inim-
itable part of the self.

e. One final aspect of moral excellences like fidelity
must briefly hold our attention.[18] This is the idea that
fidelity exists within a structured framework of other moral excellences. For example, many moral excellences re-

quire courage. There has to be courage to question a friendship and turn around to look at other standards. There has to be courage to question one's own character and moral excellences. There must be courage to remain loyal to all sorts of ideals in all sorts of trying situations. There must be courage to turn away from a friend when such turning away is necessary.

The network of excellences of which fidelity is only one dimension can be pictured in a number of different yet interrelated ways. Some of these excellences are almost wholly moral excellences or at least have their primary significant home in the moral domain. Other excellences have meaning in a number of different domains. On the level of primarily moral excellences, fidelity is interwoven with many other excellences, with loyalty, truthfulness, honesty, sincerity, respect, and courage. Excellences like truthfulness and honesty are just not a part of fidelity even though these other excellences are necessary conceptual components of fidelity. Simultaneously, fidelity is not just truthfulness, honesty, loyalty, or any other single moral excellence. In other words, it is impossible to say that fidelity is just a structure of a limited number of other excellences without its possessing a unique territory of its own. Instead, other excellences take unique coloration when residing within the network that centers on fidelity.

This issue of the relationship between the one dominant moral excellence for one situation and the structure of necessary related excellences can be seen in another light. With an orchestra and pianist playing a piano concerto, the audience reflexively seems to concentrate first on the single instrument and then on the orchestra. Yet, in a very real way, this is not the nature of the audience's experience. The music emanating from the orchestra and pianist is not dependent first on the pianist playing alone, then the orchestra and pianist playing in unison, and finally the orchestra playing alone. Rather, even when the pianist is the only instrument heard, the orchestra has a role. For the audience is braced for the orchestra to take up themes being played on the piano and at the same time, when the piano and orchestra are playing together, the audience lis-

tens in suspense waiting for the piano alone to emerge
from the orchestra. Similar to the piano playing alone, at
times, someone thinks that fidelity alone is the moral excellence that governs conduct. The moral excellence "fidelity"
is more similar to both the cases of (1) the piano playing
solo and the orchestra waiting to enter, and (2) the piano
and orchestra playing together. In this case, the orchestra
does not just form an innocuous background for the solo
piano, but highlights, nourishes, forms, and unifies the
playing. Analogously, fidelity is the solo instrument, but requires other moral excellences, its orchestra, to enrich and
develop the outstanding, necessary themes.

There are other excellences that are not designated as
moral excellences. Intellectual excellences are necessary
components forming networks with moral excellences. Aristotle stresses this and states that "choice cannot exist either without reason and intellect or without a moral state:
for good action and its opposite cannot exist without a
combination of intellect and character."[19]

4

A Conceptualization of Character

In this chapter, there must finally be a reckoning, the presentation of a conceptualization of character. Yet before beginning this conceptualization, we must note two other concerns, first look ahead to future chapters, and second, comment about the theory of human nature or the philosophy of psychology that underlies character.

The journey of this present chapter is long and involved. It can only include brief comments about education. Thus, the next chapter is devoted to what type of moral education this conceptualization of character would recommend. The issue is not one of which variety of disparate moral education implications are possible from the conceptualization of character presented here. The separation of these two concerns into two chapters is required not because of disparity between these two matters, but because of the lengthy discussion needed for both problems. Later chapters turn in yet another direction. Though this theory gives character a central role in moral life and moral education, character is not the sole means to resolve moral dilemmas or the sole basis of moral agency. At the heart of this theory is the assumption that morality, the moral life, and moral education require many diverse dimensions, not a single component. Character provides a means of refocusing moral education. The recent overemphasis on moral conflicts, divergent claims, interests, rights, moral reasoning, and abstract principles has simultaneously blurred other components of the moral life (e.g., the quality of ordinary public and private life, daily social interactions, common interpersonal relations, and the moral person or self making moral judgments and manifesting moral action). Instead of denying the existence of conflicting claims, interests, and rights, the need for moral reasoning and abstract principles, I have argued that the moral domain should be enlarged to include situations and relationships that were once taken-for-granted.

In a seminal article, Anscombe questions whether modern moral theory can do its job unless it is provided with a rather different and more adequate philosophy of psychology than is presently accepted.[1] In earlier sections of this book it was briefly suggested that earlier twentieth-century ethical theories have underlying theories of human nature and these do not posit a satisfactory view of the moral self. The two ethical theories noted represent the general trend to leave out some view of the moral person or moral self. A conceptualization of character needs some view of a coherent self that retains its selfhood through a wide variety of change. Neither the ghost nor the machine or the ghost in the machine, neither a successive bundle of diverse experiences nor a bundle of habits, neither cognitive processes nor affective components can suffice to give us the needed concept of a moral self or moral personhood. This story of self or personhood and thus moral self and moral personhood must eventually be addressed in a separate study. That it cannot be addressed here must remain a promise to be delivered at another time.[2]

A View of Character: A First Statement

A person's character[3] is dependent on the possession of coherent moral excellences that have become dispositions or habits with the potential for active moral engagement. In commonsense, everyday situations personal desires, impulses, and interests usually conform with possessed moral excellences. These moral excellences are formed from and based on a reasonable way of life that in most cases develops within some community. Though a relatively settled aspect of moral agency, character is amenable to change when such change is required, for example, because of particular types of moral dilemmas or because the moral agent self-consciously rejects certain aspects of present character.

Any brief overview of character cannot stand without further analysis, explanation, and qualification. Before accepting the above view, certain key ideas and problems must be examined. Only then can this view of character be harbored within a theory of moral education.

The Coherency of Moral Excellences

The expression "moral excellences" is used here for a number of reasons. First, though the word "traits" has a natural affinity with the original nonmoral meaning of the term "character,"[4] this etymological relationship can no longer influence the inclusion of traits in a conceptualization of moral character. The term "traits" is rejected because it still connotes older views of moral education based on an outdated faculty psychology. The use of moral excellence instead of moral trait sidesteps unfavorable psychological connotations and points in another direction. Moral excellences and virtues denote the positive moral qualities of a given way of life.[5] The idea of moral excellences is not a new one; in classical Greek, the term *"arete"* refers to excellences or virtues, but not necessarily moral qualities. In this conceptualization of character, the moral aspect of older usage is emphasized. Sidgwick uses the term "excellence" to refer to "an ideal complex of mental qualities of which we admire and approve the manifestation in human life."[6] Excellence is closely connected with perfection, with perfection referring to an ideal. Excellence is the "partial realisation of or approximation to the ideal as we actually find in human experience."[7] Moral excellences then allude to excellences in the moral domain. As we continue, we will recognize, as Sidgwick and others have, that moral excellences cannot stand by themselves unless one subscribes to an unregenerate form of intuitionism. The moral, for example, does not stand alone without reference to intellectual excellences. Moral excellences require standards and intellectual tools, a notion of the good life and some means of evaluation.

To affirm the coherency of moral excellences at the outset seems to involve problems, since coherency as a logical criterion has been criticized from a number of directions. For example, when Odysseus in Sophocles' *Philoctetes* is portrayed by Martha Nussbaum as holding "a coherent view of some interest,"[8] Odysseus is described disapprobatively. The coherency of Odysseus' desire for self-advancement and the general good, in this situation, reveals a "character with his coherent, though deficient, standard of behavior."[9] The goal to be achieved, according to Odysseus, is to bring the warrior Philoctetes to Troy to insure a successful conclusion to the war. Odysseus is not troubled by the means that might have to be used; any type of cunning or deceit is acceptable for Odysseus if he accomplishes his desired end. I do not want to question here whether Odysseus actually possesses a coherent character, though he may display a "coherent, though deficient, standard of behavior."

Three other concerns enter to clarify this example and indicate why coherency can serve as a logical criterion. First, coherency in itself cannot serve to recommend moral character. Coherency is one of a set of criteria all of which contribute evaluative tools. Second, by referring to the coherency of moral excellences, there is the realization that a moral agent such as Odysseus may possess few excellences and/or may possess such a partial realization of excellences that they cannot adequately inform moral life. Third, moral excellences do not refer only to the acceptance of some externally mandated compulsion of the type Odysseus wanted to maintain for self-aggrandizement. Moral excellences refer to the internal condition of the agent's moral being, a balancing of the internal and external, a struggle between integrity and the common good.[10]

Some might also wonder whether the coherency criterion meets the actualities of present-day moral life. Perhaps the character of Odysseus or the youthful son of Achilles, Neoptolemus, can be partially assessed with the coherency criterion. Even those living during the Victorian period would seem to possess coherent characters. But can this criterion readily and realistically be ascribed to late twentieth-century moral personhood? There are numerous examples of people who selectively manifest both moral excellences and their negations, moral faults. Perhaps some of these examples could be understood through the definition Polemarchus gives in the *Republic*. Polemarchus defines justice as helping friends and harming enemies. Whether a moral excellence is manifested, according to Polemarchus, is dependent on the context. In a moral agent's private life with family and friends, excellences like generosity, kindness, honesty, and caring are appropriate, but in business dealings, for instance, these disappear and are replaced by ruthlessness, competitiveness, an uncaring attitude, and the unexamined acceptance of a role. The justification for such contextual, selective manifestations of character may refer to what the moral agent believes necessary or prudential in the given situation. In schools, such selective manifestation of virtues also exists. Teachers may seem to be caring, concerned, sensitive people to their families and colleagues. They demonstrate respect for others and are fair and considerate if these others are administrators and teachers. Students, however, describe some teachers rather differently, as uncaring, insensitive to students' feelings, authoritarian, disrespectful, and unfair.[11]

The coherency standard does not falter on examples of people whose moral virtues do not possess coherency. Rather, this criterion is superficially sustained by the shock of spectators about the incoherence of an agent's character. The shock in itself reveals that people generally expect moral agents to have coherent moral excellences and feel betrayed or at least disappointed when the moral agent radically diverges from this standard. The problem here may be couched in a different form than the language of coherency. A moral agent may have coherent moral virtues, but like an avid slave owner or Nazi storm trooper could also have narrowed the class of human beings for whom the virtues apply. Though these moral virtues and their narrowed referents are consistent with the moral agent's preferred way of life, it will be argued later that a preferred way of life is not necessarily a reasonable way of life and if not reasonable, should not be advocated. As these cases indicate, though coherency is a necessary characteristic of virtue, it is not sufficient to conceptualize the agent's moral character or to prescribe it as a measure of the success or failure of moral education.

Instead of accepting the coherency criterion, some detractors might also argue that certain moral theories and their general moral principles would require radical changes in recommended conduct. By concentrating on the quality of moral judgments and standards, the internal condition of the moral agent becomes unimportant in the sense character theory requires. For example, a utilitarian would prescribe the action that results in the greatest good for the largest number. Thus, a moral agent who lied to foil the evil intentions of a madman could justify the actions on the basis of the utilitarian principle. By lying, the moral agent saved the community from considerable harm. The issue was not lying, but from which action the greater good would be derived. Even the chicanery of a business executive could be justified (or maybe, just rationalized) in this manner. The business executive would not allude to self-interest but the good of proposed actions for others (e.g., the health of the national or local economy, the welfare of employees, the profit and continued support of stockholders). Thus, reprehensible conduct in one theoretical framework seems purified in another. Or has it been purified? Let's leave aside the former case of lying to a madman and settle the utilitarian view of the more common case of the self-interested business executive. Neither act nor rule utilitarianism would necessarily accept the rationalization of the business executive.

An act utilitarian would say that in ordinary, taken-for-granted moral life, a moral agent should use rules of thumb for moral dilemmas.[12] A rule utilitarian would be

more specific by referring to a set of moral rules that maximize goodness for the greatest number of people.[13] These
moral rules should form the basis of moral judgments and
actions. With rule utilitarianism, one could even claim[14]
that such moral rules are exactly what comprise a community and its way of life. These rules are part of the basic
structures that underlie some community or style of life.
Both act and rule utilitarianism seem to accept something
like Rawls's distinction between justifying a practice under
a rule and justifying the rule.[15] Rule utilitarians advocate
the justification of a set of societal moral rules with the utilitarian principle, that is, which set of rules would have the
consequence of maximizing the good for the greatest
number. A moral agent would then justify a practice under
one (or more) of the rules. In other words, act and rule
utilitarians argue that rules would have been justified by
the utilitarian greatest good principle, but this justification
would not be required of each individual moral agent.
Each individual moral agent on the other hand would have
to assess which practice comes under the rule. With both
types of utilitarianism, constraints are placed on the moral
agent to avoid the types of rationalizations criticized here
and to avoid the excesses of calculative reasoning. Accordingly, both the act and rule utilitarianism would reject the
rationalization of the business executive.

Someone may now ask how these characteristics of act
and rule utilitarianism relate to the problem of the coherency of moral character excellences. With certain types
of ideals like honesty and truthfulness, some might argue
that a theory of character and moral excellences require
the upholding of these ideals in most situations. As against
this, it would be argued that utilitarianism, for example,
would assume that whether one should be honest and tell
the truth would depend on the consequences of being honest and telling the truth. In actuality, however, it was shown
that both act and rule utilitarianism would argue that honesty and truthfulness should be accepted as rules of thumb
or societal rules since these would in most cases have the
consequences that utilitarianism seeks. Though this is not
an argument for the coherency of moral excellences, it

does indicate that another moral theory does not advocate wholesale rejection of the possibility of coherency.

The coherency criterion undercuts those who accept Lawrence Kohlberg's description of character as a "bag of virtues" or a "bag of Boy Scout virtues." The "bag" metaphor suggests random, unorganized, unrelated virtues in that a bag does not have to contain anything in particular and can include all sorts of objects. The bag metaphor also does not suggest any means of evaluating the bag's contents, whether good or bad, haphazard or organized. Instead of being an accurate description of character or the virtues of character, the bag metaphor is a derogatory slogan whose content crassly negates, but does not argue against, the validity of a virtues ethic or moral character. Kohlberg's "bag of virtues" interpretation of virtues is invalid for other reasons. Character virtues are not possessed in some haphazard manner, but are organized in a coherent fashion depending in part on certain logical features of the main virtues, the form of life, community, and external, objective evaluative standards. Current empirical studies have not been particularly concerned with community affiliation or with the logical structure of virtue systems. Considerable philosophic groundwork is necessary for any assessment of the coherence of virtue systems; empirical studies alone cannot unearth this.[16] Instead of the hodgepodge of uncoordinated virtues Kohlberg criticizes, character must include a coordinated, structured set of compatible character excellences.

The coherency of moral excellences has been a feature of moral character throughout history. The dominant moral excellences or virtues of the Homeric Age, for example, were the heroic qualities of courage and manliness; for the Periclean Age cardinal virtues were temperance, justice, and courage; nineteenth-century English virtues included loyalty, generosity, sincerity, and responsibility. In each case, the moral character of anyone with these excellences was not fragmented or unorganized. Rather, moral character was organized and structured so that any excellence could not exist or function without a whole set of compatible excellences. This does not suggest that all those with sets of moral excellences were sterling individuals. Often, the fatal character flaw of some agent was based on not possessing all the requisite excellences; having the excellence(s) in a weakened or flawed form; or unexpected, uncontrollable events creating intolerable moral dilemmas. Novels often explore these features, shortcomings, and flaws of protagonists' character. At present, however, during a period of value and moral pluralism, one single set of moral excellences probably cannot be stated. Virtue systems at this time partly have to relate to community affiliation and a life's framework, both of these evaluated in part according to the criteria of reasonableness.

Coherency implies that certain fundamental moral excellences must be harmoniously integrated and interrelated. For example, friendship and fidelity also mean that an agent is expected to act in certain ways toward friends and acquaintances, such conduct based on a body of related virtues like honesty, loyalty, truthfulness, care, respectfulness, and so on. At the same time, however, it is stressed again that such moral excellences as loyalty and caring are more than coherently related excellences. They simultaneously have rootedness within a place and are related to some higher ideals than these excellences. According to the coherency criterion, a moral agent doesn't at one time lie because it is prudential and at other times speak truthfully; sometimes display kindness and compassion and in other instances be unkind and insensitive; sometimes respect other human beings and in some situations become disrespectful; sometimes be loyal and at other times disloyal; sometimes responsible and sometimes wholly irresponsible. Even though there may be occasional instances of moral slippage or ostensible changes in character, either slippage or modification of character can be explained. Explanations are not necessarily excuses, but reasons why agents modify their character or why they may decide to act in a manner not consistent with character virtues.

In everyday dealings with friends and acquaintances, with colleagues and strangers, conduct should be based on an integrated set of moral excellences or virtues. These structured, interrelated excellences are not formed in a vacuum, but depend on a number of other factors, two of which are noted here. First, there are necessary logical relationships between given virtues. Second, moral excellences are dependent on a given community, society, and culture. The logical necessity of coherence is discussed in this section. A later section investigates how community, society, and culture affect the coherency of character excellences.

In a long-forgotten study, experimenters asked subjects to note which qualities came to mind when any one character excellence was mentioned. A number of fairly generalized character excellences were mentioned to each member of a random sample. Each subject was asked to note which other excellences a moral agent with the one mentioned excellence should also have. There was considerable uniformity in the network of connected moral excellences stated by members of the sample. If a moral agent possessed any one excellence, it was also expected that the moral agent would possess a wider group of moral excellences.[17] The issue here is not the quality of the experiment, but whether it gives us some general hint to follow regarding the relationship among virtues. Are the results of this experiment just a matter of its subjects' stereotyping people after being given a single moral excellence? Or is there some logical relationship between groups of moral excellences?

The logical necessity of coherency can be sustained in two ways, first by virtue of the attributes of subordinate concepts and their superordinate category, and second, the relationship between superordinate categories. The subordinate concepts and attributes of superordinate categories are networks of family concepts and exemplars that "overlap and criss-cross," are "more or less related to one another," and yet, still reveal "deep disquietudes."[18] Though the superordinate category "fruit" seems to possess certain clearly understood attributes like sweetness and juiciness, even this relatively agreed upon category eludes simple structural components. Fruits like olives and tomatoes immediately reveal the disquietude in an ostensibly neat classificatory schema.[19] With moral excellences such as loyalty, compassion, truthfulness, courage, and humility, structures possess considerable overlapping and crisscrossing that reveal deep disquietude.

These overlapping conceptual schemas are not limited to subordinate categories, but often include superordinate categories with their own conceptual luggage. Truthfulness, for example, has both ethical and epistemological dimensions. Instead of confusing truth and truth-telling or emphasizing the epistemological over the ethical,[20] in some way the epistemological and its concern for truth criteria enters into understanding the superordinate moral excellence "truthfulness." The epistemological network is neither eliminated nor dominant, but one of the deep disquietudes of the moral excellence superordinate category. Moral excellences like fidelity and compassion are subtly interrelated with truthfulness. Truthfulness cannot be the sole characteristic of fidelity. For truthfulness is not fidelity nor fidelity truthfulness. Yet truthfulness has a fundamental role in fidelity. Compassion and care are not just passions, but have a subtle relationship to truthfulness. Especially in such cases as elderly infirmed parents and children with serious illnesses, the relationship between truthfulness and caring for becomes even more important and complex.

What of the cases when coherency is not sustained, when there seems to be some short-circuiting in the crisscrossing network of moral excellence attributes? The issue here is twofold, first whether the internal moral excellence structure remains coherent if external action is not based on those excellences, and second, whether coherency is an optimum or ideal criterion or the normal state of moral excellence structures.

The relationship between the internal and external aspects of the coherency of moral excellences includes varied features (e.g., owing to the ascription of moral excellence terms to external acts and to the internal characteristics of an agent). There may be situations in which an agent's internal moral excellences are described by one set of terms and spectators ascribe other moral excellence terms to that moral agent's actions. How can this be explained? Do the contours and dimensions of moral dilemmas sometimes require an agent to abandon firmly held moral excellences and turn from the moral ideals at the core of his or her moral being? Such action may be a matter of faltering and slippage. Such slippage may exist for many reasons, because of the agent's unexpectedly being overcome by a passion; because of an inability to understand the situation completely; because of an unwillingness to recognize the actual features of the situation; because of the conflicting claims of very different moral excellences; and because of moral dilemmas that must be resolved with other types of ethical considerations. All these challenges to the internal coherency of moral excellences require very brief comments to sustain the coherency criterion.

An agent unexpectedly overcome by passion and the coherency of moral excellences

Most moral excellences cannot be "stripped bare of all emotional elements"; some virtues have indispensable emotional elements.[21] These emotions or emotional elements are dimensions of the crisscrossing networks of attributional concepts of superordinate moral excellences. These emotions are inherently part of what it means to possess a moral excellence. In some situations, however, an agent is overcome by another type of emotion or passion. Fear or lust, for example, may so overwhelm, control, and paralyze an agent that the appropriate moral excellence does not govern the agent's moral action. How does this occur? Is this a comment on the coherency of the moral character? Yes and no. Yes, there may be little coherency of moral character and thus, character excellences may not govern the action. Another very different explanation of emotions overcoming moral excellences can be given. An agent may possess coherent moral excellences in such a narrow and limited form that some conflicting, negative emotion can gain control in specific situations. In addition, with some emotions like fear, the emotion may be so strong that it overcomes any moral character except a perfect instantiation of character like that of a Socrates.

An agent's inability to understand the situation completely and the coherency of moral excellences

Human understanding of moral situations is limited not necessarily because of self-deception, but because of the inherent limitations of human knowledge, imagination, and understanding. A moral agent at times acts in a manner that might have been rejected if the agent had understood the actual moral situation or if the agent had been more (or less) imaginative. Should we claim that these failings are actually flaws of moral character? When there is a shortcoming of moral action, should these instances be used as examples of the incoherency of moral excellences? As one possible reason for such shortcomings, we again have to recognize human weaknesses and how even the most sterling moral character with a coherent set of moral excellences may not guarantee appropriate or approbative moral action.

This weakness is not weakness of will, the failing of someone who knows what should be done but does not carry out the action. This is the failure of a person caught up in a complex situation with an extensive web of external forces and variables. This is the average moral human being with average intellectual and imaginative abilities who cannot see all possible data, alternatives, and consequences. Recognition of this problem is seen in one fairly recent development in medical ethics. Instead of saying that one single autonomous moral agent has the responsibility for judging, the formation of institutional ethics committees to make ethical policy implies that certain decisions cannot be made by one individual because they require an interdisciplinary network of experts and lay persons, physicians, ethicists, nurses, social workers, administrators, and attorneys to understand technologically generated, multifaceted medical problems. One of the main responsibilities of these committees is to make ethical policy. Accordingly, these committees formulate the rule of the practice and then various medical personnel can decide whether some practice comes under that rule and what the action under that rule should be.

An agent's unwillingness to recognize the actual features of the situation and moral excellences

There is a very different case in which an agent could understand and know the actual features of a moral situation and yet through self-deception or intellectual laziness not recognize these necessary aspects of the moral dilemma. The agent may refuse to acknowledge and in retrospect may claim not to have known about those features of the moral dilemma. What should be said about this agent and the coherency of his or her moral excellences? As noted previously, coherency alone cannot be the sole criterion to judge character or a set of moral excellences. The agent may have such a narrow, limited, and/or rigid set of coherent moral excellences that many compelling components of moral dilemmas do not affect that agent.[22] There is another way to view the problem of not recognizing all dimensions of a moral dilemma. Moral excellences must include and relate to intellectual virtues. Moral action does not imply blind obedience to some character excellences but the ability to make judgments about the means by which a moral agent can act in conformity with the ideal moral excellence. Intellectual virtues are also needed for agents to turn in on themselves and question the contours of presently accepted moral excellences and reflect about dilemmas that seem to conflict with these presently held moral excellences. Failure to understand or recognize a moral dilemma is a character failure and indicates a failure of the intertwined network of moral excellences.

The conflicting claims of very different moral excellences and their coherency

A moral agent may be torn by opposing ideals and excellences, each of which suggest rather different moral action. In an ideal moral world, the agent would discover a Hegelian synthesis to retain the integrity of all the moral excellences. Perhaps someone with sufficient time, experience, imagination, intellectual virtues, and a wide range of interlocking moral excellences would be able to discern some resolution that retains the integrity of all moral excellences. But in some situations this is not the case. Even though there is coherency among the moral excellences, this coherency does not guarantee that all proposed moral solutions or moral actions will maintain the integrity of all the moral excellences.

The problem here might be seen in two ways. In one case, the issue may be to prioritize moral excellences and decide which is the most important.[23] In another case, the problem may be the necessity to enlarge and expand moral excellences. Present moral excellences may reveal this conflict because they are not sufficiently complex.

Moral dilemmas that must be resolved by other types of ethical considerations and the coherency of moral excellences

Moral character and moral excellences do not always seem capable of prescribing appropriate moral action for all moral dilemmas. These particularly difficult moral dilemmas might involve conflicts between private and public lives or relate to the moral dimensions public roles. The conflict the agent faces is between possessed moral excellences and the moral dimensions of a public role. In some cases, the maintenance of personal integrity and sustaining one's moral excellences may be paramount and in this case, the agent may relinquish a public responsibility and follow the course dictated by personal moral excellences. At other times, an agent may use rather different moral principles to resolve the public moral dilemma, but always revert to personal moral excellences as a means of moderating public decisions and action.

At times, an agent's decision and action in a public matter may be criticized. Emotions and impulses may have led the agent in this unacceptable or different direction. The desire for glory and power may have clouded the agent's moral character, and thus the public decision was not tempered with personally accepted moral excellences. In another instance, some personality flaw may lead the agent to analyze the public situation incorrectly and make an ill-conceived judgment. These agents in retrospect may be remorseful about their judgments and moral action.

One further point must be made. The most perfect moral personhood does not guarantee that a person's life will also be perfect. Moral life cannot be cleansed of the tragedies, sorrows, regrets, and shortcomings of human beings. What is claimed here is that human beings must live and recognize such tragedies and regrets and thus, by feeling a little less perfect be a little more humble and again seek to attain a moral ideal.

As noted, coherency may sometimes seem a confining standard since an agent may possess a narrow and possibly rigid set of moral excellences. Yet instead of being a limiting, narrow standard, coherency can potentially contribute to an enlarged structure of moral excellences. In a sense, this coherency takes a cue from Hegel, who assumed coherency can admit the entire moral universe if not for actual, moral human beings then at least logically. For the average person, the range of concepts coherency refers to is limited by societal affiliation and culture, knowledge, emotions, attitudes, imagination, and various serendipitous events. Moral character need not include a narrow set of moral excellences, but can encompass a complex structure and intertwining network of virtues. How optimistic should we be about anyone's fully integrating all possible sets or an exceptionally enlarged group of moral excellences? There are two sides to such development. On one side, moral excellences do not wholly exist abstracted from the practical moral life of a moral agent. Since no one can live in every community and accept every way of life, a moral agent cannot possess a character that includes all conceivable virtues. Even though at times some of the same virtues may be included in different ways of life, these virtues are not exactly identical. The crisscrossing networks of concepts and attributes defining any superordinate moral excellence acquire different meanings and trace different paths by being related to different communities and ways of life. Second, moral excellences and networks of their attributes cannot just depend on the communities and ways of life because these may be seriously flawed. Thus, there is another standard for evaluating the various forms of coherent character excellences that agents possess.

The coherency criterion applies to mature moral character. The coherency of mature moral development cannot be expected of children. As Hampshire states, "One has only fifty or so years to think, and to act on one's conclusions, if like Aristotle one excludes the possibility of moral coherence in childhood."[24] If children are excluded from those who possess coherent moral characters and yet coherence is a mark of mature character, then moral education should aim to achieve this coherency.

Habits: The Potential for Active Moral Engagement

Recent accounts of moral development, problem solving, and reasoning shy away from assigning an active, vital role to habits. This present account of moral character again assigns habits a role in morality and moral education.[25] At the outset of this presentation, however, it must be noted that in themselves habits (or even dispositions) are not the sole psychological dimensions of character. The point made here is that habits must be included in a conceptualization of character, but they are not the sole psychological phenomenon explaining character. Two problems are addressed here to redirect the role of habits in morality and moral education. First, reasons why the abandonment of the concept "habits" is unwarranted are explored. Second, a different conceptualization of habit than the one commonly accepted is briefly sketched. Included in this second problem is attention to the relationship between character and habits.

Reasons for the abandonment of habits

Kohlberg is an excellent example of a moral development psychologist who has long rejected the cultivation of habits to induce moral judgments and moral behavior.[26] Kohlberg argues that (i) habits are a remnant of stimulus-response psychology, and (ii) habits are antithetical to self-conscious thought processes and objective moral judgments.[27] Behaviorists and associationists have long stressed the development of habits and habitual behavior. Rejecting any taint of behaviorism and stimulus-response psychology, Kohlberg shuns a concept commonly used by these rejected positions. The stimulus-response conceptualization of habit, rejected by Kohlberg, is described by Paton in the following way:

> [Habit] is generally used to designate certain forms of adjustment marked by increasing facility in execution due to repetition, and includes responses in which the motor element in the reaction is also only dimly represented in the field of consciousness. Habits may also be described as individual adaptations, or modifications in behavior due to experiences and accompanied by merely slight, if any, participation of consciousness, which only becomes a prominent factor in the cerebral process when a choice between two or more motives is required.[28]

More thoroughgoing behaviorists would not even mention a "field of consciousness" or "cerebral process," but would account for which habit was executed by the strength of earlier reinforcement and the nature of the present stimuli, by the strength of the association between behavior and reinforcement. The only psychological phenomenon discussed is habits and how they are formed through stimulus-response association. All human functioning is thus *reduced* to habits and how habits are formed. Radical behaviorists, such as Skinner, assert that the world's social and moral problems can be solved through a "technology of behavior," which jettisons personal autonomy and human freedom. Morality becomes the habits generated by stimulus-response-reinforcement conditions.[29]

Kohlberg rejects the concept "habit" in part because of its inherited behaviorist roots. At the same time, he has another reason for rejecting it and giving it no role in cognitive theory. If an agent's moral judgment is based on a moral standard or principle, then, according to Kohlberg, that judgment cannot be tainted with habits. Habits, according to his criticism, imply an unthinking adherence to conditioned or habituated moral behavior and would call into question whether the moral judgment was actually based on cognitive processes and moral standards. Habit is thus wholly extracted from moral judgments.

At first, Kohlberg expressed unbridled optimism about what moral education for the development of higher-stage moral judgments and thought processes could acomplish. In time, however, the moral discussion sessions he advocated did not prove wholly successful. Students at lower moral cognitive stages often manifested antisocial behavior like drug use, petty theft, and vandalism. Kohlberg was confronted with two problems concerning the control of student antisocial behavior: First, how could this behavior be controlled if students had not attained a level of moral reasoning by which they would judge their actions unacceptable? Second, could prosocial behavior be fostered when student behavior was not consistent with moral judgments? In this latter case, students might make moral judgments that included desirable prosocial behavior but then these students for various reasons did not manifest the actions dictated by their moral judgments. Actually, Kohlberg was not just asking about which method should be used to transmit acceptable behavior, but which psychological phenomenon would explain that behavior. This created a difficult dilemma. On one side, Kohlberg solely advocated cognitive processes and on the other side, his cognitive theory's concepts were not able to control antisocial behavior. At this point, he advocated another method to control unacceptable behavior but did not mention the psychological phenomenon by which students would control their antisocial behavior. Kohlberg advocated indoctrination and did not mention habits, habit formation, or any other psychological phenomenon that indoctrination created.[30]

Kohlberg's championing of indoctrination was inopportune. First, unlike the concept "habit," indoctrination at present has very strong negative connotations and denotations. Indoctrination is viewed negatively because of both the method and content of the process. Habit, as Dewey well recognized, remains a neutral term. In their content, habits can be positive or negative. They can include a wide variety of dimensions and can at times even be described as intelligent habits. The process of developing habits can be based on regimentation, blind adherence to repetitive behavior, or mechanistic associationism; it can be a form of conditioning or can involve intelligence and thought. Simultaneously, habits can explain repetitive behavior like typing or can be one component in intelligent problem solving. There is no reason for the concept "habit" to reside comfortably only within a behavioristic psychology or be interpreted as unthinking elements for moral behavior. Sufficient warrant can be given for habits being an integral part of all cognitive processes. Instead of being two radically different aspects of mental functioning, cognitive processes and habits require each other and are both necessary aspects of problem solving and moral reasoning. Moral reasoning and problem solving are aspects of informed habits and allow agents to question and change unacceptable habits.[31] The issue here is not whether a person possesses habits, but rather, as Dewey recognized, the quality of these habits, whether they are an integration of multidimensional experiences, whether they relate to narrow, rigid qualities and behavior, or whether they are amenable to growth and change.

Another view of habits

The remainder of this section considers a different view of habits that takes its cues from a rather different tradition than the one accepted by contemporary behaviorists. Though this discussion of habits begins with three twentieth-century writers—Dewey, Peters, and Piaget—this view has other roots and notions that cannot be considered here. While Dewey and Peters seem obvious choices, Piaget is a less likely candidate. His contribution to a theory of habit is stressed since unfortunately this aspect of his thought is usually ignored.

"Out of habit" behavior is described as mechanistic, as the following examples illustrate: a typist blindly copying documents, soldiers rhythmically marching, an assembly line worker continually attaching a part to the frame of an automobile. Even "out of habit" behavior cannot be separated from intelligent habits as neatly as some philosophers have attempted to do. For example, there seems to be "out of habit" behavior that one would not wish to confuse with marching soldiers, assembly line workers, or repetitive typists. What of a ballet chorus's precision dancing or a pianist playing a memorized piece or making a recipe many times? Are all these instances of "out of habit" behavior described in the identical manner as the typist typing and the soldier marching? Or again, must we wonder whether a rigid boundary can be drawn between types of behavior? Since it does not seem to involve any intelligence, out of habit behavior has been rejected as a basis of morality. But "out of habit" is not the only way of conceptualizing habit, as philosophers and psychologists have long recognized.

Habits can be intelligent and inform self-conscious moral action. Piaget, for example, refers to the positive role of habits in moral development: ". . . [the child] very soon contracts habits which constitute individual rules of a sort."[32] Piaget thus speaks of the habit being a mirror image of some individual rule. The mirror seems a fair metaphor here since Piaget says that habits "constitute rules *of a sort*"[33] (my emphasis). Of a sort means that the reflection (the habit) may be blurred, enlarged, diminished, and thus may involve varying personal interpretations of a rule. Piaget also recognizes that "these new habits of thought lead to genuine deductions . . . and to deductions in which the child grapples with a given fact of experience, either present or past."[34] By speaking of habits as "habits of thought" that "lead to genuine deductions," Piaget gives the concept "habit" something much more than an unthinking foundational role in morality and moral reasoning. Habits have a fundamental role at every level because they involve thought. Finally, Piaget even connects a quality like cooperation with habits: "In so far as habits of cooperation will have convinced the child of the necessity of not lying, rules will become comprehensible, will become interiorized, and will no longer give rise to any judgments but those of subjective responsibility."[35] Piaget's use of habit is not idiosyncratic or accidental, appearing only in a single work. Similar usage occurs in his other writings. For example, elsewhere he states, "Thus at all levels imitation is the continuation of accommodation of the schemas of sensory-motor intelligence from perception and habits to interiorised co-ordinations."[36]

What is Piaget saying about habits in these passages? Habits, for him, have two functions in relation to self-conscious thought and intelligence, the first dependent on their place within cognitive structures and the second dependent on how they are formed. First, Piaget is not making a rigid distinction between habits and intelligence or habits and thought processes. Through imitation and repetition, a child first develops habits that are externalizations of rules and structures and ways of solving problems. Children eventually interiorize these external rules and habits by forming new schema to modify older structures. The development of these newer structures does not imply the destruction of habits but their transformation. They become deeply embedded within structures. Through this type of development, a child who was first only a participant becomes, to use Strawson's idea, a "participant/observer."[37] In sum, Piaget advocates a fundamental place for habits within the very cognitive structures the child develops.[38]

Second, Piaget also asserts that these habits form through activity the active creation and recreation of structures to interpret, understand, and act on the world. Habits are not the imprinting of ideas or forms of behavior on the child nor are they the passive acquisition due to an association between stimulus and response. Instead, habits form through the child's activity, through an interaction between the child's present structures and way of interpreting the world and the physical and social world. Through ongoing interaction within a world, the child transforms various phenomena and rules into structures that include habits based on the child's own quest to understand the world. Interestingly, Piaget doesn't expect the characteristics of sensory-motor intelligence to cease with higher cognitive development. "Sensory-motor intelligence, which during the first two years coordinates perceptions and actions . . . continues to play a fundamental role throughout the rest of the period of mental development and even in the adult stage."[39]

Habits also enter into Piaget's discussion of the development of moral judgments in children. When analyzing a child's moral judgments of objective versus subjective responsibility and the stage of moral realism, Piaget states, "since thought in the child always lags behind action, it is quite natural that the solution of theoretical [moral] problems . . . should be formed by means of older and more habitual schemas rather than the more subtle and less robust schemas that are in the process of formation."[40] With the moral as well as other cognitive areas, Piaget recognizes that habit and the habitual have a foundational role. Though they cannot provide the most mature means of resolving moral problems, habits and habitual schemas remain vestiges embedded within later structures. Akin to Aristotle's and Dewey's notions of habit and morality, for Piaget, early rule and habitual schemas developed through active interaction within a social and physical environment. Though they involve cognitive dimensions, habits and habitual behavior are prior to self-conscious thought about moral dilemmas and judgments.

An important facet of this view of habits dates back to Aristotle: human beings become moral by being moral. In other words, moral life and moral action precede moral thought in that children must first act morally, be members of a moral community, and thus develop adequate, appropriate habits of a particular quality. Being a certain moral person, acquiring moral personhood, having certain moral habits gives a child the background with which to think about these moral habits and if necessary, question their adequacy.

Habits relate to moral character in another way. In a number of ways, they provide a means to insure active engagement in moral life. First, internal moral being is not some stationary structure that will be completed at some time. Rather, throughout the person's entire life there should be growth and change, this dependent on the range of moral dilemmas confronted, the different communities joined, changes in social and intellectual life, and probably most important, increased understanding of the characteristics of moral ideals. Second, the relationship between the internal and external is dynamic because character and moral excellences also require active moral engagement. By using the term "engagement" instead of behavior, other aspects of moral life are included. The moral agent does not only behave in an appropriate manner when confronted with a moral dilemma, but also must become intimately engaged within the situation as a whole. Engagement implies not just that the agent does something and affects the outer world, but that the agent by being immersed within a moral situation and a moral universe acquires strength and understanding from that situation and universe. Any moral dilemma is part of much larger moral situations with rather untidy boundaries. For the sake of logical neatness moral agents more or less restrict a moral dilemma to manageable dimensions. Furthermore, both moral dilemmas and the larger situations occur within moral communities and a moral universe. These concentric circles mean that a moral agent engaging within any circle is nourished by the meanings and ideas of these circles. In other words, though any single moral dilemma may seem unique and may be a particular concrete problem, it is interconnected within a much larger structure, that of a moral community and moral universe.

Even after a moral dilemma has been resolved or some moral interaction completed, an agent will still be engaged in the larger moral situation and moral universe. How that one moral dilemma was resolved has reverberations for how the agent lives and understands these larger circles. For example, a teacher may ill-advisedly say something unkind to a student. Sometimes there are sharp, harmful words; sometimes there is only a look or a shrug or a turning away from a student in need. In any of these cases, the teacher may realize what she said or did; she may wonder whether her action had any ill effect on the student. Even if the teacher apologizes and thus makes restitution, this does not wholly end the situation. In a sense, by negating her accepted moral character and cherished virtues, the teacher also scars her moral personhood. For that teacher needs to be engaged on an ongoing basis in a larger moral situation to know whether the ill-advised language was a foolish, emotional mistake or a regular occurrence. Finally, the absence of overt, direct moral action does not imply that a moral agent ignores the moral situation. The moral agent may engage in various processes to understand the moral denotations and connotations of the situation. In either case, engagement implies embeddedness within the ongoing moral situation. Character requires that in "normal," everyday moral situations the moral agent acts in recognizable ways, recognizable in that spectators would connect the agent's actions with character excellences.

Consistency Between Moral Excellences and Desires, Impulses, and Self-Interest

The consistency criterion contributes two conditions to character. First, the acceptance of certain moral excellences based on a way of life also implies the channeling of emotions, desires, interests, and impulses in a compatible direction. Desires, interests, and impulses do not remain raw, unorganized material, but become intimately related to an agent's character, moral excellences, community, and way of life. The consistency criterion is used in an even stronger sense. For moral excellences to comprise an agent's character, suitable desires and interests must integrally be part of these excellences. For example, a Homeric hero did not on the one hand possess a moral excellence like courage and then a separate interest to act courageously. Rather, the moral excellence "courage" included the interest and desire to be courageous. Moral excellences like compassion, care, sympathy, and kindness inherently possess emotional elements.

The relationship between moral excellences and emotions is much more complicated than indicated thus far. On one side there can be a relationship between a moral excellence and an emotion (or emotions). In this case, the agent possesses the moral excellence and has suitable emotions to manifest the excellence in appropriate situations. On the other side, the moral excellence itself possesses emotional components. The following are different ways of seeing the relationship between moral excellences and emotions: (a) The moral excellence may have very limited emotional components but requires suitable interests, desires, and emotions for its manifestation in action. The agent must possess suitable interests, desires, and emotions for a moral excellence to be considered as suitable for a particular moral situation. Without appropriate desires and emotions for the moral excellence to be an operative factor, the moral excellence would wither. Thus, the possession of requisite desires and emotions is a necessary condition for a moral excellence. (b) A moral excellence may have very strong emotional compononts but still require suitable interests, desires, and emotions for its manifestation in action. In this case, the moral excellence itself has dimensions that are fundamentally emotional in nature. For example, compassion, care, and sympathy among others do not just involve cognitive components but are heavily overlaid with emotional dimensions.

At times, however, a moral agent may experience desires, impulses, or interests that are inconsistent with accepted moral character. Some of these inconsistent desires or interests may motivate an agent to question whether it is necessary to modify some aspect of her character. In other instances, there may be some faltering, some shortcoming from the moral excellences the agent cherishes. The agent follows the calling of the desire and in retrospect may regret this compromise of character. Such concessions to inconsistent desires, impulses, or interests do not imply rejection of accepted character, but may at times be a failure of will. To state that interests and desires are normally consistent with moral character and simultaneously that they do not always function in this harmonious, peaceful manner at first glance seems strange. Similarly, it seems odd to assert that inconsistent desires and interests can serve to change character and simultaneously that they overcome accepted character. Instead of these relationships between emotions and moral excellences being unexplainable, they reveal different characteristics of desires and interests, and they show how desires and interests can overcome a moral agent, are basic features of character excellences, and finally, are motivational forces to modify presently accepted character. There is no requirement that emotions have been laundered and refer only to worthwhile qualities, objects, action, and ways of life. Emotions may well harbor unacceptable qualities. Decisions must thus be made regarding whether the desire or emotion should be followed or shunned.

Desires and emotions as an integral part of moral excellences

Some desires and emotions function as an integral part of the moral excellences of character. An agent who is compassionate, sympathetic, and caring also possesses the emotional components of these moral excellences. Sympathy, for instance, does not have only cognitive but also emotional dimensions, both of which are difficult to separate from each other. With sympathy and compassion, an agent feels pain when another is ill or suffering, pities the poverty-stricken, feels anguish about the unnecessary pain other human beings and animals suffer. But no one would be described as sympathetic or compassionate merely because of possessing certain appropriate feelings. The actions of that person would have to be described as sympathetic and compassionate. Sympathy and compassion cannot remain emotions that overwhelm. They cannot be spectator emotions. These excellences must contain dimensions that provide reasons for making certain judgments and the motivation for doing certain types of action.

Yet as mentioned previously, desires and emotions can have a looser relationship with a moral excellence. An agent who is honest and whose character includes the moral excellence "honesty" also possesses the desire to be honest. There will be emotional repugnance when others are dishonest or the agent thinks that dishonesty is possible in a particular situation. What would an alternative be to this relationship between character and emotions? If an agent's impulses, desires, and interests were always extremely different from character and the agent never questioned or evaluated either the desires or the character, then that person would have what R. D. Laing has termed "a divided self." On one side, the agent would be pulled by the demands of character excellences, and on the other side by the equally powerful impulses and desires. This type of ongoing disharmony would not just create unhappiness, alienation, or confusion, but probably serious emotional problems as well. What is asserted here is that in normal life whenever there is a schism between character and the affective, between character's moral ideals and emotions, there has to be adjudication between these two contrary claims. There needs to be some decision about the adequacy of the desire versus moral excellence. If an agent continually follows the call of fragmented, unrelated desires rather than some moral excellence, then that agent cannot claim to possess some moral excellence. Sometimes, however, the emotional pull of the contrary object is a temporary, passing fancy akin to a daydream with no action involved. Sometimes the desire or impulse makes the agent wonder about the validity of accepted character excellence and thus causes some form of evaluation of the character emotions vis-à-vis those pointing in a rather different direction.

At the same time that human moral life cannot be the pull of the many-headed monster, it does not always remain a tranquil, peaceful, harmonious relationship or some haphazard relationship among emotion, desire, interest, and moral excellence. Something very different is suggested here. Each moral excellence is not only an entity unto itself or a virtue with internally related dimensions. A virtue's defining features are not just cognitive and logical. Without possessing emotional dimensions, moral excellences would have no impact on an agent's judgments and actions. Instead of there being a separate affective domain to fuel the cognitive, as Peters suggested, the affective and cognitive are inextricably interwoven. Instead of character excellences, as Peters claims, being the style by which one carries out a moral judgment, character includes the style, emotions, desires, and moral excellences that make the moral judgment and ensuing action possible. In addition, moral excellences interrelate with and overlap each other. This interrelationship and overlapping also means that emotions that fundamentally seem dimensions of one moral excellence can have implications for another moral excellence.

Conflicts between desires and moral excellences

Character excellences and desires (or interests) may conflict in various situations. Since the emotional elements are an integral part of the moral excellence, a conflict between desire and the moral excellence is also a conflict between two or more emotions or desires. Thus, when a conflict occurs between moral excellences and emotions, it is also a conflict between the emotions of the moral excellences and other sorts of emotions and desires. There may be at least three different types of conflict here. First, there may be contrary emotions directed toward the same person and/or object. Anger about someone's actions may cause conflict with compassion for that person. Fear about something like embarking on a wholly new experience may conflict with the attitudes necessary to care for somebody. Second, there may also be the emotional pull of the character excellence and on the other side, the conflicting desire for some other object or state of affairs. In this case, there may be the emotions necessary to care for family as opposed to the desire to succeed in a professional career. Third, there may be emotions that overwhelm an agent and thus conflict with emotions that would have been held in a cooler moment. These conflicts describe various types of moral dilemmas. Instead of examining how these moral dilemmas would be resolved, I briefly look at the various ways emotions might function in these cases.

Emotions as warning signs   Impulses, desires, or emotions may serve as warning signs that a moral dilemma may exist. At times, the agent's present emotions may serve this purpose by highlighting some dilemma. A nurse treating a patient already feels compassion for that patient. That compassion in turn contributes to the nurse's recognizing a new moral situation. At another time, a novel situation arises that then produces unexpected emotions. At still other times, when two moral excellences conflict with each other, conflicting desires may also occur.

An agent lives within the normal experiential stream. Perhaps there are problems, but these are primarily intellectual problems, repairing a car or trying to understand instructions in a manual. And at times, there are no apparent problems. An agent enjoys a heightened aesthetic state, has what Dewey calls "*an* experience," for example, by attending a concert or by walking at the seashore. A radical change in emotional texture may signal the onset of some sort of moral dilemma.

Under what conditions may this change in emotional texture occur? This is a difficult question to answer since there is no formula to specify in what situations and for what reasons the emotional texture may change. Changes in emotional fabric may be one reason why children's moral education must proceed from moral action to moral reasoning. With moral action, a child is not introduced to thoughtless or nonemotional action. The moral action is not without both cognitive and affective dimensions. With moral action, children are introduced to both cognitive and affective worlds. A child helps an injured animal. The child begins to grasp what it means to help the animal, extends the helping action to other animals and even to human beings, feels sympathy for the animal and unhappiness about its condition, feels relief about the improvement of the animal's health, comforts and coaxes the animal, feels proud about success and sad about failures, and feels sorrow if the animal dies. In this situation, no matter its brevity or length, a child also develops both the cognitive and intellectual dimensions, the affective and emotional components of a moral excellence.

At another time, emotions or desires signal moral dilemmas that are fairly specific and well within the range of

dilemmas that the agent commonly recognizes. A close relative needs medical attention or a friend needs to confide
in someone. How does an agent realize that these are moral
problems? Emotions are felt when seeing how the relative
suffers; the friend's voice hints of her problems and creates
a desire to listen. On the other hand, there are more unusual situations. New emotions, feelings, and desires are
felt and these often signal a moral dilemma. Someone who
loves animals and who has had many household pets is
walking through the city and passes many indigent, homeless people. There isn't the slightest feeling of sorrow or
sympathy; no emotion wells up and motivates the person to
ask how these many unfortunate people might be helped.
Yet suddenly the agent spots an emaciated cat sitting on a
wall. She stops. There are feelings of sadness and distress,
compassion and care. But suddenly these emotions and
feelings unexpectedly extend from this one suffering cat to
all the suffering human beings who had never explicitly
been noticed previously.

Emotions that overwhelm   Emotions can function in a
very different way. Sometimes emotions overwhelm and
paralyze an agent as during a natural disaster when someone seems emotionally numb, when a tragedy befalls someone who then reacts hysterically, or when an agent is overcome with fear. Though emotions or passions function in
this manner, one measure of an agent's character and moral excellences may be whether a strong passion is con-
quered. An agent may conquer great fear to exhibit courage; courage might not be ascribed to someone who was
wholly fearless and boldly proceeded to act without a
worry.[41]

Emotions as motivations to evaluate the moral self   At
times, some object, event, or action appears attractive and
awakens desires and emotions. When these newly awakened emotions and desires are inconsistent with accepted
moral excellences and their respective emotional components, there must be assessment of the situation and/or the
agent's moral excellences. This assessment can move in a

number of directions. First, an agent may decide that the newly awakened desire must temporarily be followed. In some situations, the actions based on the desire may have few cognitive components, in which case the agent may be dragged along by the desire. Following the desire here is incompatible with accepted moral excellences and may not be based on a fully cognitive decision. If a moral excellence is continually negated by the lure of contrary emotions, judgments, and actions, it would be impossible for the agent to claim to possess the original moral excellence. Through gradual erosion, the moral excellence ceased to be a vital force governing the agent's moral judgments and actions.

Second, instead of generating the gradual deterioration of a moral excellence, desires and emotions may function in a rather different way. They motivate an agent to question the adequacy of the configuration of a moral excellence or examine the crisscrossing attributional network underlying a moral excellence. The issue here is not the moral excellence itself but the way an agent or community defines or views that virtue. Finally, when assessing the comparative claims of a newly awakened desire and an accepted moral excellence, the moral agent may decide that the claim of the original moral excellence should have greater import.

Emotions, desires, and changes in character

There are even more extreme cases of contrary emotions, passions, desires, and interests that may motivate an agent to question more than a single moral excellence or contemplated moral action. An entire way of life may be at stake. This is a more radical but yet not wholly uncommon situation. Nora in Ibsen's *A Doll House* questions her entire way of life and her role as a docile wife. Similarly, Vera Britten in a rather different manner rebels against the customs and mores of her family and social group that denied a university education and professional life to women. In both cases, these women's desires and interests, their feelings of frustration and anger, were radically different from the moral excellences it was assumed they should possess. Rather than maintain consistency between desires and character or interests and character by denying the validity of their newly awakened desires and interests, both women rejected the ways of life on which their character was dependent.

Radical transformations in a way of life do not seem dependent on common or easy decisions and are not accomplished without considerable difficulty and even pain. Yet in another sense, we may challenge the idea that changes in a way of life or membership in new communities always require a total restructuring of character. The person's moral being and character's fundamental structure may still be dependent on earlier primary community affiliation. Instead of a wholesale destruction of earlier moral excellences and changes of character, these modifications of life-style may require the realization that the original moral excellences were shallow replicas of what the moral excellence actually could be. Thus, rather than being radical changes in moral character, these changes in life-style may nourish and enhance the original moral excellences. But still the problem remains of how someone modifies moral character. Later, we return to this problem. Just as someone can evaluate present character, accepted moral excellences, habits, and way of life, that moral agent can also evaluate her desires, impulses, and interests. Whether this evaluation occurs and the quality of such evaluation depends in part on what type of moral education the agent receives.

Communities, Ways of Life, and Their Reasonableness

No one virtue, no single set or even limited number of unorganized, fragmented excellences can form the basis of optimum moral character. Since the coherency standard is a formal characteristic, it does not imply particular moral excellences. Simultaneously, coherency does not necessarily refer to a narrow field or limited number of character excellences. In addition, moral excellences do not develop in a vacuum, without some appropriate social life by which a given moral community is pictured by its constituents. How can we judge which sets of excellences should be included for adequate moral character? Some recent theorists have posited the priority of the individual over the community and thus argue that an individual chooses which goods, interests, emotions, and moral excellences to adhere to. This view creates an impossible problem for moral education. The individual is seen only as a decision maker who is the sole agent writing on a blank slate that then will contain those moral excellences, interests, emotions, and goods that agent desires to possess. A community according to this view is one of the goods that agents might choose. An agent might choose community affiliation to insure attaining other goods, not because of the worth of the community.

Human beings cannot enter a supermarket of moral excellences to shop for a suitable collection of virtues. Moral excellences and virtues are derived in part from communities; among other characteristics, moral excellences and virtues provide defining marks of communities. The relationship between communities and moral excellences is complicated. Though at first sight some excellences ostensibly seem inconsistent or incompatible with other excellences, few limitations can actually be attached to how many excellences or which moral excellences can be included in the structure of an agent's character. Moral excellences, sets of virtues, and moral character cannot be evaluated according to pristine logical categories or formal principles. They do not exist in themselves, but are always embedded within an historical moment of some community, which has translated moral ideals into actual, concrete ways of life. Seemingly identical virtues acquire different interpretations and implications for morality and moral personhood when embedded within different communities.

Instead of settling for any single set of moral excellences, each community would provide its members with those groups of moral excellences consistent with the community's basic values. Moral excellences do not exist without a community or way of life and the community or way of life cannot be maintained without the moral excellences. Some of the social and educational problems created by a pluralistic society might be settled by the advocacy of a first level of moral education in communities. The advocacy of the moral excellences of a community being transmitted to children creates various problems for schools and society. For example, how can various communities live in harmony? What would be the relationship between the moral life of the larger society and the moral excellences fostered by communities? Are all the moral excellences of communities equally valid? At the end of this section and in the next chapter, we return to these questions.

Though the expression "way of life" or "life narrative" implicitly may seem to refer to individualistic, solitary pursuits, every way of life is connected with some sort of community. Some mistakenly posit a conceptualization of way of life or life narrative without including the role of community. It may be, as other theories advocate, that individuals in the quest for unique life narratives may join communities. But this much weaker sense of community affiliation is not the community-individual relationship advocated here. The joining of a community is not the basis of this present discussion, since such joining is based on a mistaken idea of how human beings are educated and develop. Education and development first needs to take place within communities and only then might these morally developed people choose to affiliate themselves with other communities.

Someone may question whether adults may eventually leave a primary community. Certainly, someone like James Joyce may physically leave a community and exile himself from his primary moral roots. But this is not a wholly accurate portrayal of Joyce or anyone else who seems to leave a primary community. Whether Joyce ever psychologically or spiritually left his primary community is a very different question. By physically leaving it, he seems to have lived in an idealized form of that community throughout his entire creative life.

The problem of growing up within a moral community rather than eventually choosing a moral community raises a variety of theoretical issues. The way that these various issues are handled depends on one's conceptualization of community. In addition, different views of community have very different implications for practical moral education. The term "community" is used in numerous ways. Some theorists wholly ignore the concept, in part tacitly assuming it no longer can serve the needs of this age. For some sociologists, for example, there seemed to be more profitable ways of describing primary groups and social entities. Others use the concept "community" to refer to neighborhoods, pressure or interest groups, associations, or some nebulous, undefined group of people. The aim of this section is (i) to discuss a number of ways of viewing community; (ii) to choose the notion of community that best meets the needs of this theory of moral education; and (iii) to resolve a number of residual problems such as what the connection is between a primary community and a person's way of life, what the relationship is between communities, and what the relationship might be between the larger society and an individual community.

Michael Sandel recognizes three conceptions of community, the first two being an instrumental account and a sentimental account. These two accounts, Sandel claims, are accepted by Rawls. Sandel then posits a third conception of community, the "constitutive community," which, Sandel argues, is required by both Rawls's and Dworkin's theories.[42] Each of these three accounts is examined; the third is modified to include features Sandel does not explicitly stress. Throughout this conceptual surgery on these various views of community, the dimensions of community accepted as basic to this theory of moral education are delineated.

The instrumental community

According to Rawls, an instrumental community exists when a group of agents have similar "shared *final* ends" (my emphasis) that can be achieved through mutual cooperation and the acceptance of necessary burdens. This is basically an individualistic account of community that assumes agents have "self-interested motivations" that they seek to achieve. These interests can best be fostered and satisfied by membership in an association through which agents collectively seek the desired end. While the instrumental community is a tool to fulfill a group of individuals' "shared *final* ends," that association must be governed by the principles of justice. Three components are crucial to the instrumental conception of community that make it unacceptable for the form of character and the character education advocated here. These unacceptable elements are first, the priority of individuals over communities; second, the idea that communities exist because of members' shared interests and purposes; and third, the view of rationality that underlies the instrumental community.

In instrumental communities, individuals are prior to communities   Since they decide which communities to join, individuals and their unique interests are prior to any community. Though it seems obvious that individuals may join a variety of communities during a lifetime, this idea of joining is not without its difficulties. Joining a community is not like joining a team or a club in which members may have mutual interests. Belonging to a community requires that the person be rooted within the community, accept its moral excellences, be changed by its underlying values, understand its historical roots in that the member becomes the next link in an historical chain, possess the skills the community cherishes, comprehend the community's metaphors, symbols, and art, adhere to the community's rites and rituals, and understand the jokes the community laughs at. Since this type of belongingness and membership in a community is not gained by trivial or limited education or by mutual interests, individuals would have to expend considerable emotional and cognitive energy to become new members of a community.

According to the instrumental view of community, each individual has particular interests and motivations. Affiliation with a community becomes desirable because the community serves the individual's instrumental and prudential purposes. One problem here is where and how individuals acquire their particular interests, desires, and motivation that cause them to decide to join particular communities. Are all these interests, desires, and motivation formed individually and solely by means of cognitive, rational processes? In other words, does the individual approach potential interests and desires with a completely rational but *tabula rasa* self and then choose which are the most appropriate interests and motivation? In this case, the rational tools would be formal abilities and the blank slate would describe the content at the outset of decision making. The problem here cannot be resolved by turning to logical criteria, but rather requires examination of the person's actual life history.

There are two ways of looking at human beings. Those deciding about which communities to join without previous communal membership can be called "individuals." The term "individual" refers to a single entity who is separated from all other human beings and thus has few if any inherent bonds or attachment with others. What description of a human being would imply the making of rational decisions about interests without any other prior communal bonds? Bonds in themselves would be suggestive of some interests and purposes. The term "person" is used here as distinguished from individual and suggests that a community member is not an abstract, disconnected being who rationally decides on self-interests and purposes. This is not to say that the community or others determine the person's interests and purposes, but that communal affiliation affects personal interests and purposes.

The term "person" imparts a different focus to the relationship between a community and its members. By first being members of a community, human beings become persons who are mutually related to other persons of the community and who internalize the meanings, values, and morality intrinsic to the community. At a later stage in life, someone may decide to join another community. By first having primary affiliation within a community, this person can later become a member of another community, of groups and associations. But this decision is not made without a first-level primary community affiliation and is not purely a rational decision based on instrumental purposes. The motivations, purposes, and interests of persons in this second group, association, or community are in part based on their character. This character was formed in their primary community affiliation and is not just dependent on a self-conscious rational decision. Second, some communities may be specially formed for various purposes and yet not be artifical constructions. These secondary communities may be dependent on the characteristics of various professions and specializations or may be created to fulfill special functions.

Instrumental communities exist because of the shared interests and purposes of their members   Rawls assumes that an instrumental community exists because its members have shared interests, motivations, and purposes.[43] Any attempt to describe a community solely in terms of its members' interests and purposes must meet incredible barriers. Even within a community that satisfies members' purposes and interests, other factors make the association of human beings a community. Other forms of human interpersonal relationships are required for the association to be a community. For example, communities have historical roots that transcend the relationships, interests, and motivations of its members and at the same time, these histories nurture and inform relationships, interests, and motivations. The histories of communities are complicated matters since no history can be fully abstracted from larger human history. Even if members of a community cannot fully articulate and discuss the community's history, this history informs their lives in many ways, through the quality of relationships among members, through the language spoken, the values transmitted to younger members, and the community rituals and rites.

As important as the historical component is another dimension of communities that Rawls generally underplays, this being the types of interpersonal relationships existing in communities. Interpersonal relationships between community members can be described in a number of ways that have little to do with individual interests, purposes, and motivation. Rather, members of a community acquire loyalty to other members and to their community as a whole not for any ulterior motive but because of their attachment within the community. Members of communities have affectional ties to other community members since they all share within this bonded network.

The instrumental community requires one particular view of rationality   Fundamental to Rawls's notion of instrumental community is a particular conceptualization of rationality. In this section, we note why this is a flawed account of rationality. Why is one type of rationality recommended by the instrumental account of community? If the individuals forming an association have similar ends and motivations and accept the burdens connected with the association, these individuals had to determine these ends and motivations in some way. They also had to assess whether their personal ends were worth the burdens of the community. In other words, personal ends and interests had to be balanced against communal burdens and responsibilities. Decisions regarding ends and the assessment of burdens, Rawls would say, are based on one type of rational thought processes. Rationality, according to this view, is the means of deciding on the good for the individual. The good for Rawls is not Plato's Form of the Good or Dewey's end-in-view, but rather a plan of life. "The formal rule (of rational deliberation) is that we should deliberate up to the point where the likely benefits from improving our plan (of life) are just worth the time and effect of reflection."[44] Similarly, Rawls follows Sidgwick's notions of rationality by connecting deliberative rationality with the good of a life plan, when stating that "a person's future good on the whole [is] . . . what he would now desire and seek if the consequences of all the various courses of conduct open to him were, at the present point of time, accurately foreseen by him and adequately realized in imagination."[45] Rawls further extends this idea of rationality in another section that discusses choosing the "good for life plans." It is crucial to realize that Rawls's account of rationality in this form applies only to the good, not to the right, to life plans, but not to justice as fairness. Even if Rawls were to provide additional analysis of rationality for choosing the good for life plans, this would not affect the theory of right. For the rationality of the theory of right is prior to the rationality of the theory of good.

Rawls's notion of rationality and the good dependent on rational life plans leads to an instrumental account of community. The life plans of individuals provide their primary interests and motivation, which in turn then require an instrumental community for their fulfillment. Since they cannot fulfill life plans by themselves, agents must contractually bind themselves to some association. Any association, however, does not just dispense goods to its members and thus fulfill the motivations and interests of its members. Maintenance of the association requires that all members accept certain burdens (i.e., act in ways that might not further their own interests, but further the interests of the association as a whole). When accepting the burdens of the community, an individual would assess whether the communal burdens would so erode life plans that the life plan no longer meets the conditions of deliberative rationality. In this case, community membership would not further the agent's life plans and interests. One may also wonder what an agent would do if at one time the trade-off between communal burdens and personal life plans were tolerable, but as time passed communal burdens far outweighed the personal benefits accrued. The community no longer can fulfill the agent's life plan. Agents, in other words, are willing to accept the burdens of the association only as a trade-off, a condition for fulfilling their own interests. There is no fundamental commitment to the association or to the members of the association except when these fulfill one's own life plans and interests.

Thus far, we have seen that deliberative rationality serves in a number of ways, both to assess the comparative benefits and burdens of community membership and in the first place to decide on one's good through a rationally chosen life plan. When an agent uses deliberative rationality to choose one life plan among numerous other possible life plans, that individual is actually using a type of calculative reasoning. According to this type of reasoning, an individual weighs each life plan to determine which one can be fulfilled, which will not require excessive or intolerable effort.

The deliberative rationality of the instrumental community is very different from the way someone who has prior community affiliation would evaluate the good and the merits of comparative life plans. The reasoning of someone with prior community affiliation and relationships would be influenced by the community, its values and moral excellences, its symbols and metaphors, and its notion of the common good. These factors would have little or no import for deliberative rationality. The notion that community life and values influence an agent's idea of a personal good and desired life plan is not a matter of brainwashing or manipulation,[46] but involves the nurturing of younger members to become fully mature persons. Assertions that all communities indoctrinate or manipulate members do not take us very far in understanding the relationship between communities and their members and how new members are initiated into communities. Unquestionably, every human being is educated and nurtured in a way that influences who and what the mature person is. As Pascal well recognized, moaning about why I was born here rather than there and why I was born now rather than then resolves very little, but only tells us something about the human condition. The fact that someone is born in this community, in this place, and at this time tells us something about what values, history, roots, social relationships, symbols, rites, metaphors, and education the person might acquire. Whether this nurturing and formal education are indoctrinative or manipulative in a negative sense depends on other qualities. Without adequate nurturing and thus induction into a human society and moral community, infants will not become persons, human organisms will not become human persons, human beings will not become moral persons. A network of relationships and early, primary community membership create who the person is and thus what the person judges worthwhile and good.[47]

The sentimental community

The sentimental community also is fundamentally individualistic. While this community may often involve sacrifices by members, it is still individualistic since member cooperation is based on individual needs and the ties of sentiment.[48] These ties of sentiment again relate to the interests and goods of the individuals in the association. In the case of the sentimental community as well as with the instrumental community, the plurality of individuals is prior to unity, the individual prior to the community. At the same time that there are other differences between these two forms of community, there are also similarities. For example, according to Rawls's account of "the morality of association,"[49] a sentimental community can evolve out of an instrumental community. Individuals first choose to be members of an instrumental community because community membership can further their life goals, their personal good, and their life plans. At first, any new member of the community has purely instrumental attachment to the other members of the community. But in time, this member through familiarity, sharing burdens, and working together with others for the attainment of common personal goals acquires sentimental bonds with other members of the community. At this point, the community is no longer merely an instrumental but a sentimental community as well.

Rawls's notion of associations that others may interpret as communities is extended to a wide range of exemplars, not only the family, but also school and neighborhood. In addition, Rawls includes "such short-term forms of cooperation . . . as games and play with peers."[50] Also there are larger associations, where individuals come together to achieve self-interests. In these associations, individuals may also develop feelings of goodwill and friendship[51] since through these arrangements agents learn appropriate virtues and ideals.[52] Thus, the association becomes a sentimental community as well. What began as an instrumental community eventually also becomes a sentimental community. The inclusion of an extensive range of exemplars of associations, from family to school to business association, simultaneously has advantages and disadvantages. One advantage is that Rawls recognizes, as do Lawrence Cremin and John Goodlad in a more explicit way, that there are various educational networks that foster the learning of skills, ideals, and virtues. Such moral education can occur in families, team sports, schools, and the workplace. On the other side, however, some of the criticism directed against Rawls's notion of community derives from his extension of the notion "association" or "community" to all sorts of diverse social groups. For example, the family and team sports are two very different types of associations as are the school and team sports. Children do not join families because of some interest or purpose. Children are born into families that already accept values, rules, ideals, and virtues. Children not only acquire these from their families, but also become rooted within the family and attached to family members. If anything, the family provides a child's first steps toward moral personhood. A sports team in comparison is a very different type of association: members change and thus players do not become attached to any one individual; the primary interest is the games, not necessarily the players; children may join or leave team sports dependent on many factors, whether they are interested in the game or whether their game improves; children, as Piaget noted, can change the rules of games in a rather different way than might exist in families.[53] Associations such as schools and team sports are also very different from each other. Schools in most cases are compulsory, team sports self-chosen; schools may intentionally and purposively structure a specific environment in which to achieve the goals of moral education; the primary goal of team sports often concerns the game, not some collateral experience. Though the very general notion "association" seems to serve certain theoretical purposes for a theory of justice and its subordinate notion of good, association and its many diverse exemplars also confuse various issues. Instead of accepting either the instrumental or sentimental community that is derived from these various types of associations, another conceptualization of community needs to be sought.

The constitutive community

After challenging the adequacy of Rawls's instrumental community and sentimental community, Sandel posits a third way of looking at the notion "community." This third way he calls the constitutive account of community. According to Sandel, the constitutive community

> is not just a *feeling* but a mode of self-understanding partly constitutive of the agent's identity. On this strong view, to say that the members of a society are bound by a sense of community is not simply to say that a great many of them profess communitarian sentiments and pursue communitarian aims, but rather that they conceive their identity—the subject and not just the object of their feelings and aspirations—as defined to some extent by the community of which they are a part. For them, community describes not just what they *have* as fellow citizens but also what they *are*, not a relationship they choose ... but an attachment they discover, not merely an attribute but a constituent of their identity.[54]

By being nurtured within a community, a human being not only becomes a member of that community, but also acquires an identity and thus becomes a particular person. Acquiring an identity within a community is not a linear affair in which a number of conditions and experiences affect the human being. An interacting matrix of communal experiences, conditions, and events nurture and create the identity of a community member. Among other matters, these include the community's symbolic system, its music and art, its values, its mores and customs, its history and ideal type human beings, and its rites and rituals.

This view of the relationship between community and person leads to many problems. A few of these include the following: If a person's identity, feelings, aspirations, and

interests are formed within a community, does this imply
an absence of individual freedom and personal autonomy?
If moral education occurs within this form of community,
can this moral person qua community member attain a
moral vista that expands to include an enlarged or universal moral community? When the member of this primary
community moves into public life and joins other forms of
communal associations or groups, how do the values and
moral excellences of the primary moral community relate
to those of the new associations? Since moral education is
first given in children's primary communities, how can the
public school accommodate the diverse moral concerns
and excellences of these different communities? These
questions form the basis of an ongoing struggle that moral
education, communities, and human beings encounter. In
this section, these questions are only partially answered.

   This account of the constitutive community can also
be viewed from a rather different perspective, that being "a
way of life."[55] Way of life does not refer to the life plans of
a few especially favored groups or apply to membership in
some specialized profession.[56] The idea "way of life" has a
much wider application than many theorists note, this notion referring in part to the communal affiliations persons
endorse. In other words, by endorsing a particular community affiliation, someone also accepts a way of life consistent with the community's values and ideals. At present,
for example, many American farmers may not retain
ownership of their small family farms. These farmers do
not bemoan the loss of a livelihood, but the demise of their
way of life. This destruction of a way of life also implies the
destruction of community structures. That way of life and
its community structures are not dependent on earning a
living and working the land, but on relationships to the
land, to animals, nature, to other farmers, to other community members, to churches and community institutions, to a
set of values, and to an underlying historical tradition. People living this way of life are not individualistic or embedded within an instrumental community or even a sentimental community. Rather, farmers as well as other members of
this constitutive community mutually reach out through

time and space to form a network of persons. Their identities and values are created by virtue of their membership in a particular type of community. According to the characteristics of a constitutive community, the members of farm communities see a similar moral reality. Michael Walzer endorses this idea by claiming that "goods have different meanings in different societies. . . . A solitary person could hardly understand the meaning of the goods or figure out the reasons for taking them as likable or dislikable."[57] The numerous goods, including moral, aesthetic, and religious goods, that farmers for example strive to achieve may seem similar to those desired by other communities. On one side, the meaning and articulation of these goods depends on the primary communal affiliations and way of life of farmers. Thus, when we say that identity, feelings, aspirations, interests, and motivation are dependent on the person's primary community affiliation, we recognize that in certain ways a community also structures the meaning of moral goods. Yet on the other side, this idea of the diversity of meanings must be tempered more than Walzer would accept. In some important ways, the goods communities cherish, what they consider the good life and morally good, are not wholly diverse and without any connecting features. The goods of diverse communities share certain root meanings.

During earlier periods, the expression "way of life" was not an exceptionally common means to describe the life narratives or histories of a human life. But such ways of life can be derived from the community values, moral excellences, and models of human life accepted during various ages. The ideal of the Roman orator did not just represent the way of life of one group of individuals. The monastic life of the medieval religious order did not merely describe one life narrative. The dominant way of life for each period influenced the character excellences of each larger community. To sustain community values and the prime model of human life, the ideal of the Roman orator dictated that other people in society live particular types of life. The major theme of their life narratives was dictated by the major theme of the community's life. There might have been variations composed based on the theme, but not changes in the theme.

Someone may argue that these examples are not accurate exemplars of current use of the expression "ways of life," that ways of life refer to individualistic life plans, styles of life, and life narratives. At present, some might say, any such uniformity no longer is acceptable for many reasons, for example, because of diverse religions and ethnic groups, each of which may cherish rather different moral excellences. In addition, someone else may argue that the excessive individualism and privativism of this age must foster a very different way of looking at ways of life, that individuals choose their own unique ways of life. While these aspects of current American society to some degree exist, they are not the entire picture. More important, excessive individualism and privativism should not be the model on which to base a conceptualization of way of life. The position here is that there must be a balance between communal affiliation and individual way of life, that communal life and individual ways of life interact and interrelate and are not two rigidly separate means to describe a human being's life.

If there were exceptionally diverse community values and life models, the difficulty of character education would be even greater than already expected. But is it really the case that there is such excessive diversity or are certain basic forms of many moral excellences accepted by seemingly diverse groups? For example, to say that a child is born an American does not just designate citizenship. There are also distinguishing moral excellences that are or should underly being an American during the end of the twentieth century.[58] These excellences are part of the present American national character, have developed from the beginning of our history, and are still in the process of changing. Though many authors point to the challenges, to a crisis, to conflicts and problems in the American system and how this reveals itself in the national character and the virtues of its people, these authors also reveal the great potential for revitalization and change.[59] In addition to a child's receiving a country's national character, the child is initiated into a certain community, into subsocieties, into ethnic and religious groups. Such nurturing within a matrix of community and society associations is dependent on parental primary and secondary affiliations. Though there may be considerable variation in the various communities different children are initiated into, these communities govern children's fundamental values and moral ideals. At the same time, however, we cannot view communities as entities unto themselves without any relationship to each other and to the larger society. They survive and flourish within a larger society and exist at this time and in this place. They do not write their own unique moral history detached from every other social, political, scientific, and cultural influence. Their moral excellences and values are influenced by both the community's, society's, and culture's history.[60] As the child develops into young adulthood, there is the possibility of choosing variations on the major themes of the society and community, and these variations provide the basis for particular life-styles and the writing of a life narrative. But to make rational decisions about one's own life-style does not imply that the person wholly eliminates every aspect of already accepted community excellences and values. The person choosing a life-style does not create a wholly new one, which is not shared with any other people. Yet even with these limitations on the possibility of developing a wholly new and different life-style, there is some merit in saying that each person lives a unique life style. Living a unique life-style is painting the same view in a different style, the playing of a variation on a well-known musical theme. With the development of a life-style during a given life, the person's character *may* be enhanced, enriched, become deeper, more complex, and be restructured to include a reconfiguration of moral excellences.

One further problem remains to be discussed in this section, this being whether all communities are equally acceptable or whether some standard is necessary for judging communities. Even if readers have suspended judgment about communities and ways of life until this point, they may now question whether there is a flaw in a position that celebrates the diversity of communities. By speaking of diverse communities, ways of life, and how sets of moral excellences and virtues are attached to different communities and ways of life, we preserve the notion of moral and value pluralism. However, detractors may very well claim that such pluralism is an inadmissible form of relativism. Their argument might include comments that this view of community, with its pluralism and relativism, may be descriptive, but it is not normative. By being descriptive, this view of community would thus seem to accept any form of community. While the position presented in this section thus far may very well be used to describe actual pluralistic or relativistic ways of life, these different ways may not be equally approbative. I do not argue that during any particular historical period, every community and every set of moral excellences accepted by communities are equally valid. Some communities, it can be argued, should be inadmissible, according to rational, humane conceptualizations of moral life. A theory of moral education has to be normative and not just accept the matter-of-fact. In two ways, this view of community sidesteps this criticism, first in relation to an external, objective standard and second, according to certain internal conditions of the community itself. First, as will be discussed in a later chapter, moral excellences cannot just be tested according to community standards. Rather, moral excellence refers to another standard, representing the approximate manifestation of a variety of moral ideals.[61] In the last chapter of this book, we return to this issue and examine moral ideals and their relationship to moral excellences and moral education.

Second, the possibility that all communities and ways of life are not equally valid or that some are disapprobative leads to other criteria, these relating to what it means to describe a way of life as reasonable or approbative. The problem of how to judge whether community and its ways of life are disapprobative is complex. The answer to this problem, however, does not suggest that eventually I foist a single preferable model of community or its ways of life on readers or will list preferable community attributes in hierarchical order. The criteria noted here relate only to what some may call a weak claim that during any given historical period, some communities and ways of life will be reasonable and others unreasonable. But in actuality, as will become apparent, this is neither a weak nor minimalist claim.

Some communities and ways of life are reasonable; others are unreasonable and thus unacceptable, according to this theory of moral education. By which standards or on what basis is a way of life judged reasonable? Just as no individual lives in abstraction from some society and an historical period, so no community or way of life survives by itself. Every way of life is confined within a larger society, within an historical stream and spatio-temporal period. Within American pluralistic society, in particular, any way of life is influenced and limited in some manner by the larger society, by other communities, and by the nature of this historical period. This does not mean that eventually there is some complicated amalgamation of communities or ways of life, but just that in contemporary social, political, technological, and cultural life, communities encounter and collide with one another. No community survives in total segregation from all other communities. For their very survival and enrichment, communities require contact and interaction within a larger national and global society. There can be no harmonious general social and political life unless communities can meet in some agreeable, comfortable public setting. Communities themselves cannot survive unless there are general provisions within the larger context for their nurturance and protection. The nurturance and protection of any one community must imply the nurturance and protection of other communities.[62]

How then can we judge whether a community is reasonable? I believe we can begin with three general standards: (a) Inner coherence and conditions for self-generation. (b) Beliefs and values that accept the existence of other ways of life. (c) Relationship to the overall historical stream and present historical context.

Inner coherence and conditions for self-generation

The inner coherence characteristic also refers to one criterion of an agent's character. Though communities may change very slightly and seem excessively traditional and conservative, all communities require some means to maintain themselves in the face of external and internal change.

Acceptance of larger society and other ways of life

This standard is not as simple as it may seem on the surface, for the acceptance of the existence of other communities cannot mean that some other communities are accepted or envied. Unquestionably, members of any community see its own customs and mores, values and beliefs as superior and furthering the good life. But even so, there should be no active intrusion into other communities and no inquisition to convert recalcitrant outsiders. Rather, any community's "right" to exist and flourish should be explicitly warranted by all other communities. In some cases, these comments would not hold since those communities dependent on professional specializations would not usually be antagonistic to other communities.

Acceptance of the larger society and its social and political structure implies that any single way of life accepts that the larger society, its mores, customs, laws, morality, and political system guarantee the best possibility for the survival of the community and its way of life. Thus, members of the smaller community see the larger society as a vital means of nurturing communal life. This in no way means that members of a community must passively accept all the conditions of the larger society. Through engagement in the civic life of the larger society or through political activism, some members of a smaller community may struggle to modify the larger society. This delicate problem must be examined at another time.

Relationship to the overall historical stream and the present historical context

Every community exists at some spatio-temporal juncture. It has a past, a history, and assumes it will have a future. What is the developmental stage of the community? Has it continued to grow and flourish, questioned itself, and applied corrective surgery? Someone may point to particularly conservative, traditional communities as examples that seem to confound this characteristic. But this is not the case. Even groups like the Amish in this country have had to use more contemporary means to guarantee the continuance of the good and healthy life. What has happened is that ways of life have continued to accept the basic tenets, values, and beliefs that underly the fiber of their being. But at the same time the way these tenets, values, and beliefs are interpreted vary, if even ever so slightly, with the historical context.

In this chapter, we have examined a view of moral character. The possession of moral character includes having coherent moral excellences. These moral excellences are superordinate excellences that include criss-crossing networks of exemplars and attributional concepts. These other concepts advance beyond the normal domain of the moral and include epistemological and logical dimensions. Moral excellences are often capable of being understood as dispositions or habits that insure active moral engagement. The view of habits suggested here steers clear of stimulus-response associationist psychologies and instead sides with earlier philosophic conceptualizations and Piaget's notion of habits. However, habits and dispositions cannot be the whole story of character. Other elements must be included. Moral agents' desires, impulses, interests, and emotions often conform with their moral excellences. Though there are times when desires, impulses, interests, and emotions conflict in some way with accepted moral excellences, all these occurrences cannot be described as negative or unacceptable. Emotions that conflict with accepted moral excellences of course can have negative results that a moral agent regrets and that scar moral lives. However, emotions can also have a positive function, such as signaling the onset of a moral dilemma or motivating a moral agent to question the adequacy of moral excellences. Finally, it was argued that character and moral excellences require a certain form of primary community life. Though agents may eventually join various associations, moral agents become members of a moral community and acquire moral excellences by living within some primary community.

5

Character, Community, and Education

By living in an intimate, communal society and thus being a member of a moral community, children acquire habits, dispositions, interests, feelings, desires, language, knowledge, attitudes, symbols, ways of treating other human beings, and thus an embryonic form of morality. The more important issue here is not whether some thinkers would use the derogatory terms "inculcation" or "indoctrination" for this process of becoming a moral person and a member of a moral community. It might even be argued that all initiation into society and a moral community is some form of inculcation and indoctrination. Instead of disagreeing about the negative denotations and connotations of these terms, it is accepted that education in societies and communities also involves the transmission of certain moral views and values. This transmission some writers might call inculcation or indoctrination. The terms are unfortunate. What alternative could be suggested other than educating children in communities and society? Would those who insist on negative descriptions want to educate children with no roots and no ties? Would they expect that at the age of reason, children will be able to reason abstractly without any taint of the concrete or particular that is nourished in communities? Any such view could only be an exaggerated figment of the imagination. And the creature would not be a human being, but some aberrant organism.

The problem we must study here is how moral education involves two faces—one, the transmission of moral excellences by a moral community, and two, moral education within a large public environment such as the school.

Communities and Moral Education

The Good Life, Communities, and Public Policy

Some might be aghast at the assertion here that communities transmit moral knowledge, skills, attitudes, sentiments, and excellences. Critics would wonder whether the stress on community life and the noting of various aspects of communal moral education are posited as a jest. Critics would point to the recent disintegration of so many communities and question whether the present writer slept through a period that witnessed the demise of constitutive communities. This criticism can be answered in the following way. It is true that at present there have been major shifts in communal life, that some communities have disappeared, and some have been scarred beyond recognition. Does this mean that constitutive communities with historical roots and moral traditions have almost wholly disappeared? Does this mean that newer constitutive communities cannot be formed? An examination of some of the recesses of human life and society suggest that perhaps scholars ignore the communities that have survived the strains of twentieth-century social, scientific, and value revolutions. At present, about one-third of the children in the United States are still raised in such communities.

In relation to these surviving constitutive communities, we must address various issues that refer to these communities' ability to provide moral education for their children. First, someone may argue that such communities have a right to exist and their survival requires that they effectively provide moral education to a younger generation. Instead of couching this argument in terms of a language of rights, there is a different way of beginning. We need to question under what circumstances human beings achieve the good and moral life? Is the maintenance of community life one avenue for achieving the goals of the good and moral life? Present criticism of the quality of moral education and of public morality is hollow if certain questions are not answered or if answers only camouflage the problems. Formal education alone cannot resolve the problem of societal morality. The development of reasoning about moral dilemmas in itself cannot be the sole way to promote morality. Many public figures and policy makers assume that schools can resolve all the problems of American society. There are few attempts to examine whether other institutions of society and whether communities should also be expected to contribute in positive ways to moral education. When John Goodlad and Lawrence Cremin refer to educational networks,[1] they refer to all the other places and institutions in which human beings are educated. These other places—communities, institutions, associations, groups, media, and the like—can no longer be ignored. They are places where moral education occurs. Policy makers and theoreticians now need to investigate how various places outside the school can promote moral education.

Someone may wonder why these other places are ignored and not seen as foundational to moral education. One reason for this present omission is that moral education theory and policy have been dominated by one single view of what moral education should be. Even many of those who claim to move beyond the Kohlbergean hegemony of the previous decade still adhere to Kohlberg's basic notions. There is continual reference to abstract reasoning and formal standards as the basis of moral education.[2] These thinkers continue to posit a questionable conceptualization of human nature and reasoning and they ignore fundamental dimensions of the moral life. Unlike the questions asked during the last five decades, philosophers are again asking the question that was fundamental for earlier thinkers. This question is, What is the good life? The good life is inextricably tied to the moral life. Moral education also needs to be broadened to include this question. This question about the good life cannot be answered by schools alone. Schools cannot provide the sole means to transmit and engender morality.

Moral education must begin with induction into a moral community that will give children an intuitive vision of the good and moral life. This induction includes in embryonic form many dimensions of mature moral life. Young children who act and live within a moral community gain unarticulated understanding and skill in this moral world without necessarily gaining moral self-consciousness. A vision of the moral world is best provided by communities and parents who are already members of communities. The question society as a whole must ask is whether it is sufficiently concerned to provide the tools and policy to foster the good life and morality as it develops in communities and in the broader arena noted here. Does society want people who are moral and possess a vision of moral ideals and a moral universe? The issue of moral education is not just an issue resolved by families or schools, but depends on more general, broader social and political policy. In other words, rather than assuming any single institution, political group, or social association can assure the moral climate of society, moral education is a multifaceted endeavor involving all major communities, associations, and groups, involving political and social life, and personal decisions and responsibility.

If society is committed to the belief that communities should initiate children into a moral world, then society must ask which political and social policy can nourish communities and guarantee their survival. What political and social policy will foster the health of communities without requiring these communities to become fanatic political pressure groups? Some of the recent fanaticism and political pressure of communities may well be based on fear of this new age, fear of the changing values of society, and fear that their own communal values and ways of life may be crushed. These communities may see public policy as protecting and nourishing the autonomous individual and privatism and denigrating the worth of communities. Concern with how public policy might promote communities may also neutralize some of the more irrational and potentially fanatic forms of political and social pressure. Any social policy to nourish communities raises other problems. One of these problems is where community interests and a community's moral world should end and where the common good of a larger, more universal public morality should begin. Can a boundary be drawn between the community and the public moral world? The boundary between community and public morality creates especially difficult problems and probably ones that are presently causing excessive political and social consternation. If society as a whole turns away from these various questions and does not foster rational and serious discourse on these issues, then communities will fight for their survival and rely on political partisanship and pressure techniques.[3]

Moral Education in Communities

Emphasis on communities and communal ties in the first place assumes that moral education at an early stage would aim to induct children into the traditions, values, and morality of the community. Children would acquire the moral excellences of their community. Through education within a community, children would become members of a moral world. Numerous examples of analogous induction into a community can be given. These examples provide insights into how novices become full-fledged members of communities and can also suggest how communities induct children into their moral worlds. An initiate in some religious order, an apprentice in an art studio, or a doctoral student in a science laboratory is introduced and gradually accepts appropriate excellences, character, and rules of the religious order, the community of artists, or the scientific community. Induction into these and similar communities occurs by having the agent surrounded by and embedded within that community, by the novice taking part in the community's rituals and rites, by imitating exemplar skills and moral behavior, by recognizing the ideal types respected by the community, by having behavior corrected by older members of the community, by having an implicit (or explicit) mentor system, by being guided to develop know-how and acquire appropriate skills, by listening to the stories of the community's history and its moral heroes, and by acquiring knowledge and understanding, appropriate attitudes, and feelings. Through these and other experiences, novices acquire the knowledge and understanding, the skill and expertise, the attitudes and feelings necessary for membership in the community. Membership in a moral community is not achieved by attending courses that explain the community's moral rules and rites, its moral standards and behavior. Induction is not achieved through formal courses to motivate student moral discourse and discussions. Rather, through active participation and engagement within the life of a community, by actually living and practicing the skills and morality within some particular community, the novice becomes a competent member of a moral community.

Those who want to become professional painters or dancers, scientists or physicians, violin makers or singers do not create communities for themselves. As Rawls and others have recognized, these artists and scientists seek already formed associations to achieve their goods, purposes, and interests. These associations or communities already exist and have their own histories, traditions, common language and symbolic system, implicit requirements for membership, standards of skillful performance, knowledge, and attitudes, values and morality. The full-fledged members of the community already possess attachment bonds with other members of the community and with the community itself. Membership in these communal associations is not automatic, but requires some sort of induction, initiation, and training by which the novice acquires the values, skills, knowledge, and moral excellences of the community.

A child's moral education should begin within some primary community. The term "primary" is used to refer to the child's first community membership. For children, induction into a community is both similar and dissimilar to the novice's induction into a professional community of experts. The induction of a child into a moral community is different from novice induction into a professional community in that the novice's interests, desired good(s), and purposes govern the choice of the community membership sought. Children do not choose which communities they will become members of. They do not choose whether to become members of a moral community and moral world. Whereas novices who want to become experts join instrumental communities, children are born into constitutive communities. Membership in a moral community is one criterion for being human. All human beings need to join a moral community. Novices already are members of such moral communities, whereas children by being born and living within communities become members of a moral community. Yet in some ways, it is unfair to distinguish too rigidly between these two types of communities. Though novices may see a community as instrumental to their desires, interests, and purposes, the community itself may actually be a constitutive community in that its members' identities are constituted by the community.

A child's induction into a constitutive community is similar to a novice's induction into an instrumental community in two additional ways. First, both types of communities have similar techniques for transmitting the community's values, moral excellences, skills, and knowledge. Through induction into a community the child acquires an intuitive understanding of what it means to see other human beings as cherished members of a larger moral community. Benevolence and altruism are among the many sentiments children may acquire. What else does a community transmit to children? What aspects of moral life do children learn and understand through induction into a community? Only a few of the many moral dimensions transmitted by communities are noted here: admiration for moral heroes; the practice of actual moral life as it occurs in the daily, ordinary aspects of communal living; the development of skill in carrying out moral actions; recognition of the struggles and tragedies of moral life and,

simultaneously, respect and admiration for moral grandeur; intuitive understanding of moral excellences; assistance in the first developmental steps in acquiring moral
excellences; acquiring the responsibilities of moral life;
being loved, nurtured, and cared for by cherished members of the community and thus learning how to love, nurture, and care for others; becoming attached to and bonded within the community, this bonding being one dimension of membership in the moral world of the community;
learning the symbols and metaphors, the forms of moral
discourse, the rites and the rituals that make up and define
the community and its moral world. This transmission occurs through being cherished and nurtured, through living and breathing, speaking and listening, acting, participating, and experiencing within the community. The
child becomes a member of the community's moral world
both through the great leaps of momentous events and the
small steps of unnoticed, unrecognized events.

There is a second way to look at the problem of the
survival and nurturance of communities. At different times
in human history, new communal structures have formed.
These newer communities may even begin as instrumental
communities, but in time they eventually may become constitutive communities. With changing values, changing
family patterns, new technological developments, questions about values, and shifts in demographic patterns,
there are also changes in communal structures and align-
ments. In other words, newer and undreamed of communal groups and structures could be developed. These need
not just be small, elite groups of fortunate people, as Her-
mann Hesse assumed in *The Bead Game* or in a different
way, Alasdair MacIntyre seems to suggest as beyond virtue.
Rather, new groups of people in instrumental and sentimental communities need to be provided with the power,
social strength, and means to nuture what could become
constitutive communities.

For some moral agents, the character acquired during
this early period remains a primary aspect of moral life.
Even if community moral excellences still seem acceptable
in adult life, they acquire different meanings through the

diverse styles and moral lives of various moral agents. However, some might still wonder whether during the late twentieth century a primary community's moral excellences can remain the basis of mature moral character and govern all moral judgments and action. Though the instances seem few to intellectuals analyzing present changes in morality and human life, there are still a considerable number of people who live their moral lives within the confines of communal moral excellences. However, the point made by some philosophers is quite different. They claim that moral agents must make autonomous and principled decisions to resolve moral dilemmas. Moral agents cannot use moral excellences that have been transmitted by communities. According to these philosophers, an agent using such moral excellences would not be making a judgment but only following morality dictated by some group or custom. This common assumption has serious defects. First, it assumes that the only people who can be moral are those who have a most highly developed form of reasoning and use formal principles. Second, it assumes that morality exists only when autonomous, fully self-conscious judgments are made. Anyone who acts without autonomously making reasoned judgments with formal principles is not a fully moral person. Third, this common assumption involves an incorrect understanding of how moral excellences, communities, and reasoning function in morality. If a person possesses moral excellences, this does not imply that the person acts without reasoning or judgment.

At times, an agent may modify communal moral excellences. With development, more mature or ideal forms of moral excellences emerge. For many persons, there eventually will be entrance into additional communities. This will often be entrance into the public domain and into the larger political world where different, more complex moral problems exist. At times, the character and moral excellences of the original community cannot wholly meet the needs of these new communities, of public life, or complex moral dilemmas. This does not negate the formation of character in a primary community during early childhood. With this character, a human being becomes morally rooted and from this perspective acquires a vision of a moral universe. From this perspective, a moral agent also should have the potential to modify, restructure, enlarge, change character, and make informed moral judgments.

Families and Moral Education

Though newborn babies are helpless and require nurturance and care, they possess abilities, potentials, and reflexes that allow them to reach out and relate to their world. The first moral lessons begin during infancy and continue in early childhood. The world provides the written music, the notes and musical phrases of these moral lessons; the infant directs and interprets this music; the infant combines disconnected notes and musical phrases into a new whole that eventually becomes his or her moral life.

An infant's world is not merely an extreme form of egocentricity. A larger universe that extends through time and place is reflected within the child's narrow world. The mother nursing her infant and the concerned father fondly consoling the sick infant may not at first be known by the infant. But through their constant attention, the glow of their love and warmth, an infant receives the first lessons of morality.

On one level, the positive resolution of Erikson's first psychosocial crisis "trust" describes one aspect of these first lessons:

> The ontological source of faith and hope which emerges I have called a *sense of basic trust:* it is the first and basic wholeness, for it seems to imply that the inside and the outside can be experienced as an interrelated goodness.[4]

> For the most fundamental prerequisite of mental vitality, I have already nominated a *sense of basic trust,* which is a pervasive attitude toward oneself and the world. . . . By "trust" I mean an essential trustfulness of others as well as a fundamental sense of one's own trustworthiness.[5]

While speaking of how the development of trust affects the ego,[6] mental vitality,[7] conscious experience,[8] human vitality,[9] and faith,[10] Erikson in his major writings does not explicitly relate the development of trust to morality.[11] However, the implications of acquiring "a sense of basic trust" for later morality and moral education can be discerned. For example, a "lack of concern for the interests of others . . . (may result from) the agent's having been psychologically damaged as a result of emotional deprivation in childhood."[12] The degree of emotional deprivation, the possible lack of trust, and the level of mistrust can influence the morality of the adult moral agent. In an extreme case of such deprivation, the psychopath is found.

How is morality and moral development related to the resolution of this first ego crisis, trust versus mistrust? For example, the mental vitality required for resolving complicated moral dilemmas is related to trust in that a moral agent must trust herself in numerous diverse ways even to embark on the voyage necessary to resolve the moral problem. Furthermore, moral action requires trust in oneself. The moral agent must trust in her own competence and be willing to carry out a moral judgment and to act, even when moral action is fraught with uncertainty. Without trust, the moral agent will withdraw from the moral scene and be fearful about her ability to resolve the problem. When turning to the other dimension of trust, trusting others and trusting the world, we see another way that the sense of basic trust relates to morality. If someone does not trust other people or the world in general, why would that person enter into the moral domain in any way but a timorous manner? If a moral agent does not trust other people (e.g., believes that those others are hostile, manipulative, or self-serving), would that agent be concerned with the welfare or interests of others?

While denying that trust is dependent "on absolute quantities of food or demonstrations of love," Erikson stresses the importance of "the quality of the maternal relationship."[13] Similarly, psychologists, lead by Bowlby, have highlighted the importance of attachment bonds between primary care givers and infants.[14]

An infant's world is not just a subjective or wholly egocentric universe, but contains the symbols, meanings, and messages that are the raw material for the child to fashion into his own world and his own being. In some cases, however, that world may be too distant and separated from the infant. The infant reaches out to embrace the world, and the world's meaning and substance elude his grasp. For other infants, the world is oppressive; it suffocates their attempts to breathe and experience. In this case, some narrow, confining portion of the larger world becomes the infant's world and this limited segment infuses the infant's entire being. But no matter who the infant is, using different styles, the infant extends himself, interprets the world, gives it meaning, and incorporates these meanings into his being.

How can we interpret the first awakening of the infant and how relationships with the world stir within the infant? How can we describe how these stirrings eventually form not only the person's psyche and innermost self, but also her moral world and moral being? The world does not remain William James's "buzzing, blooming world" for long, but instead must be transformed into a caring, warm, concerned, recognized, and structured world if that infant is eventually to become a moral person and a full-fledged member of a moral community. During these early years, important moral education occurs. Even when personal moral agency is nonexistent, moral education and the development of morality occurs; it occurs from birth, not merely at some arbitrary "age of reason."

Character is formed through a reflexive interrelationship between a human being and that being's environment. Even though an infant at birth possesses potentials, these are not components of an inherent moral script that automatically unwinds with increasing age. Even genetic makeup does not *determine* moral character. Simultaneously, the child is not a tabula rasa on which the environment writes its moral messages. Dewey argues that habits and thus character are "outgrowths of unlearned activities which are part of . . . [one's] endowment at birth."[15] At birth, these impulses are "as meaningless as a gust of wind on a mudpuddle . . . , a blind dispersive burst of wasteful energy,"[16] and yet these impulses acquire meaning, according to Dewey, through social interaction with a responsive environment and responsive people. Similarly, Piaget refers to the unorganized, unstructured sucking reflex that becomes the infant's first introduction to the world. The infant's reflexes, impulses, and genetic endowment gradually become an organized structure of certain aspects of the larger world, his world reflected through nurturing care givers and society.

It is not blatant romanticism to claim that infants reach out to the world and silently urge a parent to hold and caress them, love and nurture them, talk to and feed them. We cannot underestimate the role of infants' reflexes and impulses in fostering moral development. Through these reflexes, the infant turns a head toward a parent and the parent hears the unsaid words, "Here I am, your child, to be held and fed, loved and educated. I will discover the world through you. You will introduce me to the world." These words are not just a flight of fancy. They are believed and cherished by parents. While we can speak of how these reflexes evolve and that they disappear within a few months of birth, still they serve another purpose. The new parent does not merely see the infant as a helpless being in need of caring, but as a responsive person who reciprocates caring behavior. Parents interpret such reflexive behavior by saying, "She likes me; look how she holds on to me."

During the first months of life, an infant's development is often interpreted by parents in terms of personal affection and attachment. This is not a far-fetched interpretation, for infants' preference for the contours of a human face, their eye contact, and turning to see where a sound comes from strengthen attachment bonds between child and parents. The cooing and babbling between child and parent are not just educational necessities for language development, but also are among the first steps of the dance of morality. All the neonate's reflexes and the infant's abilities and experiences occur within a social world, with other people, primarily between infant and parents.

These parents, however, are part of some society, ethnic group, religious group, or other intimate community. Parents are actually the vehicles for presenting the values and morality of the community and society.

Few would doubt parents' effect on the morality of their children. And yet, it is also commonly recognized that traditional forms of families are in disarray, that there is considerable divorce and large numbers of one-parent families, and that many mothers have entered the work force. We might argue that this is one sign of the tremendous changes occurring in society. But if we expect to improve moral life or provide adequate moral education, then there must be attention to what alternative family forms might be and to what type of social policy might insure the moral education of the very young child that previously had occurred only in one setting, the traditional family.

Schools and Communities

We must begin this section on moral education in schools with additional comments about the communities that children come from and the relationship between schools and these communities. Those who have stressed the schools' responsibility for moral education may argue the following:

> Communities may inculcate children with expected forms of behavior and social rules, but these should not be confused with the moral education schools should engender. Acceptance of communal rules and values applies to small kinship systems, what Tönnies called the *gemeinschaft*. The aim of moral education in schools is something quite different in that it should refer to justice and fairness, to the rights and interests of a much wider group of people. The reasoning and principles of formal moral education programs should apply universally.[17] Moral education given in public schools thus requires a different framework

and form than that of communities. It is acceptable for communities to induct their children into the moral universe of those communities, but public schools cannot take this course.

Other voices may join in this criticism and say that there must be a wall separating the public school from community, separating induction and moral education.[18] Some may also say that whereas a community will have agreed upon moral standards and values, the public school cannot advocate a single set of moral standards or values. These critics would claim that present society with its rampant individualism requires that moral education in public schools concentrate on abstract reasoning and formal principles. According to this position, communities no longer have moral vigor. Solitary individuals make up society, and these individuals have the sole responsibility of making moral judgments. Therefore they must be given the tools to make these judgments. Their moral reasoning must be improved. They need to acquire moral principles (e.g., neo-Kantian formal principles or a utilitarian maximization of good principle).

Still others champion abstract reasoning and formal principles for an altogether different reason. They claim that moral education that fosters such reasoning and principles does not conflict with a community's fundamental values and morality, but places communal morality within a larger context. Abstract moral principles would sidestep the problem of concrete, particularized moral standards by advocating a form of reasoning and abstract principles. Cognitive processes and rational thought would be the focus of moral education. The content of actual moral decisions would not be as important as the justification of the judgments (e.g., deciding which moral standards should be used in making a moral judgment). However, formal criteria and abstract reasoning cannot serve either communities or curb excessive individualism. Communities are unhappy with highly generalizable, abstract moral principles and argue that principled ethics actually sustain a certain view of morality that they find unacceptable. Instead of being neu-

tral regarding moral content and moral decisions, moral
education based on abstract reasoning and formal, highly
general principles is often destructive of community life.
On the other side, moral education that subscribes to formal ethical principles is deficient for those who have never
been raised in communities. A moral education based on
abstract reasoning cannot correct excessive individualism.
Before agents are willing to subscribe to any morality or
ethical principles, they must view other human beings as
members of a moral community. These others cannot be
outsiders to be manipulated in the quest for private interests and personal success. Recognition of others as
equals within a moral community is not dependent on
learning to reason abstractly or using certain ethical principles. Rather, the reasoning and principles require prior
membership in a moral world and this criterion is fulfilled
by communities.

Instead of advocating either community moral education alone or moral education based on highly abstract
moral principles, another approach to morality and moral
education can be taken. Moral education must include a
variety of approaches, two of these being character education based on community affiliations and the development
of rational means of solving moral problems.[19]

Saying that both communities and schools must have
a role in moral education creates many problems. Children
from very different communities with different values and
moral excellences may attend the same school. How can a
school approach the question of moral education under
these circumstances? Are the only two alternatives to be
recommended either the development of abstract moral
reasoning or moral neutrality? Since both these alternatives are rejected, another course and a different relationship between community and school needs to be briefly
sketched.

The School as Bridge

It has been said many times that the school is a bridge
between the family and the larger society. Thus, the school
becomes a meeting place for communities and an intersec-

tion between communities and the larger society. For various reasons, schools in recent years have lost touch with communities and communities seem to have little to say about the moral education their children receive in school. How could some balance again be reinstated?

Let's look at one proposal and see how the school and community might jointly further moral education. Numerous philosophers have argued for the priority of moral action over moral reasoning and for the need of moral education to juxtapose moral action and moral reasoning. One form that this could take is to institute a program of public service, by which students tutor and play with younger children, work in senior citizen centers, entertain and give concerts in hospitals, assist the handicapped and help in social organizations, assist in day care centers and nursery schools, teach religious school, and help those confined to their homes.

The range of a public service program, however, is not the issue here. More often, the issue has been whether a service program should even exist. For example, toward the end of the Vietnam War it was suggested that instead of military service, young people should be required to serve two years in some capacity that could include social service. More recently, when considering the "Nation at Risk" and other national reports, some states again considered this question of a service program. In this case, their concern in part was with civic education. The mandating of service programs was to insure civic responsibility. Students in these programs, it was believed, would develop greater awareness and practical understanding of a common social good. Again, this idea to mandate that students contribute a certain number of hours in social and public service was abandoned. A number of public and private schools, universities, hospitals, youth organizations, and churches have service programs. But these are different from what had been proposed. In these various institutions, children and young people volunteer to help others. No one is required to serve.

For a short time, one Northeastern school district mandated service as a graduation requirement. However, when this mandate was challenged and criticized by taxpayers, the board of education withdrew their earlier mandate. The program became voluntary. Service was acceptable providing adolescents chose whether to volunteer for the program. Was this the taxpayers' real criticism? Might the problem have been that a very small group of people, administrators and members of the school board, made the decision to mandate the policy.

The decision to develop a public service program could have been made in another way. There could have been sufficient discussion that included the various community constituencies of the school district and thus taxpayers, administrators, teachers, adolescents, and other concerned persons. These would be discussions, not the hearings that boards of education often have. The difference between discussions and hearings is great. With hearings, each interest group presents its case in the most exaggerated form possible. The goal is to present the most forceful persuasive brief for one's position. There is little or no attempt to find common meeting grounds or solve a common problem. The advocacy of discussions is not a call for each individual or group to do nothing but present his or her unexamined opinion. The discussion noted here refers to networks of communication, to groups of people working to resolve a common problem. In this case, specific skills and knowledge are necessary. The school may need some neutral person with appropriate interpersonal and group skills to conduct these meetings.

These discussions might not only include questions about whether there should be some service program, but also what such service should include. Service might not just be monitored or administered by schools, but by other institutions, agencies, and organizations. Unquestionably, the people of the school district might reject the idea of service, develop a pilot project to test the consequences, or try a service program in some limited form. They may see certain experiences, volunteerism, and work as service, whereas the school previously had not included these as part of the service program. In this case of community involvement in the decision-making process, the idea of some form of service may well have broad support. Instead of waiting to see whether various communities criticize a policy, the school insured that communities contributed to it. Finally, there is also the question of school leadership needed to implement such policy. When decisions are made, school leaders need to have the courage and integrity to implement the policy. This does not mean that a public service problem continues without any evaluation or modifications, but instead that school leaders are committed to the process of developing moral education programs and to the decisions emanating from such policy groups.

Communities and Agreement About Moral Education

It is often assumed that the presence of a number of diverse communities implies that there can be no agreement about the moral behavior, moral standards, and moral ideals fostered by schools. Assuredly, there are differences in the morality and moral excellences accepted by different communities. But admitting this is not the same as saying that there are no agreed upon moral standards, moral behavior, or moral ideals. What is needed at this juncture is for communities and parents to come together with educators to ascertain where there is agreement. In this quest, parents, communities, and the school become partners. This relationship is not easy to maintain, but the alternative is for schools to claim to be the experts and for parents and communities to remain political pressure groups fighting the unacceptable decisions of educators. The advocacy of partnerships may be particularly difficult in excessively large or comprehensive schools. The answer here is not necessarily a return to neighborhood schools. Other directions could be taken to insure that schools are of a size that allows for extensive community involvement. The control of school size may allow for the fostering of the ethos that Gerald Grant and others claim would improve moral education in schools. The issue here is providing much greater communication networks among diverse groups.

Educational Aims: Aims of Education and Aims of Moral Education

It has not been fashionable to posit far-reaching, long-term educational aims and ideals. Recent criticism of American education and the reports that recommend educational policy have had no time for educational aims. There has been only criticism of declining test scores, a weakened and fragmented curriculum, how American education does not meet the economic and technological challenge of the present age, and the inability of American youth to match the performance scores of students in other highly technological countries. Without reference to educational aims, there have also been statements about what direction specific educational reform should take. Cries about educational excellence have been little more than persuasive slogans without theoretic underpinning or practical denotation.[20] State mandates to test at every level of public schooling and new curriculum requirements have had no relationship with long-term aims. The vision of the "educated" person has not just been clouded, but has disappeared as the concern of any constituency.[21] Different constituencies march to different drumbeats.

General, long-term educational aims and the goals of moral education are closely related members of the same family. Moral education and its goals not only involve moral virtues, but intellectual virtues as well. The goals of moral education move in many directions and encompass the following: improvement of students' character; the further development of the moral excellences students have acquired in communities; the developing of the emotions, interests, and desires necessary for the possession of moral excellences and for making moral judgments; the fostering of the intelligence and reasoning necessary to evaluate character, enlarge moral excellences, and resolve a wide range of moral dilemmas; the acquiring of knowledge and the means to obtain additional knowledge that contributes to the resolution of complex moral dilemmas. The more general aims of education must also include these same dimensions: questions about the good life, intellectual and moral virtues, the development of the individual, and various criteria—moral criteria, epistemological claims, and aesthetic standards.

One example of general aims of education indicates why long-term, general educational aims are needed and how the goals of moral education and general education are related. After defining culture as "activity of thought, and receptiveness to beauty and humane feeling," Whitehead then posits a first statement of what education should aim to produce—people "who possess both culture and expert knowledge in some special direction."[22] Through this aim of education, Whitehead integrates the generalist and specialist, the intellectual and the moral, the intellectual and the aesthetic, the past and the future. The "receptiveness to beauty and humane feelings" describes the aesthetic and moral aspects of culture, and the "activity of thought" refers to the reasoning and intelligence that cultures and human beings require to insure the good life and then improve life. But Whitehead does not limit the aims of education to this one terse statement. He stresses the importance of appreciating ideas and the interrelationship among ideas. Among the various passages that relate to these educational aims is the following:

> You may not divide the seamless coat of learning. What education has to impart is an intimate sense for the power of ideas, for the beauty of ideas, and for the structure of ideas, together with a particular body of knowledge which has peculiar reference to the life of the being possessing it.[23]

Finally, Whitehead advocates the development of the aesthetic characteristic "style" that includes both "attainment and restraint." With style, the person possesses the power to attain the desired end without distraction, with restraint and with control over diverse events. Style "pervades the whole being."[24]

Many policy makers and philosophers of education would argue that long-term, general aims of education now have little currency. Except for sounding pleasant at the beginning of a school handbook, they tell little about what should be done in classrooms or about what curriculum recommendations should be or about which methods should be used. The better way, these critics would claim, is to stop arguing about irrelevant aims of education and begin mandating specific subject requirements that relate to the economic needs of a nation and the work needs of students. It is true that general educational aims do not provide specific educational policy and practice. This does not imply that schools who accept one set of broad, general educational aims would have identical programs. In their practical instantiations, different schools might have very different programs and practices. But all the schools would have programs and practices that in some way reflected the broad educational aims.

What would such aims do to the current arguments about educational excellence and the improvement of schools? Why would broad educational aims be one means of tempering present arguments? Instead of arguments, criticism, and mandates being fragmented and relating primarily to political and economic concerns, there could be a refocusing of educational discourse. By placing educational discourse within a different framework, a different set of recommendations might emerge.

What of the other primary problem that must concern us here, the relationship between general educational aims and the aims of moral education? General educational aims refer to characteristics that generate the good life. For Whitehead, the good life involves the enjoyment of beauty, the beauty of ideas, the attainment of desirable ends without distraction,[25] humane feelings, activity of thought, and the seeking of various perfections. These various dimensions are also basic to the moral life. The various perfections one seeks in the moral life are related to moral excellences, which are not just the virtues implanted in young people by communities. Any moral excellence can be evaluated against a standard of what it would mean for that moral excellence to be a perfection. Activity of thought is necessary to evaluate present moral excellences, to change them, to decide whether they can provide the right or best standard to resolve a moral dilemma, and to judge what action a moral excellence requires in a particular situation. But there is another relationship between general educational aims and the aims of moral education. All formal education is moral education. Even at times when moral education becomes a specific course of study within a school, it is still inimicably interconnected with the larger aims of education. Moral education and its goals are not subsumed under the more general goals of education and are not a component of the larger domain of education. Rather, moral education and its aims are embedded within and overlay all of education.

School Communities

Someone may ask how those many children who have never lived in communities or whose family and community life have been unsatisfactory can acquire the moral excellences that it is assumed families and communities transmit. In these cases, schools can supply the missing community life and transmit suitable moral excellences. In addition, schools also have the responsibility to provide an adequate setting to continue to nourish the bonds and moral excellences of community life for those children who already possess an appropriate foundation of moral excellences. One way of accomplishing this is for schools to be communities. This has been a common recommendation of many educational theorists. Dewey, for example, advocates that schools should be communities.[26] The present recommendation that schools be communities resembles many of these earlier proposals and yet diverges from them. For the community being referred to does not merely refer to a democratic communal structure of a scientific laboratory. The community advocated here possesses the moral excellences, values, symbols, rites, heroes and heroines, celebrations, traditions, history, and rootedness to make the school a place where identities are formed. With these characteristics, the school would not just be a bureaucratic institution or merely a group of individuals with rights, but would be a constitutive community. As mentioned previously, such school communities are best maintained when the number of students in the school is limited.

Entrance into the school community

New members entering communities are initiated in some manner. For infants and children, there are a series of events that mark each step in their entrance to communal life. There are birth certificates, baby naming ceremonies, birthday parties, and parties for special holidays. A school community could have similar ceremonies for those entering the school. In elementary school, for example, there could be ceremonies for those entering kindergarten or first grade and those who have recently transferred into the school. The nature of these ceremonies would vary with the school community, but the ceremony in any one school community would remain the same from semester to semester and year to year. In this way, all members of the school community would come to recognize the meaning of the ceremony.

History and traditions

Communities in society have histories, roots, and traditions. Some of these are "official" in that they are recorded. Some are part of an oral tradition handed down to each new generation. These oral tradition roots include stories that may after a while wander from factual truth. These stories are not designed to give members factual information about the community but represent the values and moral excellences cherished by the community. A school community can take advantage of this powerful vehicle for transmitting communal ideals and excellences to newer members. A history, stories, and traditions can be created for this purpose. These do not necessarily have to be fictions. Yet like the histories of their larger community counterparts, these histories and stories are not purely factual. They can be constructed from the history of the place, from the experiences of alumni who attended the school, and from the memories of teachers and administrators.

They can include the happiness and sadness, the joy and hard work, the struggles and creativity that actually made the school a community.

Symbols, rites, and celebrations

Symbols, rites, and celebrations do not refer to some of the halfhearted practices that now exist in public schools. And yet in the weaker forms of these practices we find examples of what could be enlarged and modified to give students and even teachers a feeling of community affiliation. Schools close on national holidays, on days that democracy, participatory communal life, and freedom in all its many social and political forms should be celebrated. Instead of having appropriate ceremonies and educational experiences to deepen understanding and appreciation, students stay home, watch television, and accompany parents on shopping trips. The significance of the holiday is dissipated. When noting that symbols, celebrations, and rites should be included in the school community, there is recognition that these should be endemic to the school community and should be derived from the larger society.

The school community and moral education

At this juncture, someone may ask whether the above examples and discussion relate to moral education. Can the school community that creates an ethos through the above structure and practices also expect the development of adequate moral character by students? Any model of how to create a school community would have to extend much beyond the few ideas presented here. There would have to be attention to other matters like how to resolve more complex moral dilemmas, how to attend to infractions of school community moral life, what are the respective roles of teachers, administrators, students, parents, and other concerned persons, how the curriculum and teaching methods relate to the school ethos, and whether educational aims and educational philosophy contribute to the creation of this school community structure.

Teachers and Character Education

Teachers often claim that moral education and moral development theories have few implications for their teaching. In this section, there must be some attention to how the classroom teacher can affect the moral education that students receive.

Though character refers to internalized moral excellences the student possesses, character also refers to external standards, (e.g., community beliefs about moral excellences and their views about the ideal dimensions of these moral excellences). The teacher's problem in implementing a program of character education is manifold. There are students with diverse moral excellences, communities that may see moral excellences in different lights, the moral excellences the teacher accepts, and moral ideals of the moral excellences. These four are exemplars that indicate the internal and external aspects of moral excellences. Both these aspects of moral excellences must be considered when a teacher attempts to implement a program of moral education.[27] In this section, only one example is given to indicate the direction that character education in classrooms could take and how teachers can resolve the internal and external dimensions of moral excellences.[28]

Wonder and imagination have been seen from Plato to Whitehead as essential components of the intellectual and moral life, as a means of turning from the inner dimensions of the self to the outer dimensions of the universe. Wonder has been described by Edith Cobb in the following way:

> Wonder is, first of all, a response to the novelty of experience. . . . Wonder is itself a kind of expectancy of fulfillment. The child's sense of wonder, displayed as surprise and joy, is aroused as a response to the mystery of some external stimulus that promises "more to come" . . . , the power of perceptual participation in the known and unknown.[29]

When Whitehead speaks of philosophy beginning in wonder "and when thought has done its best, the wonder remains," he refers to many of the same ideas Cobb mentions. There is expectancy of something more, expectancy that one can know the unknown, surprise in suddenly realizing that there is something other than what was known and believed, the mystery posed by this veil over the unknown. It is a promise that can be fulfilled. The two important points are that wonder is the conjoining of the known and the unknown, and when the previously unknown is known, the wonder remains. There is a new conjoining of the previously unknown now known with a new unknown.

Whitehead's idea of the rhythm of education provides an appropriate method for the conjoining of known and unknown dimensions of moral excellences. Three stages make up this rhythmic method: romance, precision, and generalization.[30] As Whitehead notes, there must be care not to construct a rigid border between these stages. Instead, these three stages represent ". . . a distinction of emphasis, of pervasive quality—romance, precision, generalization, are all present throughout."[31] Before noting how this method can be used for moral education, the characteristics of each "pervasive quality" are noted. According to Whitehead, "The stage of romance is the stage of first apprehension. The subject-matter has the vividness of novelty; it holds within itself unexplored connexions with possibilities half-disclosed by glimpses and half-concealed by the wealth of material."[32] The student is surprised by the novelty and mystery of the unknown and thus no longer focuses on what is known or already believed. There is the desire for something more. In what may seem an uncharacteristic comment, Peters notes how American teachers seem to destroy such moments. Peters had been observing an American class in which a teacher read Gray's "Elegy." After reading the poem, the teacher immediately posed a problem for the students to resolve.[33] Peters expressed regret. The teacher's voice had been so beautiful. The reading of the poem had, if we are to use Whitehead's ideas, allowed students to recognize that there were "unexplored connexions with possibilities half-disclosed by glimpses." Students had entered the mystery of the unknown. But then there was immediate reversion to a problem and problem-solving technique. Why couldn't it be otherwise? Why, according to Peters, were American educators so intent on problem solving? The moment had passed and the romance was destroyed.

The stage of precision is the stage we know so well. It is the stage of increased knowledge, of exactness and facts. This is the way of a large portion of present education and the way of standardized testing. There is nothing inherently wrong about exactness and facts. They "become barren without a previous stage of romance: unless there are facts which have already been vaguely apprehended in their broad generality."[34] The final stage, "generalization," is "a return to romanticism with the added advantage of classified ideas and relevant technique."[35]

Now finally we must look at how this method, these stages, can be used in moral education. In the first place, with this method students are continually reminded that there are external standards and external knowledge as well as already accepted standards and knowledge, that there is a meeting of the subjective and the objective. Thus, this method gives students a certain attitude about the relationship between the inner and outer, the subjective and objective, and beliefs and knowledge. It is an attitude that can influence how students see morality, moral excellences, and moral dilemmas.

Let's now move to a more direct example of how this method might be used in moral education.[36] For our example, we can take the many moral questions and dilemmas raised regarding environmental issues and environmental pollution. Before beginning with this example, two points are noted. First, there must be concern about which moral excellences and moral beliefs relate to these problems. Is it compassion, caring for, sympathy, justice, honesty, and/or courage? Or might which excellences apply depend on the student, community, moral excellences and ideals, and the general features of the moral dilemma? Second, how one begins also depends on both the students and the external standards. Students cannot entertain the mystery and wonder of the unknown if there is no basis for grasping this mystery. This is not a vicious circle, but the well-recognized idea that an educator must begin by knowing where students are and knowing what they understand. For this example let's assume that this rhythmic growth cycle develops through elementary school. In other words, instead of examining the smaller rhythmic cycles of a single lesson or unit, we pass from cycle to cycle throughout elementary school. Finally, it is well to quote Whitehead on what this adventure of rhythmic cycles will be. The aim of education as it relates to style and power, in science and in morality,

> takes the various forms of wonder, of curiosity, of reverence, of worship, of tumultuous desire for merging personality in something beyond itself. This sense of value imposes on life incredible labours, and apart from it life sinks back into the passivity of its lower types. The most penetrating exhibition of this force is the sense of beauty, the aesthetic sense of realised perfection.[37]

The romance of the study of environmental issues might include students maintaining a school garden. This would not have some ulterior motive as might be the case when students are directed to keep careful scientific records about how different conditions affect the growth of plants. With gardening as an example of romance, students become directly involved in cherishing and caring for the environment. Moral action precedes moral thought. The moral action here is taking care of the environment through the nurturing, cherishing, and beautification of a garden. There may be more to romance. Younger children may concentrate only on gardening. Older children returning again to romance after completing rhythmic cycles within cycles may turn to other forms of romance (e.g., painting pictures of the beauty of the garden in different seasons and at different times). From this too, there is a dim awareness of the wonderment of nature. From this, there is recognition of something beyond.

What precision is possible to gain greater understanding of environmental issues and ecology? Younger children do not turn from their gardening and look at some artificially constructed problem. They do not seek fragmented facts that are unconnected with the initial romance and their search for something beyond. Precision can take many forms, and with gardening as with other similar examples there is a conjoining of many aspects of the self and the world. Children gain patience, become diligent, and intuitively understand the personal characteristics necessary to care for the environment. They experience frustration, but learn to continue to struggle with the hardships of nature to maintain their garden. Habits and attitudes develop that contribute to the moral self. Precision may develop in other ways. For the young child, there can be the study of the names of various flowers and other plants. For the older child, there can be the study of the various parts of plants and flowers and an investigation of the life cycle that contributes to plant life and by which plant life contributes to human life. At another time, precision can come from the child's natural questioning of why certain flowers never grew or why some withered and died. At this point, the scientific method could be introduced with students investigating in more rigorous, systematic manner the conditions under which plants flourish. In this investigation, there may also be questions of how pollution affects plants.

Finally, there is generalization, where students possess the skills, attitudes, habits and dispositions, knowledge and ideas by which the environment and nature are experienced as a unified whole. With each subsequent cycle in the development of the character excellences, students will possess a broader, more complex means to nurture and respect the environment. They will not have some disinterested set of facts or resolve some artificial problems. These students will possess the habits, moral excellences, understanding, knowledge, attitudes, and interest to live a moral life in which ecological concern and environmental pollution are central.

This example demonstrates that moral education is not limited to a single course or unit on moral problems. It cannot be a conservative enterprise in which students are blindly indoctrinated and inculcated with absolute rules. It cannot be the learning of an authoritarian dogma. Instead, the moral education advocated here requires a radical change in the nature of public education's aims, structure, curriculum, and teaching method.

6

Two Voices Are There: . . . Each a Mighty Voice

In the cadences of moral theory and moral education, two voices have sometimes sung harmonious duets, sometimes sung unconnected, discordant songs, and sometimes only one voice has been heard, the other overpowered by the fervor and strength of a single dominant voice. These two moral voices have recently been classified as altruistic emotions and neo-Kantian principles, as men's language of rights and women's language of care and response. Though the composers of two voice theories now seem amazed at their new awareness of the duet's beauty, this is not the first time these two voices have been heard.

Even Plato, that confirmed rationalist, wrote songs for these two voices. Though abstract, universal, eternal Forms are the only assurance of moral knowledge, they are not the only voice included by Plato. He discerns another voice: the person searching for knowledge and the Forms does not achieve this prize through rational means alone, but is driven by *eros*. *Eros* is the motivational force to generate the quest for knowledge. The cognitive and affective are thus forever joined. Plato's utopian city-state does not require many laws since its citizens would live together not as autonomous individuals, but as friends with the bonds *philia* generates. Citizens of this city are not autonomous

167

moral agents who each seek a separate way and who ponder self-chosen moral principles; they are friends bound by the ties of love and community. For Hume, feeling and sentiments are even more fundamental phenomena; rational moral judgments and reasoning act in the service of sentiment. When utilitarians posited a greatest happiness for the greatest number principle, they recognized the need for a moral agent to possess altruism. In this moral theory, altruism was joined to a calculative principle to ensure a certain quality moral decision and action. Altruism was the fuel to charge calculative reasoning.

A disjunction between the affective and cognitive, between emotions and principles has recently dominated mainstream Anglo-American ethical theories and moral education policy. Moral principles and rules won the affections of theorists and assumed a dominant role in moral education theory. The other voice, emotions, feelings, and sentiments, was stilled and remained in the background as a dissonant sound noticed only by a few theorists. Within the last decade, however, this stilled voice has again been heard singing a different song. In this chapter, I examine these two voices and focus on why in themselves these theories and voices cannot be the basis of moral education.

Moral Principles and Moral Education

Introduction

Two types of moral principles, utilitarian and neo-Kantian formal principles, have vied for preeminence in midtwentieth-century Anglo-American ethical theory. Before assessing whether either of these moral principles should have a role in moral education, we need to recognize what claims each makes, what types of moral education policy and practice each might recommend, and whether either already has a good track record to insure its inclusion in a theory of moral education. We begin with utilitarianism and then consider in a much longer section the claims of neo-Kantian formalism.

According to utilitarianism, the principle "the greatest good for the largest number" undergirds moral judgments and public policy decisions. This principle actually includes two standards, a principle of aggregation that refers to the greatest amount of good, and a principle of distribution that would spread the good as broadly as possible.[1] The preferred action or public policy should be determined by assessing the comparative good of the consequences of various alternative actions or public policies. Whichever action or policy contributes the greatest good to the greatest number is the right action or policy. Though some actions fulfill both the principle of aggregation and the principle of distribution, often an action is preferable though on a comparative scale it meets the standard of only one of these two principles.

Nineteenth-century utilitarianism, which viewed the good as happiness, has rarely survived in its original form. The theory has undergone various modifications. Some theorists now would prefer a society to posit basic moral rules that would maximize the good and that rational people would accept.[2] Others argue that some rules of thumb must exist so every trivial aspect of moral life does not require extensive calculation of comparative goods.[3] According to this version of act utilitarianism, moral agents would not have the time and might even go mad if every minor moral matter required extensive analysis of "probable consequences." Whether advocating rule utilitarianism or act utilitarianism, a utilitarian would still endorse the greatest good principle to underlie general societal rules or rules of thumb. Even with contemporary changes to soothe uneasy critics, utilitarianism has continued to receive an unfavorable press. There are arguments that a utilitarian calculus of contending goods cannot designate the actual allocation of various goods; questions about whether a large number of goods for a small elite would equal a few goods given to the entire population; disagreements about whether both the principle of distribution and aggregation have equal weight and how to decide whether one of these two aspects of the utilitarian principle should have priority; and condemnation of calculative reasoning because of its recent dire practical consequences for public policy.

In two ways utilitarianism may affect moral education: first, through educational policymaking, and second, by providing the underlying theoretical assumptions for a moral education program.

Educational policymaking

Educational policymaking cannot be isolated from an explicit program of moral education. When deciding which standards should underlie moral education, theorists should also be concerned that the same moral standards or sets of moral standards are used to assess educational policy decisions. One cannot hope to motivate or teach students to respect and care for each other; accept that human beings and animals have rights; believe in the importance of social justice, equality, freedom, and personal responsibility; or follow the light of moral ideals, if these dimensions are not part of educational policy. On the surface, many educational policy issues seem far cries from the concerns of moral education, but a few brief examples indicate the close relationship between moral education and educational policy.

How should policy makers decide what curriculum should be mandated or recommended? Can decisions about what knowledge and skills should be transmitted be made without some sort of evaluative and moral underpinning? What sort of assessment, evaluation, or grading occurs in schools? Do teachers and other members of the school staff have decision-making roles? How are disciplinary and punishment decisions made? All these and other questions relate to the quality of moral education the school provides. Educational policy and moral education may seem unlikely relatives in that each includes rather different dimensions; moral education is in part dependent on psychology and teaching methodology, while educational policy possibly is dependent on political and economic factors. Yet they both meet in philosophic territory and in particular through their use of moral standards for decision making and their similar methods for resolving issues. If educational policy decisions are based only on economic considerations, pressure groups, legal decisions, and politics, students will quickly become aware that moral principles apply only to a very small area of human life. Students will realize that economic resources and political power are of even greater importance than moral principles and that these two former domains underlie public decision making.[4]

The hidden curriculum, we now commonly recognize, often presents messages that are contrary to explicit aims of moral education. Students may be more influenced by the hidden curriculum messages than by explicit moral education. The social and intellectual environment and ethos of the school often contribute more to students' moral development than specifically designed moral curriculum.[5] In other words, a student is often impelled by the deeds of school personnel and school policy rather than words, by what is implicit and underlying rather than the explicit surface messages. If educational policy and thus the hidden curriculum are not based on the moral standards advocated for moral education, an explicit moral education program may well have little or no impact.

The issue we must now investigate is whether a utilitarian calculus could underlie educational policy decisions. Like all social institutions, schools have limited resources and goods. These must be distributed among diverse populations, to teachers, staff, and various groups of students. There must be decisions regarding resources for curriculum, the physical plant, audiovisual and technological equipment, health facilities, special materials, and extracurricular programs.[6] When schools question how to allocate scarce goods, they may also assess the consequences of such allocations. Should a school allot considerable resources to gifted and talented students in the belief that this small group will now benefit more from these goods than other students? The gifted, it could also be argued, will later contribute more significantly to society and thus eventually increase the overall quantity of good throughout the population. In this case, both the principles of aggregation and distribution would be met. At the time they use the scarce resources, the gifted would produce the largest aggregate amount of good and then in the future their contributions to society as a whole would produce the widest distribution of good.

One could reject the distribution of scarce resources to the gifted and say the school should allocate these limited resources to the handicapped to increase greatly the good of a group that previously had received limited goods. One could further justify this decision by saying that these students' natural handicaps severely limit their enjoyment of the common goods other members of society generally experience and enjoy. Since there are many more handicapped students than gifted ones, the distribution of scarce educational resources to the handicapped would satisfy the distribution principle at the present time. There would be no necessity to wait for the future satisfaction of the distribution principle. Some would even argue that this short-term satisfaction of the distribution principle is preferable to consideration of long-term future consequences since long-term future consequences to satisfy the distribution principle cannot be accurately assessed.[7] In addition, since the more numerous handicapped had experienced so few goods, the allocation of school resources would satisfy the aggregate principle by greatly increasing the aggregate good. Others might reject both of these two distribution options and argue that these scarce goods should be distributed to the entire student population in the belief that intelligence and the potential to profit from educational resources are more or less equally distributed among all human beings. In this case, though all students would receive fewer resources, a much larger number of students would benefit.

Problems with the utilitarian calculus extend beyond the difficulty of weighing respective equations with varying goods and different populations. How does one assess the comparative worth of different goods desired by different students and their parents? Are different goods equivalent and of equal worth? Since schools have only limited resources, decisions have to be made about which resources should be chosen and how they should be distributed. These resources, according to the utilitarian principle, should produce the greatest good for the greatest number. Thus, one must have a notion of what the good is. Should there be considerable expenditure for science and computer equipment in the belief that these resources will increase student good in the form of enjoyment of the educational experience and simultaneously increase the general good of society by sustaining technological and economic growth? If the school commits its limited economic resources to these goods, which other resources and goods should be curtailed? Should it be the arts or should it be sports and other extracurricular activities? Some have assumed, for example, that the arts are frills to be enjoyed by a small segment of society or to be included if all other necessary basic curriculum requirements are fulfilled. Others view the arts in a very different way and argue that instead of being a frill, the arts contribute to the sensitive, humane, and cultured life of the entire society.

Similar difficult questions have been raised about athletic programs. Some critics have said that athletics should not be the central concern of students, but should have only secondary importance. Of primary concern should be cognitive development, grades in basic subjects, or standardized test scores. Athletic participation should be open only to those students who successfully complete school requirements. Others claim that athletics engender school spirit, keep students from dropping out, and can be a career choice for some students. Therefore, overly stringent academic requirements should not be attached to athletic participation. That these questions are not easily answered in any philosophic court is not the concern here. The only concern is whether utilitarian calculative reasoning can resolve these issues. Let's briefly look at the issue of school sports programs. With what policy is the greatest good served? If the only concern is calculative reasoning, the televison and live audience's enjoyment of college sports outweighs concern about the future life of one player who fails required courses and will not be graduated. This position satisfies both the aggregate and distribution principles.

However, college sports associations do not accept this comparative weighting and calculative reasoning. Their rejection of the aggregate and distribution principles for deciding athletic policy must cause us to wonder whether they are using rather different standards than those of the utilitarian calculative reasoning and the greatest good for the greatest number principle.[8]

This question of the comparative worth of different goods poses a difficult problem for utilitarianism. If one has to make decisions about the comparative worth of contending goods, what criteria should be used? This problem cannot be decided according to which consequence contributes the greatest amount of good. Let's say that alternative judgments to resolve an educational policy dilemma have different consequences, each consequence with different amounts of different goods and evils. Even if one can calculate the different amounts,[9] there is still the problem of the different goods. Can the same measuring rod be used on different outcomes, on $a, b, c, \ldots n$? Could one unit of a intrinsically be worth more than many units of b and c? Or is one unit of a worth more only to a small population that would prefer that one unit rather than many units of b and c combined? Mill referred to this knotty problem when saying he would rather be an unhappy Socrates than the happiest of pigs. Even the nineteenth-century good "happiness" was not always an overriding consideration, but had to be evaluated by a different standard.

Moral education practice

The problems discussed thus far pertain to educational policy and indirectly to moral education through the effects of educational policy and the hidden curriculum. What sort of moral education program could be based on utilitarianism? Would educators teach students some type of mathematical moral reasoning, how to calculate the relative worth of goods and quantitatively assess the good of alternative consequences? How would students judge whether a good was a good? Should students assess the good for society, for the greatest number, for themselves?

Should needs or desires, happiness or pleasure determine what is good? What criteria can be used by students to determine whether the desired is the desirable? What type of moral education would induce students to question the meaning and nature of various comparative policies and their respective goods, whether these goods be pleasure, happiness, justice, and/or knowledge?

A perusal of present theories of moral education and their practical proposals reveals that utilitarianism is no longer considered a viable alternative. Are educators at present disinterested in utilitarianism because of its various theoretical problems and the difficulty of implementing it in practical moral education programs? Before assuming that theoretical and practical problems make utilitarianism a poor candidate for moral education recommendations, we must remember that this theory provided the underpinning for educational and social reform in nineteenth-century England. We must thus wonder whether the theory is inherently as flawed as critics would like us to believe. Or has the relative eclipse of moral education programs based on utilitarianism occurred for other reasons, a new understanding of the theory's weaknesses, the unfortunate ways utilitarianism has recently been interpreted in practice, or changes in the social context in which the theory is applied? Finally, with the explicit avoidance of the taint of utilitarianism in educational policy and moral education, does utilitarianism still implicitly underlie much of commonsense moral education and moral practice?

Whereas utilitarianism at one time provided an excellent basis for improving social welfare, instituting public education for an increased number of people, and undergirding moral education, late twentieth-century society seems to need a rather different theoretical underpinning. The context, the social, political, and educational conditions, changed so radically from the nineteenth to the late twentieth century that another form of principled morality was sought to meet the needs of this different age. We now have to turn to the principles and moral theory that has recently dominated center stage for educational theorists and only then question whether an ethic of abstract principles can be the sole basis for educational policy and moral education practice.

Recent moral education writings have been more comfortable with neo-Kantian abstract, formal moral principles. In moral development theory, Lawrence Kohlberg has been the leading proponent of a rule-based theory that asserts moral judgment development is sequential and described by qualitatively different stages. With moral maturity, moral judgments are based on abstract, generalizable, and universalizable moral principles. Rawls's theory of justice now stands at the apex of Kohlberg's developmental theory and functions as a regulative standard and ideal for moral development and moral education.[10] The central issue for Kohlberg is not whether someone believes a moral action is right or wrong, but what sort of moral reasoning underlies that moral judgment. The questions of *why* a moral judgment is right or wrong and *what* moral standards justify the judgment are crucial in assessing an agent's moral development stage. Though the moral standards used at lower development stages seem a far cry from the neo-Kantian principles of the highest stage, lower-stage moral judgments and standards are related to principled morality. These lower-stage moral standards are parasitic on the higher moral-developmental-stage judgments and criteria; the higher-stage judgments are wholly justified by abstract, general, universalizable moral principles.

One can ask why Kohlberg's theory became popular when it did, why philosophers and educational theorists alike were at first persuaded by its arguments and evidence. What were the political, social, and cultural conditions that contributed to this theory's success? What educational problems existed that made Kohlberg's theory a frontrunning candidate for educational theoreticians and practitioners? These questions relate to the notion that a theory is not necessarily confirmed or disconfirmed on the basis of its conceptual soundness and empirical evidence, but at times certain social, political, and cultural conditions contribute to its acceptance.[11] After we examine why Kohlberg's theory flourished during the seventies, we study its main features to uncover reasons why this theory cannot provide the underpinnings for moral education practice.[12]

Kohlberg's Theory and the Historical Context

The cultural and social conditions of the thirties and forties did not provide a hospitable climate for the flowering of Piaget's moral development theory. Though at this earlier time educational commissions listed moral standards that schools should inculcate in students, only a few thinkers argued for radical changes in moral education. With the Second World War, people patriotically worked together to make the world safe for democracy and freedom; they rarely questioned the nature of Western democracy, freedom, equality, or their own moral lives. Schools as well as other social institutions tacitly assumed that American society was dominated by a single ethos that guaranteed the good and moral life. With inbridled enthusiasm to defeat known enemies, problems of morality and moral education did not surface. Though the end of this war at first seemed to herald a carefree, enthusiastic period when the dreams and hopes of millions would be fulfilled, a rather different destiny waited in the wings. People were unaware of these latent cataclysmic cultural, social, political, scientific, and technological changes and could not imagine how life, morality, and values would be radically transformed. Few wondered whether adequate theoretical tools existed to cope with the moral consequences of these changes.

Lawrence Kohlberg posited his moral development theory at the same time that all segments of society were finally shocked into recognition of the radical changes in every area of human life.[13] Eventually, Kohlberg's theory was heralded as a means to improve the morality of society. Whereas the eighteenth-century social agenda that Condorcet and others acclaimed for education failed, it could be said, because they did not possess adequate tools to implement their utopian scheme, education, for Kohlberg, in the second half of the twentieth century possessed the conceptual tools needed to regenerate the morality of a new generation. Unlike Piaget's theory, which applied only to children under the ages of twelve or thirteen and thus was not relevant for high school and college students, Kohlberg's theory also included this older group and therefore had implications for every level of formal education.

The political, social, and intellectual environment of the sixties and seventies nourished Kohlberg's theory. Previously hidden minorities, invisible men, and disenfranchised women militantly battled for rights, for a share of the goods that society had previously given to the more fortunate and powerful. Instead of being a melting pot, ethnic groups insisted the United States was a salad bowl, that each ethnic group had unique values and different moralities and a right to pursue its own way of life. Kohlberg claimed his theory accepted such pluralism and yet simultaneously included formal, universal moral principles. He resolved the problem of pluralism versus univerality, one all-encompassing set of moral principles and the considerable diversity of moral data, what is seen as the problem of the relationship between the one and the many, in the following way: The outward, explicit moral standards, mores, and beliefs of each separate ethnic group are surface data that do not reveal moral principles or modes of reasoning. The surface moral data of all societies can be classified into twenty-six categories,[14] which only indicate the sorts of moral situations, actions, and problems that all societies include within the moral domain. Even if these moral data can be squeezed into a finite number of categories, each culture or society exhibits considerable surface diversity of moral conduct and mores. Below diverse surface data, however, morality takes on a different look. The important characteristics of this other aspect of morality are the logic of moral reasoning and the moral standards used to make moral judgments. All sorts of diverse moral data can be manipulated with identical general moral standards and principles. Just as the same limited number of algebraic formulas and logical techniques are applied to an infinite quantity of problems, so Kohlberg expected a limited number of abstract moral standards and logical techniques to resolve an infinite number of moral dilemmas. At the highest stage, according to Kohlberg, moral agents universally use formal, abstract moral principles to make universalizable moral judgments. Diverse, radically different ethnic and religious groups thus maintain their unique surface morality that ostensibly seems unique and incompatible with the moral data of other groups. However, all these diverse groups actually use the same logical techniques and hierarchical sets of moral standards to solve diverse moral problems.

For schools, this developmental stage theory promised to resolve a most difficult problem, how to provide moral education for children from diverse ethnic and religious groups, each of which claimed to have a very different morality. Since public schools had to respect moral pluralism and yet provide moral education, they confronted a new problem. During earlier periods, in fact from its very inception, the public school was seen as a common meeting place where children from many immigrant groups and all socioeconomic levels would meet to be inculcated with the American ethos and society's generally accepted morality. Horace Mann, the architect of the common school, continually emphasized the moral lessons this institution should transmit. In the "First Annual Report" of 1837, for example, Mann stressed that the newly created common school not only was to impart knowledge, but was also to form "propriety of demeanor" and imbue students "with the principles of duty." In the "Third Annual Report" of 1839, Mann recommended that the "indispensable, all-controlling requisite of moral character" together with students' "good behavior" would be assured if teachers were unblemished, "of pure tastes, of good manners, of exemplary morals." Mann's moral message became a part of the language arts curriculum, with millions of nineteenth-century children reading the moral tales of McGuffey's readers. The religious thrust of both Mann's educational policy recommendations and McGuffey's readers were not invisible underpinnings, but boldfaced statements of one preferred religious nature of morality and human life.

Some would now point to how closely Mann's moral ideas were tied to the economic needs of society. Others would say the purported hegemony of moral standards was an illusion.[15] The harmonious picture of the common school being the agent for mass assimilation had flaws. Some religious groups rejected the public school program and argued that the morality and values the public school inculcated were incompatible with their religious traditions. These minority groups were allowed to go their own way and open private schools to transmit their religious values. Children of upper-class Brahmins were also protected from public school values and morality. These groups maintained elite private schools or educated children at home. Even though Mann originally believed that the common school would be a meeting place for all socioeconomic and religious groups, in the end only the masses—the middle and lower classes—received the common moral lessons of the public school.

By the time Kohlberg posited his theory, this much earlier public school moral agenda was under attack. Few agreed about what morality, moral behavior, or moral standards should be transmitted to students. Many argued that moral education could no longer be based on the inculcation of narrowly defined, specific rules, but had to foster and improve moral reasoning. Moral education, it was asserted, also had to accept a wide diversity of moral beliefs. Kohlberg's theory seemed to fill these qualifications.

The social environment was conducive to the acceptance of Kohlberg's theory for other reasons. Whereas World War II had been a "moral" war, a war that would defeat the enemies of freedom and democracy, the Vietnam War was seen by many as a blot on American honor and morality. No matter how the Vietnam War has been evaluated in retrospect, it divided the country, stirred considerable controversy, and engendered social and political unrest. College and high school students vociferously challenged the war and simultaneously questioned moral authority at every level, whether in government or in universities and high schools. The deportment, demeanor, respect, and "good behavior" Mann and so many others believed students should exhibit were challenged by rebellious youths who demanded freedom and the right to decide their own lives and morality. School and university administrators, however, were aghast at student unruly behavior and demands for freedom. They sought ways to channel student rebellion into morally acceptable directions and to reinstate control and discipline. Unquestionably, the Vietnam War alone was not the cause of youthful and societal unrest; rather, this war was a most visible symbol of unrest and radically changing values and morality. At that time, no area of society seemed free of moral turpitude: Watergate, "crimes" at the highest levels of government, increasing white-collar crime, and questionable professional practices. The variety and extent of moral disgrace seemed to discredit older forms of moral education and compromise traditional ways of positing moral development and moral maturity. Kohlberg asserted that his theory could bring order to all this chaos.

Kohlberg has not been the only thinker to advocate a moral education based on higher-order, formal moral principles. Rawls's theory of justice not only influenced how many liberal thinkers analyzed moral education and made educational policy decisions; Rawls himself delineates a truncated moral development program.[16] Even if Rawls rejects that psychology can justify a theory of justice,[17] it is not surprising that Kohlberg's highest moral developmental stage is now based on Rawls's theory. Since Kohlberg rode the wave of liberal social and political reform that Rawls's theory informed and described, Kohlberg's theory was of considerable interest to moral philosophers.[18] Kohlberg's theory with its Rawlsean underpinnings provided the vision of what many believed was the just society, a society in which there would be social justice and in which *all* human beings would be respected, responsibly exercise their inalienable rights, and autonomously make moral judgments using neo-Kantian principles. Moral education would finally improve the quality of moral life in the same way that science and technology had improved material life. Just as medicine possessed criteria for evaluating a patient's physical condition and making informed medical decisions, educators now would have analogous standards for assessing a student's moral judgments. Whether anyone looked closely enough at the theory to recognize how flawed it was or that its vision clouded other segments of the moral domain is not the issue. The only point is that during its heyday, Kohlberg's theory was seen as a panacea to cure the confusion and chaos confronting moral education.

Kohlberg, Moral Principles, and Moral Education

Kohlberg asserts that morality is developmental, each stage being based not on the content but the different form and structure of moral judgments. Morality, according to this view, is dependent on cognitive thought processes, on the way judgments are made, and on the moral standards and principles used to justify judgments. Since moral development occurs through universal, invariant, sequential, hierarchical stages, educators should be concerned about how to foster development from lower to higher stages. Through suitable educational techniques and an appropriate educational environment, such development of moral judgments can be motivated. Kohlberg stresses that moral reasoning and higher-level moral principles cannot be taught or transmitted. Preaching, inculcation, and conditioning are not methods to achieve higher-level moral reasoning. Rather, moral development depends on the quality of the social interaction moral agents engage in and the moral features of society. Development occurs because of interaction between lower-stage agents and a social environment with higher-stage moral attributes.

Though Kohlberg notes his indebtedness to Piaget, there are important differences between Piaget's and Kohlberg's theories. One difference highlights how the moral universes and dilemmas to these two thinkers are populated by very different sorts of moral data. While the *form* of their theoretical concepts and moral criteria and the underlying general criteria ostensibly seem similar, [19] Piaget and Kohlberg part company on the moral content or surface data of children's moral universes (i.e., on the types of moral dilemmas children confront). But in actuality, the different content also affects problem-solving methods and what sort of moral education is recommended. The moral dilemmas presented to children and youth by Kohlberg are often quite different from those advanced by Piaget a few decades earlier. While Piaget is concerned about clumsiness versus intentionality or exaggeration versus lying, Kohlberg often does not refer directly to these categories. Even stealing, for Kohlberg, does not apply to stealing something as commonplace as the single roll from a bakery or the piece of red ribbon of Piaget's dilemmas. Children and other moral agents, for Kohlberg, do not live in a restricted, simplistic, communally populated moral universe. Rather, children face the enormity of this present historical period's social, political, and scientific issues: cancer, radioactive drugs, starvation, and in one story, euthanasia.[20]

The difference between how Piaget's era and how the historic context of Kohlberg's period affected their respective moral dilemmas can be further highlighted by examining one of the dilemmas Kohlberg employs to ascertain a child's moral development stage. A young adolescent has worked to save money for summer camp. At the last minute, his father demands the money to go on a fishing trip. Kohlberg's subjects are asked a series of questions to evaluate their moral reasoning and moral development stage. These questions may include, Should the boy give the money to his father? Does the father have a right to ask for the money? Though on the surface this may seem a valid moral problem for a young adolescent, it may be a valid problem only within the present social and historic context. By prying below the surface of Kohlberg's moral dilemmas, we can see how they relate to the present period. As with Kohlberg's other moral dilemmas (e.g., the original Heinz story of stealing a drug to save a wife's life), the moral dilemma of the adolescent and his father has an underlying basis. The problem arises because of the financial constraints of the situation. For example, a youthful subject is asked whether the druggist of the Heinz dilemma should have charged the price asked for the drug. If Heinz had sufficient money or if the druggist did not charge such an excessive amount, the moral dilemma would not arise. In the case of a young adolescent, expensive summer camps have become ordinary goods in late twentieth-century middle-class children's lives, and a fishing trip for a father now requires money instead of being an ordinary agrarian experience. Marxists as well as many other social scientists could say that the form as well as the content of many of Kohlberg's moral dilemmas are dictated by the economic base of this society, not by what moral dilemmas necessarily must be. The form of these dilemmas includes certain assumptions about the nature of morality and the economic structure of socity. A comparison of these Kohlbergean dilemmas with Piaget's 1932 dilemmas reveals that for the most part the conflicts caused by recent economic conditions do not appear in Piaget's world.

This difference between Piaget's simplistic childhood moral universe and the adult moral universe of Kohlberg's child and adolescent is in one sense understandable. Piaget did not just fondly look back to the world of Tönnies's *gemeinschaft.* Piaget lived in that idyllic, peaceful community. The children of Piaget's sample attended community schools and lived in small towns or a livable picturesque city. Morality in these small communities was transmitted in the same way as marble game skills and rules were. Kohlberg is the product of a very different society and implicitly celebrates the death of the earlier forms of communal structure. The aim of moral education in the newer world is for human beings to become autonomous moral agents within communities of their own choosing. Children now live in a radically different world populated by the adult images of consumerism, of technology and television, of comprehensive schools and enlarged, bureaucratic societies, of revolutionary upheaval and religious strife, of war and famine, of nuclear weapons and deadly diseases.[21] Whereas Piaget's children were cherished, protected members of small communities within an idyllic, peaceful country, Kohlberg's children and youth are citizens of the world who owe allegiance on a local level to a nation-state. Kohlberg constructs moral dilemmas with very different form and content, both consistent with these complicated, adult images and enlarged society.

These differences in the moral world reveal how Kohlberg and Piaget look at morality and moral conflicts. For Piaget's child, morality remains within the confines of one's private, communal world. Kohlberg, on the other hand, assumes that moral dilemmas often occur in a public domain and require a subject to decide between conflicting rights, a druggist's property right versus a wife's right to life. Dependent on the moral developmental stage of the subject qua judge, conflicting rights are encased within a different form and structure. For Piaget the moral universe is populated by members of a network of interrelated persons within a community. Just as marble game players are concerned about continuing the traditions and rules of the game, so Piaget's communal members want to assure the continuance of the moral community. For Kohlberg the moral universe is populated by potentially autonomous individuals who must decide among conflicting rights. Moral education, in Kohlberg's world, does not concern historical traditions or the continuance of original social communities, but what criteria an autonomous moral agent uses to make moral judgments.

Another difference between Piaget's and Kohlberg's moral dilemmas needs to be noted. By involving common aspects of life (e.g., staining something with an inkblot or breaking some cups when opening a door), Piaget's moral dilemmas do not require extraordinary collateral knowledge. The moral dilemma can be resolved by using ordinarily available information. If some of Kohlberg's dilemmas were actual real life moral problems, their resolution would require considerable knowledge. Formal categories alone could not supply the tools for judgments. For example, adult subjects who have considerable medical and scientific knowledge may well question whether Heinz the husband could administer the drug to his wife and whether an incorrect dose might kill his wife rather than save her life. These reservations of adult subjects are not based on an inability to use abstract principles, but on their recognition that instead of being theoretical matters, moral dilemmas are practical problems requiring appropriate, diverse data to inform solutions. One of Kohlberg's other dilemmas addresses the problem of whether a doctor should commit euthanasia when the pain-ridden patient wants to die. Do not resuscitate and right to die cases at present pose exceptionally difficult medical ethics problems? Since adolescents may well be aware of the complexity of these medical ethics problems, their inability to respond might not depend on developmental stage, but on the nature of the problem and the various medical and legal questions it raises.

Kohlberg's moral development theory has undergone a series of transformations that have included conceptual and philosophic modifications, changes in the moral dilemmas presented to subjects, and changes in scoring techniques.[22] In a recent monograph, Kohlberg responds to important criticism and simultaneously formulates the most current version of the theory. This recent version is the focus of the following sections.[23] Even this newer version has problems that are not amenable to additional variations on the same theme. Instead, a different basic theme needs to be composed, with Kohlberg's theory perhaps being a variation on the newer theme.

Moral development, according to Kohlberg, proceeds through three levels: the preconventional, conventional, and postconventional; each level includes two stages, for a total of six stages. Only five of these stages now characterize actual moral development, whereas the sixth crowning stage acts as a generating standard for all lower stages. A moral agent's stage of development can be assessed by evaluating the type of moral judgment made to resolve various moral dilemmas and the moral standards used. Each stage is a structurally whole way of reasoning, qualitatively different from earlier stages.[24] Though Kohlberg's theory posits sequential development, moral development may end at any stage; progression to the highest stages is not required. Sequential development to higher stages is not automatic and based on internal wiring, but dependent on the quality of a person's moral education, the type of interaction between moral environment and agent, and the moral attributes of the social environment.

The preconventional level includes two stages, the first, a heteronomous stage and the second, an instrumental purpose and exchange stage. At the heteronomous stage, moral judgments are based on the acceptance of rules for their own sake and obedience to those in power or authority in an attempt to avoid punishment. Moral judgments at the second stage are based on an instrumental exchange of favors: "You scratch my back, I'll scratch yours." The moral agent accedes to another's demands, desires, claims, or interests because the other person may previously have satisfied the agent's desires or may do so in the future. The reciprocity of the second stage is based on self-interest, not justice.

Conventional level moral agents focus on how they are judged by a social group and what others say. At the third stage, the mutual interpersonal expectation, "good boy, nice girl" stage moral agents want to be liked and accepted by others. Caring, affectionate relationships with intimate others and friends are fundamental. The fourth stage includes larger social systems with the moral agent actively maintaining the mores and values of a society or group and upholding law and order for its own sake.

At the highest developmental level, the postconventional level, morality acquires a genuinely moral and philosophic perspective. Moral judgments at stage five are based on the recognition of social contractual commitments, rational calculation, and upholding agreed upon fundamental rights and values. Moral rules and standards can be changed by using democratic, rational processes. At stage six, the crowning standard of the theory, autonomous moral agents sustain self-chosen, universal moral principles that support human dignity, justice, and equality. At lower levels, moral standards are derived from external sources, from powerful or intimate others, from parents, friends, or society; only at the highest developmental level are internalized moral principles applied autonomously and self-consciously.

What moral education recommendations are implied by this theory? A first reading of Kohlberg's theory might suggest that teachers should use discipline and teaching techniques consistent with a student's moral development stage. A teacher might say to a student, "Let Jim use your extra pencil. Last week you used his eraser. One good turn deserves another." Or similarly, "In this class, we all share our crayons, papers, and books. This time, Mary needs to use your crayons, but at another time, you might need her book." These comments might appeal to students at the instrumental exchange stage two. Children are urged to share with another child since at some other time, they may need the favors of that child. In a different class, a teacher might comment, "What a good boy! I am so pleased with how you're behaving. Thank's for cleaning your desk." Or "Good children in this class help one another and share. When your parents attend open school night, they will be so pleased to hear about how good you are." Children at stage three want to form affectionate ties and would be concerned about how significant others, teachers, parents, and friends, evaluate them. According to this naïve view of the implications of Kohlberg's stage theory, a teacher's instructional and discipline methods should be consistent with students' stages. This interpretation, however, is misplaced since Kohlberg advocates a very different approach to moral education.

Instead of sustaining children's current moral development stage by using techniques consistent with that stage, moral education for Kohlberg should motivate development from a lower to a higher stage of moral reasoning. To accomplish this aim, teachers would proceed in a number of ways. First, they need to examine their hidden curriculum. Though they may verbally appeal to the criteria of stage two or three moral reasoning and standards, teachers may have a hidden curriculum consistent with stage one, the punishment and obedience stage. If this were true, students would receive a double message. On one hand, the teacher exhorts students to conform to a higher-stage standard, while simultaneously acting according to the lower stage. Instead of being motivated to reason with the higher-stage criteria the teacher verbalizes, students would recognize the practical priority of the lower stage. In the case of sharing personal property, a child may allow another child to use this material, not because of the instrumental exchange criteria, but because of concern about being punished by the teacher. Though the child acts in the way the teacher wants, the child's reasons for acting in this manner may have nothing to do with higher-stage reasoning. Reasoning remains at the lowest stage. Thus, if a teacher wants to motivate higher-stage moral reasoning, that teacher's deeds in the form of discipline and teaching techniques have to be consistent with higher-stage moral development.

Second, Kohlberg argued that teachers should motivate student moral development from a lower to higher stage through classroom moral dilemma discussions. Instead of these being homogenous groups of students, these discussion groups include students at different developmental stages.[25] Teachers and students at higher moral development stages would pose problems, questions, and alternative responses that would perplex lower-stage thinkers. Lower-stage thinkers could not resolve these difficulties with the standards of their present stage. This would engender "cognitive dissonance,"[26] which would motivate students to search for other ways, other principles and standards to resolve a moral dilemma. The standards needed would be those of the next higher stage.

During the period when classroom discussions and the fostering of moral development through cognitive dissonance were advocated by Kohlberg, curriculum material in a variety of subjects was developed to augment these moral education programs. For example, social studies curriculum posed moral problems for various units; literature curriculum focused on the moral dilemmas of various novels and plays; moral dilemmas discussed in class were highlighted with filmstrips. During these sessions, a teacher was not a didactic authority, but took the role of a Socratic midwife. There was no consideration of whether the facilitator or the Socratic midwife was valid for all educational levels. Most certainly, Socrates himself did not assume that the teacher should be a facilitator or midwife for young children.

In time, however, classroom discussions of moral dilemmas seemed flawed. First, empirical studies did not uphold that long-term stage changes always resulted from such interchanges or that there is a relationship between moral judgment and moral action.[27] Second, there was concern about students becoming proficient manipulators of moral standards and sophisticated discussants of moral dilemmas, but not acting in morally consistent ways. The question here is whether moral discourse alone fosters moral development and the improved moral life. In line with this, critics pointed to the lack of emphasis on moral practice.

Kohlberg now emphasizes just community schools within schools in which students democratically participate in making community policy and judging infringements of community rules. With this type of structure, students not only resolve moral conflicts, make moral judgments based on standards, but interact and participate within a community context that supports higher moral development standards. What can be said about this way of fostering moral development? Evidence of the "success" of these just community schools does not at present demonstrate that moral education should primarily take this direction or sustain the validity of Kohlberg's theory.

A theory of moral development must include a number of elements. Along with stages of development and their characteristics, the theory should also include[28] the *why* and *how* individuals develop from one stage to the next, implications for formal education, the structure and boundaries of the moral domain, its fundamental theoretical commitments, and so forth. Though questions of the relationship between moral development theory and formal educational practice have never been easy matters, a theory of moral development has little currency unless it can recommend explicit moral educational practices. Kohlberg now asserts that student reasoning, participation, judgments, and interaction within the just community motivates development to higher moral judgmental stages. On the psychological level, Kohlberg would follow a Piagetean paradigm and claim that with continual assimilation and accommodation, students develop to a higher moral development stage, form more complex moral schema, and eventually reach a stage of greater equilibration. How close a fit is there between Kohlberg's moral development theory and his educational recommendations? Has he discovered the means to achieve the aim of moral education his theory posits?[29]

A rather different interpretation can be given of moral education in Kohlberg's just community schools. The idea of the environment, in this case a "just community school," fostering moral development is consistent with other theories. John Dewey advocated an educational environment in which students would be motivated to think reflectively and resolve moral problems. Dewey's conceptualization of moral dilemmas, moral reasoning, and moral judgments is much broader than and very different from Kohlberg's. For example, Dewey would also argue that a communal school environment creates conditions in which students form worthwhile habits. Intelligent habits become foundational tools to engender moral growth. Why not interpret the dynamics of the just community school through a Deweyan paradigm? According to this Deweyan interpretation, by interacting within an actual democratic environment and using democratic processes, moral dilemmas are not artificial problems chosen by some authority. Since these dilemmas inherently concern students' own interests, desires, and needs, students are motivated to think reflectively to assess these dilemmas, accumulate evidence, make judgments, and act on these judgments. Each moral judgment and action, however, do not wholly complete the process, but instead provide means for entering new moral territory. By continually being involved in moral problem solving, students begin to question whether what they desire is desirable and see how past and present resolutions of moral dilemmas become resources for resolving future moral dilemmas. Higher-order principles and more complex, abstract reasoning may enter the picture, but the issue for Dewey is not to generate moral development to a higher stage that uses formal neo-Kantian principles. Rather, the issue is moral growth through the use of whichever principles, standards, and tools best contribute to the resolution of the moral dilemma.

One could interpret the just community schools in another manner and argue they are exactly the sort of democratic meetings and participation advocated by A. S. Neill. At these meetings, policy was decided by majority vote after debate and discussion. Infringements of Summerhill's democratically chosen policy and rules were also brought to the attention of the entire school. Whether the person was a teacher, another adult, or a student of any age, each member of the Summerhill community had one vote. Someone could argue that these suppositions miss the point, that Kohlberg would accept Dewey's and Neill's views about the need for democratic participation, but would say that these thinkers did not realize what sort of moral development was taking place and what sorts of moral stages occurred. This criticism by Kohlberg would not deal a fatal blow to these alternative ways of looking at moral education; neither Dewey nor Neill would have to be abandoned. Neill, for example, would refer not to moral principles but Freudian categories and happiness, happiness probably being based on Freud's pleasure principle. The reasoning and judgments of Summerhill students would fall into these other categories.

Dewey of course would not side with Neill, but would move into different territory. The structure of the environment or the context fosters a network of interpersonal relationships, social concerns, habits, and reflective thinking about common problems. If Kohlberg tests students, Dewey would agree that Kohlberg's results might fit into his theory. For the only aspects of moral thinking sought by Kohlberg relate to the theoretical structure. What if Dewey tested the same students? What would he uncover? He would discern the complexity and richness of morality, as it occurs in communal settings and as is explicated in his theory. One issue here is that the just community schools do not require Kohlberg's moral development theory. A more important issue is which theory best explains the phenomena under consideration, the moral education that occurs in just community schools. Since each theory could claim to provide an explanation for exactly the same phenomena, the main question is whether the explanations all these theories provide are equally plausible, valid, persuasive, elegant, and so on. This is not the place to explore this complicated question in depth, but it is worthwhile to note that in many ways Dewey provides a far richer, multidimensional approach io explain moral education in just community schools than Kohlberg does. Dewey's explanation would look at the affective and cognitive dimensions, the political and social interaction, how earlier habits relate to present and future development, how theory relates to practice, the many dimensions of problem solving and how problem solving can be improved, and many other vital aspects of the process. Kohlberg on the other hand would look only at moral education in just community schools by concentrating on the psychological phenomenon, on cognitive development.

Criticism of Kohlberg's Theory

Though Kohlberg cites numerous research studies to validate his theory,[30] philosophers and psychologists have not demurred from criticism. Only two aspects of Kohlberg's theory are criticized here, these two particularly important for this book's theory of moral education.[31] First, the theory's sharp separation of form and content is criticized, and second, the relationship between moral judgments and moral action.

Separation of form and content

Like other neo-Kantian moral theories, Kohlberg's reliance on formalism rigorously separates the form and content of moral judgments. Even though this separation is most clearly seen in the conceptualization of stage six, the division between form and content exists at all stages.[32] Though stage six is not sustained with empirical evidence, this highest stage remains a theoretical construct. Without it Kohlberg's theory would be of only marginal interest for two reasons. First, the lower stages, those at the preconventional and conventional levels, have very little ethical theory import. Second, without stage six, lower stages would be arbitrary, fragmented standards with no unifying form. With stage six, however, we see the most clearly articulated division between form and content. Stage six, the crowning glory of Kohlberg's theory, persists because the theory is

> an attempt to rationally reconstruct the ontogenesis of justice reasoning, an enterprise which requires a terminal stage to define the nature and endpoint of the kind of development we are studying. In other words, a terminal stage, with the principle of justice as its organizing principle, helps us to define the area of human activity under study.[33]

This change in orientation creates problems like the relationship of the highest to lower stages and *vice versa*, the parameters of the moral domain, and the theoretical underpinning of stage six. The rigid separation of form and content propounds the theory's problems. Not only is form separated from content for each stage, but the form of each stage itself then must relate to the form of the highest stage. In other words, according to Kohlberg, it is not enough to posit separate, unique stages, but each of these stages must be related in some logical manner to the theory's "organizing principle."

As noted previously, the new articulation of Kohlberg's theory includes an even sharper division between form and content than previously existed. In this vein, Kohlberg finds "a growing clarity of the form-content distinction"[34] and criticizes earlier scoring procedures as having "partially confounded content and form."[35] Thus, Kohlberg does not merely reaffirm a form-content distinction, but separates form and content more radically and emphatically than in previous writings.

When now examining sharp dichotomies in earlier philosophic writings (e.g., the synthetic-analytic dichotomy), many philosophers note that these rigid divisions and clear boundaries cannot be sustained. Abraham Edel, for example, finds that "the legitimacy of hard as against relative distinctions has been at the center of the epistemological controversies.[36] After rejecting the discontinuity thesis, Edel argues for a continuity thesis:

> A continuity thesis denies that a satisfactory account can be given of formal properties in any domain without reference to the material that is being organized and structured in the given form. The distinction between form and matter is a relative one, within some purposive context. Hence to understand why certain features are set up as formal requires seeing the way they function, the offices they are carrying out, and the criteria of success on which their stability depends.

Similarly, Kohlberg's discontinuity thesis for the form of moral cognitive judgments cannot be sustained; form does not exist without content just as content is never formless.

Moral judgments and moral behavior

Kohlberg posits moral cognitive stages and categories relating to abstract moral reasoning and formal principles. Morality is defined according to the inner logical processes of moral agents, by how they judge certain types of moral conflicts, by what sorts of moral principles and rules they use. The relationship between moral reasoning and moral action is not a theoretical one for Kohlberg.[37] For formal education, avoidance of this problem can have serious repercussions. Educators not only should strive to improve student reasoning and moral judgments, but also should seek to have students display appropriate moral action. Philosophers have continually raised questions about moral action (e.g., regarding weakness of will and thus why moral action at times does not follow moral judgments). Kohlberg mainly resolves the problem of moral action by citing very limited evidence to indicate that especially at higher stages moral action follows moral judgment.[38] However, Kohlberg does not examine the conceptual complexity and logic of the relationship between the two, thought and action (e.g., whether these are discontinuous or continuous). Moral action remains in the shadows of Kohlberg's theory.

By positing a cognitive developmental theory for moral judgments in a form consistent with Piaget's genetic epistemology, Kohlberg creates a problem that does not exist for Piaget's logic-mathematical thinking. A moral judgment in itself is not a sufficient condition to guarantee moral action.[39] The structural model, as interpreted by Kohlberg, delimits moral education and moral development to a portion of morality and wholly ignores moral action, a leading component of actual moral life. By first examining logical judgments and then moral judgments, the differences between the two will be uncovered.[40] Because of these differences, the Piagetian structural model used by Kohlberg cannot serve as a basis for moral development theory and moral education.

The solution of a logical or mathematical problem includes the following: With a logico-mathematical judgment, two forms of behavior occur: First, internal "operational behavior" manipulates variables and completes logical operations. Second, there is then verbal or symbolic representation of the final solution, what might be called the logical or mathematical judgment.

(i) Operational behavior is prior to and yet embedded within the final logical judgment. No matter the person's cognitive stage or the correctness of the judgment, the operational behavior is prior to and embedded within the logical judgment. Though there may be intuitive leaps and solutions, of the type Jerome Bruner notes in children or as described by Poincaré in mathematics, these in no way negate the internal operational component. For the child or mathematician must test the intuitive leap by working out the problem and thus completing the mathematical or logical processes. There may also be "dramatic rehearsals" of the proposed solutions with various operations and judgments tried prior to the final judgment. The embeddedness of operations within the judgment implies that a logical judgment does not occur without actual operations to reach the judgment, without actually working out the problem.

(ii) Though a logical judgment may be checked or tested with additional concrete or theoretical cases, no further behavior is actually necessary after the logical judgment. Once a mathematical or logical problem has been solved and the solution has been stated, it is unnecessary to do anything else. No other type of behavior needs to be manifested. The judgment itself implies completion of the solution to the problem and thus is the final behavior. For example, a child is asked to solve a Piagetean conservation problem. Water is poured from a short wide container into a tall narrow container. The child is asked which container has more water. The issue here is not the validity of the question Piaget asks or whether a different wording would have given other results. The preoperational stage child focuses on a single variable, the containers' respective heights, and then responds to the question by saying that the taller container has more water than the shorter container. Why? Because the taller container is bigger or larger. Using preoperational logical structures, the child could not decenter and thus focused on one variable, the comparative height of the containers. After completing this reasoning, she verbalized her conclusion to the experimenter. Once the child has articulated her judgment and given the reasons for it, reasons that were prior to the judgment, no other behavior is necessary.

Striking differences exist between a logical judgment and how moral judgments relate to moral behavior. Logical judgments as noted require a sequence of operations or behavior preceding the judgment. With moral judgments and behavior, there is a rather different sequence prior and subsequent to the judgment. The relationship between a moral judgment and moral behavior is represented by the following sequence:

(i) First, there must be awareness of a moral dilemma. The recognition of the emergence of a moral dilemma out of confused stimuli and experiences, relationships, and occurrence of the "normal" human life is a unique problem.[41] With the emergence of a moral dilemma, questions arise. "What sort of moral problem am I facing?" "What are the dimensions, characteristics, and parameters of this moral problem?" "What should I do?," "Should I do X (or X_1 or X_2 or X_n)?" This aspect of moral problems is mentioned not because it is lacking in logical or mathematical problems. Rather, it has rather different external and internal characteristics in that the problem itself and the agent's relationship to it are different. The moral problem is messier, possesses disorderly dimensions, and has consequences with all sorts of unexpected elements. Though we concentrate on some cross-sectional, shorthand description of the larger, far-reaching moral problem, this is often an arbitrary though not incorrect statement. With a logical or mathematical problem, the boundaries and statement of the problem are far neater and do not overlap so insistently into so many strange and unexpected areas.

Second, the moral problem affects the agent in a rather different way than a logical or mathematical problem. Though an agent may be motivated to solve a mathematical problem and may be excited about the quest for a creative or elegant solution, the emotional relationship to this problem is different from a moral problem. Nel Noddings's distinction between caring for and caring about is appropriate here. An agent may care about a mathematical problem and thus invest emotional and personal energy to work out a solution, but that agent does not care for the mathematical problem. With a moral dilemma often the solution is sought because the moral agent cares for the parties in the dilemma and thus invests considerable emotional energy.[42]

(ii) Once a moral agent confronts a moral problem, there is reasoning, self-questioning, the compilation of evidence, examination of relevant moral principles and rules, imaginary solutions, recognition of how the dilemma may relate to the agent's character, and wondering about one's ability to live the moral life. All these operational manipulations may be rather extensive or may be limited to a few elements.

(iii) A moral judgment "I should do X because Y" follows reasoning,[43] questioning, and wondering.

(iv) There must be the manifestation of action "X." Moral judgments precede moral action, whereas with logical problems, action in the form of operations is completed once the logical judgment is made and stated.

In the end, no matter the direction in which we turn, Kohlberg's theory of moral cognitive development is found wanting. Yet there is still another criticism of Kohlberg's stage theory and neo-Kantian formalism that must be discussed in greater detail. This is the criticism that has been marshaled by Carol Gilligan.

Enter Gilligan: A Moral Language of Care and Response

In recent years, challenges to the hegemony of neo-Kantian theory have come from many directions. In place of Kantian formalism and abstract principles, alternative moral theories have been proposed. The first sections of this book examined character and moral excellences, one of these alternative ways to conceptualize morality and moral development. Other recent theories argue that while neo-Kantian formalism may be one conceptualization of moral reasoning and the moral domain, moral theory can have other configurations. In what has been interpreted as a criticism of neo-Kantian theories, Carol Gilligan asserts that there are two moral themes, one represented by a moral language of justice and rights and the other by a language of care and response.[44]

These different moral orientations also describe the two separate moral languages spoken respectively by men and women.[45] Why begin with Gilligan's position, especially since it lacks sufficient philosophical sophistication and may have serious scientific flaws?[46] Why not begin with more sophisticated philosophic challenges to neo-Kantian deontology (e.g., those of Blum or Sandel)? Besides having considerable heuristic value, Gilligan's work has captured the intellectual imagination and is beginning to influence scholarly writings. No matter its philosophic flaws and limitations, Gilligan's ideas have met with a most receptive, sympathetic audience. Thus, we must ask ourselves not how can Gilligan's thesis be attacked, but rather what does she say that is such a congenial message?

Introductory Comments

Gilligan does not merely question the recent neo-Kantian monopoly in ethical theory and posit an alternative moral language alongside deontology. She makes a number of other claims. Her attention to a number of diverse issues is not outside the realm of topics that should be considered when investigating morality and moral development. She implicitly recognizes that varied factors have contributed to the narrowing of psychological theories of moral development. These theories can be broadened and other ways of looking at moral development can be discerned only by changing the way we investigate psychological phenomena. Thus, Gilligan's claims refer to behavioral sciences in general and not just moral developmental theory. Her claims include first, the male bias of earlier psychological theories and their deafness to any other voices; second, the scientific methods used in male-dominated theories; third, the narrowed parameters of the moral domain in earlier psychological theories of moral development; and fourth, the implications of these earlier theories for formal moral education.

First, Gilligan argues that behavioral science theories and empirical studies are flawed. Psychological theories from Freud to Erikson and Piaget to Kohlberg are based on male samples or male expectations, and then only as an afterthought women were included.[47] The issue here is not whether women lag behind men in psychological development,[48] but whether women were excluded "from the critical theory-building studies of psychological issues,"[49] whether studying *"a different voice"* would also reveal different sorts of psychological theories. An example of the shortcoming Gilligan notes is found in Piaget's investigation of boys' marble games. Boys' interpretations of marble game rules can be described through sequential stages. Piaget proudly speaks of the magnificant juridical nature of the rules of boys' marble games. When he finally turns to girls' games, Piaget tersely notes that girls progress through the same "stages" as boys, but that each of girls' games "is very simple and never presents the splendid codification and complicated jurisprudence of the [boys'] game of marbles."[50] The male sample provided the norm for evaluating Piaget's raw data and thus determined the evaluation of women's development. Similar to Mannheim's thoughts earlier this century, Gilligan's theory tacitly argues that the ideological base of behavioral science has limited the theories that can possibly be developed and how findings are interpreted.[51] In the case of Piaget, because of a male bias and male norm, a different voice in never heard. Gilligan disputes the validity of psychological theories based solely on male samples or a male "bias."[52] Instead of being a weak appendage to male-dominated psychological theories, women should be viewed separately, as developing through their own unique life cycle. In the area of moral development, Gilligan claims that Kohlberg's theory is descriptive only of the moral language spoken by men, which is based on a theory of rights and justice. Women on the other hand speak primarily a very different moral language, a language of caring and response.

Second, Gilligan tacitly criticizes the scientific methods used to sustain male-dominated theories when she substantiates her two moral language thesis with different research techniques than Kohlberg and others use.[53] Her four-pronged research approach to understanding moral language and action includes the original Kohlbergean moral dilemmas to discern how subjects respond to hypothetical problems; an examination of actual moral dilemmas confronting subjects; an investigation of how moral action affects and is subsequently evaluated by agents a year after the action; and reference to literary texts for additional support. Gilligan's use of these diverse methods has considerable import for sustaining her position and for philosophic discussions of behavioral science methods. Gilligan argues that certain scientific methods and questioning techniques so intimidate women and probably other subjects that they cannot respond to questions and cannot express their firmly held beliefs. Each of these techniques is discussed briefly since Gilligan's criticism of present experimental techniques and her advocacy of different scientific methods raises other broader issues (e.g., that the empirical research on teaching and learning may be seriously flawed).

The original Kohlbergean, hypothetical moral dilemmas and another voice

Kohlberg assessed the moral development stage of subjects by asking them a set of hypothetical moral dilemmas. Gilligan does not just criticize the form and content of these dilemmas, but also other aspects of this evaluation technique. She sides with Socrates' criticism against hypothetical moral dilemmas and argues that they cannot reveal a person's deeply held moral beliefs and how a moral agent would act in an actual moral situation. More important, she discerns that women perceive the Kohlbergean interview "as an interrogation," instead of a dialogue.[54] The interview qua interrogation itself takes on moral dimensions with a radical shift in the interpretive framework of the dilemmas and responses. The interviewer interprets the dilemmas and questions asked in one way. Thus, the interviewer also interprets the subject's responses or her lack of responses in relation to interpretive conceptualization of the dilemmas and questions. The subject on the other hand interprets the dilemmas rather differently and thus also answers the questions asked according to her conceptualization of the moral dilemma. The interviewer does not recognize the subject's different model of interpretation. The questions raised here by Gilligan are multidimensional. Are interviews in the behavioral sciences seriously blemished because of the interpretive models assumed by the interviewer? Does the interview format itself contain shortcomings in that some subjects feel so intimidated by the process that they cannot reveal their actual responses to questions? What is the relationship between experimenter and experimentee? Is it a subject-object relationship rather than a subject-subject relationship?

The actual moral dilemmas confronting subjects

Gilligan attempts to overcome the shortcomings of traditional interview techniques by asking subjects about the actual moral dilemmas they confront. When advocating this method, Gilligan also asserts that subjects themselves will reveal how they structure moral dilemmas, their modes of reasoning about these dilemmas, how they made moral judgments, and the various problems they encountered when manifesting moral action. The point she recognizes here is that moral dilemmas are not so labeled in the experiential stream of an agent's life. Rather, an agent must decide which situations are moral dilemmas. How this original decision is made depends on factors that hypothetical moral dilemmas cannot consider. This use of actual moral dilemmas described by moral agents is related to another issue: how moral action affects an agent and is evaluated by a moral agent.

How moral action affects moral agents and is subsequently evaluated by those agents a year after the action

Gilligan asks women contemplating abortions a series of questions.[55] A year after their abortion decision, in a follow-up study, she again questions these women about their action. Her concern here is how these women evaluated their decision in retrospect, whether the moral action contributed to their growth, whether there has been a change in moral stage, and whether they see morality in a different way.

Something else is also depicted in these actual moral dilemmas and in the follow-up study. Those who have spoken about the case study method of moral education have noted that there are "hot and cold cases."[56] Robert Hall and John Davis, for example, question "whether to deal with issues which are of current public concern on which, therefore, students are likely to have strong preformed opinions or to choose cases which are equally problematic but more remote from students' immediate concern."[57]

The abortion study vis-à-vis a hypothetical moral dilemma such as those posed by Kohlberg can be interpreted through the distinction between hot and cold cases. Both types of cases cannot be seen as "equally problematic." They may be equally problematic to philosophers and psychologists, and thus to some outside observer. But this is not what is at stake for Gilligan. The question here is what is problematic to the concrete moral agent? What is a "hot" versus a "cold" case for a specific moral agent? And further, what makes a dilemma a "hot" versus a "cold" case? The reason a case, such as a decision about an abortion, is hot is not just because it is current, but because of considerable emotional and personal involvement with the dilemma. The cognitive and the affective are inextricably interwoven in making any such decision. At times, the affective in its many dimensions controls what situation becomes a moral dilemma and at cooler times, the cognitive takes over and governs the actual situation. The decision itself like moral life is mixed, a mixture of many contributing factors. In order for behavioral research to understand and describe such phenomena, it must address this mixture and not just examine one aspect of it. More important, by concentrating on the one aspect of the mixed life, the behavioral sciences might actually even miss the one aspect being studied.

Evidence from literary texts

What should the behavioral sciences aim to accomplish? Which moral phenomena should they attempt to explain, describe, or predict? How should they go about investigating how moral agents perceive moral situations, structure the moral domain, make moral judgments, and translate these judgments into moral action? Gilligan tacitly claims that literary texts can tell the behavioral sciences something about the phenomena they investigate. Though no single literary text is explored in depth in the manner that she investigates the responses of the women in the abortion study, such literary works can have a much more salient role in the exploration of psychological phenomena.

Such a role in the behavioral sciences still needs to be analyzed (e.g., in a manner similar to how Martha Nussbaum reveals how moral philosophy can be enriched through careful analysis of a single literary text).[58] In summary, more diverse techniques can reveal other ways of looking at psychological phenomena. Gilligan would thus argue that the use of multidimensional techniques and a change in experimenter-subject relationships can surmount various difficulties with traditional behavioral science methodology.

   Third, earlier psychological theories of moral development narrowed the parameters of the moral domain. Gilligan seeks to expand and change the moral domain not only by positing two moral languages, but in addition by genderizing these two languages. According to Gilligan, men speak a language of rights[59] and women a language of care and response. Through diverse experimental techniques, Gilligan discovers that men and women interpret the parameters of the moral domain in two distinct ways. Looking at the same situation, men and women see different situations and describe very different moral dilemmas.[60] This is an important point. For if Kohlberg's neo-Kantian moral developmental theory carves out only a portion of the moral domain, an exceptionally vital portion of morality may be omitted and may elude his cognitive theory's net. Kohlberg's narrowing of the moral domain can be illustrated by turning to one of his moral dilemmas: In his much quoted Heinz dilemma, there is the question of whether a husband should steal a drug to save his dying wife. A druggist who invented the drug charges an exorbitant price that the husband cannot pay. Since the druggist will not allow the husband to pay the price over a period of time, the husband has to decide what to do. He steals the drug. Subjects are asked, among other questions, whether the husband, Heinz, should have stolen the drug and why the theft was right or wrong. Men see this dilemma as a problem of conflicting rights, lexical ordering, and logical reasoning. Its resolution is akin to solving an algebraic equation. Women on the other hand interpret this same dilemma as a problem of caring, communication, response, and relationship. Whereas men view a moral agent as making a judgment without outside interference or assistance, women speak of networks of relationship and communication. Not only is Heinz's wife brought into this network, but also the druggist. The two different ways of interpreting the problem indicate two rather different configurations of the moral domain. In one case, the domain includes issues of rights and justice, while in the other it is primarily dominated by caring relationships, communication, and responsiveness. These two configurations of the moral domain parallel the parameters of the two moral languages.

Fourth, Gilligan's thesis of two moral languages must call into question the implications of earlier theories for formal moral education. In other words, Gilligan's thesis creates problems for Kohlberg's assertion that the aim of education should be development.[61] It is not that Gilligan would disagree with development being the aim of education, but she would chafe at the development Kohlberg postulates. She would argue that Kohlberg's notion of development applies only to one-half the picture. Since Kohlberg's conceptualization of development is flawed, his aim of education is also flawed. His theory might very well force women to develop in an alien fashion. Gilligan would agree that development should be an aim of education and moral development the aim of moral education, but would argue that the conceptualization of moral development needs to be enlarged beyond Kohlberg's narrow confines. If women's development is different from men's, schools would not only have to reexamine their implicit acceptance of overly narrow educational aims but implement educational practices consistent with Gilligan's broader view. To be fair to all its constituencies, moral education would have to pay attention to women's moral development as well as men's.

Dimensions of Two Moral Languages

The story of two moral languages must begin with those recent thinkers who have nourished such ideas. Other recent theorists seem to have moved in the same direction as Gilligan, however, without mentioning gender and thus without positing this gender boundary to divide these two ways of looking at morality. R. S. Peters, for example, posited what might be called a fuel model of morality according to which the affective is drafted into the service of the cognitive[62] and sympathy, empathy, and compassion are means to motivate moral reasoning. At the same time Peters attempts to escape a questionable feature of neo-Kantian theory, he embraces the English and Classical tradition's emphasis on both the cognitive and affective dimensions of morality. In addition, Peters takes seriously both the cognitive features of Piagetean psychology and the affective, nonrational of Freudian ego psychology. With the fuel model, the affective in the form of compassion, empathy, and sympathy is not retained as a separate, uniquely valid way of resolving moral dilemmas, but is fuel for the cognitive language of rights. In one sense, being fuel for the cognitive is not a derogatory role. To interpret Peters as giving the affective or the cognitive the primary role in moral judgments would be a mistake. It would be the same mistake as arguing that gasoline or a car, an appliance or electricity are of primary importance. A car and an appliance will not work without a suitable energy supply just as a particular energy has little meaning without appropriate appliances or mechanical devices. Similarly, for Peters, the cognitive without the affective or the affective without the cognitive cannot be the basis of moral judgments.[63]

Another view of this dichotomy is offered by William Frankena, who distinguishes between two types of moral theory: an ethics of virtue and an ethics of principle. The ethics of principle stresses rules, moral law, ought and ought not, whereas an ethics of virtue refers to character, dispositions, and virtue. "Deontic terms and judgments are more like legal ones than aretaic terms and judgments. . . . Aretaic judgments [are] about agents, persons, motives, personal qualities, or dispositions or traits of character [and] . . . are basic or prior to judgments."[64] Frankena only examines the adequacy of an ethics of virtue in which the one ultimate virtue is love; thus the ethics of virtue is relabeled the ethics of love. An ethics of love is aretaic and an ethics of principle is deontic; the basic virtue of Frankena's aretaic ethics is love: "Love and love alone is intrinsically good, good as an end, etc. Love and love alone is good as a means to happiness, self-realization salvation, etc. The loving man and only the loving man will 'flourish' *qua* man. Love and love alone is truly beautiful."[65] Thus, the basic commandment of the aretaic ethics is "Be loving."

Instead of searching, as Peters does, for some relationship between two realms, Frankena assesses the merits of one ethical orientation alone for making moral judgments. By positing this dichotomy of moral theories, Frankena must finally conclude that love cannot be an ultimate standard for moral judgments especially when the moral dilemma involves conflicting rights and claims. Frankena argues that one cannot decide which alternative right or conflicting claim love should sustain. This, however, is not the real problem. The real problem which Frankena never investigates, is the dichotomy of moral theories and the tacit ultimate moral standard he accepts.

Lawrence A. Blum[66] posits a dichotomy of moral theories for another purpose.[67] Twentieth-century moral philosophy, according to Blum, is primarily derived from Kantian first principles and thus stresses cognitive processes, autonomous moral agents, and freely chosen, universalizable moral principles. Without rejecting the saliency of a Kantian ethic, Blum argues that moral philosophy can also be based on sympathy, compassion, and, in general, altruistic emotions.

Gilligan takes this story of the dichotomies of moral theories one step further. She argues that the two moral languages are genderized, with men speaking one moral language and women the other. Men characterize moral dilemmas as conflicts between competing rights or obligations. According to the language of rights, moral dilemmas are resolved through hierarchical standards, logical reasoning, and lexical ordering of alternatives. The philosophic basis for this form of lexical or serial ordering is analyzed by John Rawls to rank order competing moral principles. Instead of intuitively choosing which principles have priority, Rawls asserts:

> We can suppose that any principle in the order is to be maximized subject to the condition that the preceding principles are fully satisfied. As an important special case I shall, in fact, propose an ordering of this kind by ranking the principle of equal liberty prior to the principle regulating economic and social inequalities. This means, in effect, that the basic structure of society is to arrange the inequalities of wealth and authority in ways consistent with the equal liberties required by the preceding principle.[68]

Serial ordering at first seems questionable, even to Rawls, in that it does not readily resolve questions of conflicting principles. However, after examining alternative methods of deciding this priority question, Rawls concludes that lexical ordering is more promising than other decisional tools. Such lexical ordering is established through use of the original position, decision making behind a veil of ignorance. Similarly and with equal aplomb, a young boy in Gilligan's sample claims that some things have priority. One might also imagine that this child even believes that anyone in a similar situation or behind a Rawlsean veil of ignorance would accept this priority.

With the abstract and universal principles of men's "formal logic of fairness," a moral agent is not a concrete individual whose desires, wishes, emotions, and life history affect reasoning or judgments. Rather, the moral agent is akin to a variable in an algebraic equation, a placemark, no better or worse than any other person in the situation. The universalizability of moral judgments, according to neo-Kantian deontology, implies that the moral agent is able to put himself or herself into the role of others and that all persons (including the moral agent) have equivalent weight.

Women's language of caring and response starts from a very different base. Moral dilemmas are particular, unique situations in which all parties retain their individual identities. Caring and relationship occur between particular, concrete individuals. Moral situations are bound by time and place, existing within historical and sociological contexts. Unlike the impersonality of men's language of rights, women's morality concentrates on personal, concrete situations. The language of responsiveness revealed in women's reasoning stresses networks of relationship, connection, caring, interpersonal communication, and avoiding harm to and betrayal of others or oneself. Instead of being individualistic, the language of response views the single individual as an abstraction, even a fiction. An individual acquires meaning only in relationships with others.

Criticism of Gilligan's Views

Some critics marshal the evidence of social history to argue that Gilligan's thesis should be rejected.[69] The social consequences of Gilligan's two moral language thesis is unacceptable for anyone arguing that women deserve a greater share of scarce goods, justice, rights, and equality. According to these cautionary words, Gilligan posits exactly the categorical division that was traditionally foisted on women. In other words, traditionalists have continually argued that women belong in the home or the private domain, because of their unique nurturing ability. Thus, women should not enter the public domain, should not enter the workplace, where nurturance is at present of little value. Gilligan's thesis, it is argued, would sustain this point of view and accept a dichotomy now rejected by the women's rights movement.

This criticism of Gilligan can be seen more clearly by turning to Virginia Woolf's *To The Lighthouse.* Family and friends are having dinner. Mrs. Ramsay listens to her husband and the other men speaking of Voltaire and Madame de Staël and images of cubes and square roots emerge. Woolf has Mrs. Ramsay think, "She let it uphold her and sustain her, this admirable fabric of the masculine intelligence, which ran up and down, crossed this way and that, like iron girders spanning the swaying fabric, upholding the world." Maybe feminists like Gilligan would also describe masculine intelligence and the male moral language in this way. But what of feminine intelligence? Would

Gilligan be satisfied with Mrs. Ramsay's children and her
Boeuf en Daube with its "savoury brown and yellow meats
and its bay leaves and its wine"? There were also other
sides of Mr. Ramsay and the masculine intelligence he represented and other ways of seeing Mrs. Ramsay. What of
Mr. Ramsay's "astonishing lack of consideration for other
people's feelings" and his concern for civilization's depen-
dency on great men? Did Mrs. Ramsay possess a hopeless
vagary of mind that could hardly be understood? Was her
concern for the average human being's role in civilization
and for the importance of what her children said and did
merely a matter of vagary? Or was it, as Gilligan would
argue, a different way of thinking, what should be termed
female intelligence? Could Mrs. Ramsay have entered the
world of masculine intelligence and vice versa? Or does the
manner in which Woolf depicts these two intelligences
create rigid barriers between these two forms of intelligence and two radically different ways of looking at the
world? Critics would say that Gilligan's two moral language
thesis has created exactly this type of dichotomy. It con-
demns women to the world that Mrs. Ramsay knew so well.

Though Blum's position does not include the gen-
derization of two ethical paradigms, his view faces problems similar to the one Gilligan's two moral languages confront. Blum applies each moral philosophy to very different types of moral problems. Altruistic emotions, according to Blum's examples, apply to the private domain or to
people with whom a moral agent has a close relationship.
For example, Blum includes cases like the sympathetic and
unsympathetic college instructors, the friend in the hospi-
tal, clerical worker friends, and the dying astronaut and
her colleagues. As Santayana comments, "in a moral perspective, nearness makes all the difference." Nel Noddings's "feminine approach to ethics" contains the same
problem noted here. Noddings recognizes that caring in
the form of *caring for* takes place in a constrained context
of "concentric circles," "the inner, intimate circle" being
those we love and with whom we have close affectional ties
and its bordering circles "those for whom we have personal
regards."[70] One can imagine, as Noddings does and as

Blum would probably accept, that these caring bonds and altruistic emotions can sometimes extend to the stranger. But in the main, altruistic emotions, caring, and responsiveness seem well entrenched in the private domain and on its peripheral edges.

Since altruistic emotions and caring for primarily refer to the private domain, a Kantian morality of right and justice retains its preeminence in the public domain. Though this claim is not made by Blum, it is tacitly accepted in that he does not consider more general, broader social and moral problems of the public domain. For Noddings, however, the problem of morality in the larger public domain and concerning strangers is more complex. Though she does not reject caring *about* others, Noddings sees no way moral agents can insure that caring *about* others will have positive or predictable outcomes. Caring *for* with all its many intimate, face-to-face qualities also cannot guarantee outcome or consequences. A moral agent can experience anguish and suffering, sorrow and tragedy while attempting to care for another. "Caring requires engrossment, commitment, displacement of motivation" and recognizes that an agent cannot do everything.[71] It is the "proximate other" that the agent must concentrate on. However, an agent cannot care for everybody, cannot love everyone, cannot have the world's human masses as the proximate other.[72] What can one do? "One contributes five dollars and goes on to other things."[73] As with many other similar dichotomies, (e.g., knowing that and knowing how), the caring for and caring about dichotomy has unfortunate flaws. For example, at what point does one draw the line between caring for and caring about? At what point does the proximate other become a distant other? At what juncture *should* the distant other become a proximate other? Should the line be drawn in terms of the intimates of home and family, neighborhood, friends and acquaintances, colleagues and professional relationships? What of those who live in another section of the moral agent's city or people the agent has little to do with or probably will never know? What of the homeless who live on the street? What of the old, the hungry, and all those whom Bertrand

Russell so pitied? Can the lesser, secondary caring dimensions of caring about resolve the difficulties of all these many millions of unfortunates? Are these millions outside an agent's moral realm and thus can be the concern only of national governments and international organizations that dole out some respite? If caring for in the form Noddings posits were to become the dominant ethic and the dichotomy between caring for and caring about is taken to its logical extreme, we may have to question who will nurture, sustain, cherish, and respect all the unknown, deprived, and disenfranchised people of the world. Gilligan's two moral language thesis possesses this same problem. How would women's language of care and responsiveness, as posited by Gilligan, resolve the political, social, and economic problems of these unfortunates? The examples given by Gilligan, Noddings, and Blum do not suggest that the moral standards they posit can resolve moral dilemmas in this wider domain.

Criticism of the two moral language thesis could come from a different direction as well. Some might ask why Gilligan's thesis in its present form should be given anything but short shrift. The issue here is that what Gilligan is saying is certainly not unusual. No matter what sensitive chord Gilligan has struck by tacitly criticizing neo-Kantian theory and positing in its place two moral languages, even a brief examination of the history of philosophy demonstrates that in some ways her thesis is not unique. For example, women's moral language can be compared with Martin Buber's[74] I-Thou relationship and Max Scheler's[75] view of authentic sympathy. Though not an explicit or full-blown ethical theory, Buber's dialogical relationship has very strong ethical undertones. According to Buber, an I-Thou relationship takes place between unique human beings, each retaining his or her selfhood. The other is not experienced as "impersonal scientific knowledge"[76] or as a "loose bundle of named qualities."[77] I-Thou relationships are not just fleeting, pleasant subjective occurrences. They change the subjective self and the way the I sees and experiences the objective world. When people are treated or are experienced as generalized others or Its, their uniqueness disappears.[78] Noddings, for instance, has drafted Buber's I-Thou relationship into the service of "a feminine approach to ethics" in which caring for is the ideal. For Noddings, caring for is the master and the ideal, the generative standard and foundational quality of moral life and decisions; traditional forms of reasoning and moral principles are servants drafted in the service of caring for.

Instead of assuming that Buber actually constructs the same type of dichotomy as Gilligan, we must briefly look at other aspects of Buber's two relationships. It is not just that Buber does not genderize the two relationships. He argues that the good and human life cannot exist without I-Thou relationships, but that one cannot survive without I-It relationships. I-Thou relationships influence the quality of subsequent I-It relationships. Does this imply that the I-Thou provides the moral component for the I-It relationship? Even though I-Thou relationships change the way agents see the world by changing the I's being, I-It must have another moral component. Though Buber does not fully discuss this matter, I-It relationships can be quite different. Since so much of life is spent in I-It relationships, there must be a moral overlay and component for them. The two forms of relationship Buber posits and their respective implications for moral life are very different from Gilligan's two moral languages. For Buber these two relationships imply two different stances toward reality and other people. They imply a view of the person and selfhood. Gilligan refers to language to explain how two different genders justify moral judgments and actions. Buber speaks about who the person is.

Another viewpoint compares Buber and these newer two moral languages views. By separating caring for and caring about, Noddings questions whether grandiose or beneficent gestures to unknown others is the substance of morality. Buber also celebrates the efficacy of face-to-face relationships:

> Life can only be determined by each situation as it arises. Each person has his chance. From the time he gets up in the morning until the time he retires at

night he meets with others. Sometimes he even meets himself. He sees his family at breakfast. He goes to work with others. He meets people in the street. He attends gatherings with others. Always there are others. What he does with each of these meetings is what counts. The future is determined far more by this than by ideologies and proclamations.[79]

Isn't this what Noddings argues when giving primacy to the proximate other? Isn't this what she means when speaking about who this proximate other is? This proximate other "is the one who addresses me, under whose gaze I fall. He is the stray cat at the back door, Carl Tiflin's Mr. Gitano, the hired man in Frost's "The Death of the Hired Man," my student, my colleague, my stranger at the door selling his religion."[80] But Buber's authority cannot give additional credibility to Noddings's ideas. Nor can Noddings's eloquence recommend caring as the sole approach to morality. The difficulty is not with I-Thou dialogical relationships or with caring for. Rather, the problem is that these ideas narrow the moral domain and moral standards in a way that cannot be acceptable. Morality does not just involve proximate others, whether these be friends, family, "the hired man," the stranger one accidentally meets in the street, the colleague and the student, or the straggly cat at the back door. The moral hand must be extended to all those one does not know, will never know, and will never have to face as a proximate other.

Someone may question why this hand must be extended, why morality must extend beyond what the moral agent can partially control, why caring for as an ideal, attitude, and emotion cannot be the whole of morality. The answer to these questions does not take a Kantian turn to note the capriciousness, partiality, or transitoriness of emotions and feelings.[81] For Noddings, Blum, and others have demonstrated that feelings and emotions can be vindicated and viewed in a much more moderate way. The problem simply is that the category of those who are recipients of moral action is excessively narrowed. In the past, the category of those falling within the moral domain and deserving to be considered in a moral judgment was narrowed to eliminate slaves, at times women, at other times the handi-capped, and others who were not judged to be fully human. Animals and ecological concerns could hardly be included within most traditional views of morality in that animals and ecological problems did not possess the entrance credentials for membership in the moral domain.[82] Buber does not investigate the moral dimensions of I-Thou and I-It, in all probability because even I-It relationships that must be an aspect of human life require a moral dimension. Noddings on the other hand tacitly omits too many from the moral domain. This cannot be accepted.

Gilligan's two moral languages must also confront the many difficulties that other perennial philosophic dichotomies have faced. How does one assign moral dilemmas to one of the two languages? In other words, can all moral dilemmas be resolved with each language or are some dilemmas inherently or uniquely related to one language and other problems to the other language? How should the boundaries between the two languages and their respective domains be affixed? If the division is between the private and the public, another dilemma occurs. Can the private and public domains or for that matter the two moral languages be separated in such a decisive manner?[83] Many thinkers would argue today that decisions made in the public domain overshadow and even control what moral life, dilemmas, and experiences occur in the private domain. For example, because public policy at present accepts legalized abortions and public funds support such abortions, women can make the highly personal, private choices Gilligan investigated. However, if public policy were to change and abortion were outlawed, a very different situation would occur for anyone contemplating an abortion. In this changed venue, public policy decisions and legal constraints completely change the dimensions of the original dilemma Gilligan's sample confronted. By concentrating on care in the private domain and only rarely noting its relationship to the public, Gilligan creates an untenable dichotomy.

One example Gilligan gives highlights this conflict between the public and the private. Hilary, a lawyer, confronts the dilemma of whether to use the moral language of care or the moral language of justice and rights when she questions in a court case whether to disclose evidence to help the opposing side. Revealing the evidence would sustain her moral language of care and response. Her eventual decision, however, is not based on the language of care but on the language of rights. By not furnishing the valuable evidence, Hilary adheres "to the system, in part because of the vulnerability of her own professional position [and thus] . . . failed to live up to her standard of personal integrity as well as her moral ideal of self-sacrifice.[84] The question of how the "system" may influence moral decisions is difficult to answer. In the first place, one would have to know what the "system" is. Hilary and Gilligan apparently assume that the "system" attorneys work within primarily has adversarial and competitive features. Therefore, the virtues of this practice would include competence in adversarial and competitive techniques and abiding by the rules that govern the adversarial competition. Both Gilligan and Hilary are mistaken in assuming that these are the only features that can inform the legal "system." One law school, for example, is experimenting with a new model of the legal "system" and lawyers' roles within it. In this case, the adversarial view is abandoned and there is an attempt to find alternative means to settle disputes. Neither Gilligan nor Hilary envisages that other moral components can inform judgments within the legal profession.

The example of Hilary raises the problem of separate moral domains for each language. If Hilary cannot use women's language of care, concern, and responsiveness in many professional, public situations, when would her primary moral language be used? To which domain would women's versus men's moral language apply? In what situations would Hilary use women's moral language? Would the language of care and response primarily apply to the private domain and the language of rights to public, professional life as in the situation noted? Though a problem in one's family would most probably be resolved with the moral language of caring and response, would a woman necessarily have to use the moral language of justice to advance a professional career, to insure equal rights, or obtain a fair share of scarce goods in the public domain? If so, Gilligan's thesis could have unfortunate, far-reaching implications. For example, women would have to sacrifice their indigenous moral voice to attain equal rights, professional success, and political power. Only in the small corner of their private lives would the whispers of the language of care still be heard.

Women's Moral Language: Another Interpretation

Gilligan's concentration on caring, compassion, response, and communication recognizes dimensions that need to be included in human life and morality. By concentrating on these qualities, Gilligan ameliorates some of the recent unfortunate deterioration of the private and domestic domain and of public and professional life. Neo-Kantian first principles were never proposed to decide how to conduct family life, treat children and elderly relatives, relate to spouses and friends. The deterioration of these intimate relationships can be explained in many ways. During the recent hegemony of neo-Kantian moral theory, there were no forms of moral discourse and few moral standards to address these problems in one's private, intimate world. Gilligan, Noddings, and Blum have sought ideas to remedy this omission. In certain ways, however, the discoveries of Gilligan and others have fallen short of the type of moral theory and educational recommendations needed today. To understand how Gilligan's thesis falls short, we need to note another limitation of recent ethical theories. Gilligan is very concerned about women not harming themselves. Instead of looking at the logical components of the caring language, Gilligan seems to be led by the unfortunate plight of many women. However, a moral theory must leave room for the possibility and actuality of sacrifices. With sacrifice, there may follow pain and sadness. The parent who cares for and nurses a child with a degenerative disease most often cannot simultaneously strive to achieve success in a career or compete for professional advancement. The adult son or daughter who cares for and nurses an elderly parent puts aside those other areas of life where he or she would derive deep personal satisfaction. The caring person often must sacrifice his or her own deeply cared about endeavors. As Noel Annan noted in a rather different context, "No victory is won without casualties; and there will be those who will question whether it was a victory."[85] The conflicts and decisions, the sacrifices and pain, the victories and tragedies of moral life are hardly recognized by Gilligan.

In addition, it is not just the private domain that has suffered during this period. No matter what its tacit adherence to rights, justice, and fairness, the public domain and its various social institutions have acquired numerous negative features. In other words, the quality of life in the public and professional domain has also deteriorated greatly. While positing women's moral language of care and concern, Gilligan does nothing to criticize and ameliorate the dominant public moral language, men's language of justice and rights. Instead of accepting this latter moral language in its present form, what is now needed is a refurbishing and reorientation of its conceptual parameters.

Actually, it is exactly here in the public business and professional realm that an ethic of care might gain credibility. With the case of Hilary, the attorney, we might question what sort of morality in the public domain would sanction the priority of a moral agent's professional position over the merit of someone's legal claim or a defendant's guilt or innocence. Many would point to the adversarial system of much of the public domain, which Hilary believed she had to accept. Critics would argue that this adversarial system must be modified, and one way of accomplishing this is to include care and response in a public morality's conceptual dimensions.[86] This direction has been advocated by Hampshire, who would replace calculative reasoning and perhaps even current neo-Kantian and adversarial positions with the view that public decisions need to be tempered with other qualities like the affectionate ties of local place and responsiveness to those crying in pain. In this case, one of Gilligan's two moral languages would not be assigned to the public domain. Rather, the language of care and response would continually provide brakes for limiting the excesses of abstract, formal public moral decisions.

Gilligan's two moral language thesis as well as the theories of Noddings, Blum, and others can thus be interpreted in a rather different way. This other way of interpreting these newer theories requires some further comment. We can ask why there has been this recent emphasis on caring and responsiveness, empathy, and altruistic emotions. Why also have these moral qualities been separated so stringently from neo-Kantian and utilitarian moral categories? Sounding an early warning about excessive reliance on calculative reasoning in all its many forms, Hampshire when arguing about the failure of utilitarianism states:

> Persecutions, massacres, and wars have been coolly justified by calculations of the long-range benefit to mankind; and political pragmatists, in the advanced countries, using cost-benefit analyses prepared for them by gifted professors, continue to burn and destroy. . . . mechanical, quantitative thinking, leaden loveless minds setting out their moral calculations in leaden abstract prose, and more civilized and more superstitious people destroyed because of enlightened calculations that have proved wrong.[87]

Instead of their "natural feelings" or "unreflective intuitions,"[88] providing a brake on cruelty and callous governmental excesses, policy decisions based on calculative reasoning had horrifying, tragic consequences. The same comments can be made about public policy and decisions in other institutions (e.g., many businesses have made decisions that endangered the lives of numerous unknowing workers and consumers). At the same time that policy makers speak about equal educational opportunity, schooling for urban minority groups is in a shambles and in no way is equal, no matter what the abstract, calculative educational decisions.

Hampshire argues that human beings have always accepted the two faces of morality, one the formal, abstract moral theories of justice, right, and good and the other the more personal, context-ridden bonds of the affection of the local place and intimate interpersonal relationships. For many reasons, one of these two faces has vanished from common life or has been excessively diluted. Would thinkers be as interested as they are about Noddings's caring ethic or Gilligan's thesis of two moral languages if these affective, caring, responsive, empathetic, altruistic concerns were presently being addressed in an adequate fashion? Gilligan, Blum, Noddings, and others have enthusiastic audiences because these writers address a practical problem in present society and human life. Autonomy, for example, which had once been softened by human affective bonds, by feelings, altruistic emotions, and care, has been torn loose from its responsive roots. As an abstract concept without connecting roots, autonomy quickly has been transformed into a newer form of individualism. This view of the degeneration of autonomy into privativism and individualism is not the only problem that has occurred with the concept "autonomy" as it is derived from neo-Kantian ethical theory. How does an ethical theory that stresses autonomy as a fundamental concept explain how the many people who are not autonomous can be respected and cherished moral agents? For example, when schools assume their main purpose is to educate students to become autonomous moral agents, what happens with those many students who will never be fully autonomous? What happens to ethical theory if it is admitted that many human beings may not be fully autonomous agents in the sense that neo-Kantian theory has conceptualized this idea? What Gilligan and others seem to stress is that moral theory needs to take into consideration these other problems. Included in this newer moral theory is consideration of the limitations of autonomy.

Though the separation of the two faces of morality may have been cultivated in some recent moral philosophies, in actual moral life many had assumed these two faces remained. The face of the private, intimate community may have been hidden from the sunlight but still informed and provided the nurturance and intuitive sensitivity for the more austere public moral face. In recent years, critiques have unearthed the loss of the moral rootedness of local place and intimate community. Many problems about public moral life can be resolved only if agents are inducted into the moral life of a community prior to entrance in public life. A few examples will underline this idea. Women in the workplace are often confronted with seemingly irresolvable dilemmas, on one side the call of children and home and on the other, the responsibilities of the public workplace and the desire for professional advancement and personal fulfillment. How does one solve this type of conflict, which cuts across the two domains and includes the two moral languages? How can women reconnect their moral selves so that they are not torn in two directions?

In the workplace, whether in industry, white-collar business, public schools, hospitals, or universities, there have been questions about the quality of life. What goals and policy are primary? Though in business, for example, economic considerations are important, this single dimension should not negate caring and compassion as elements in business decision making. Health facilities that should inherently be caring institutions have been criticized as impersonal, callous, and uncaring. In the personal, private realm, there are even more perplexing problems. Divorce has become commonplace together with the emergence of a new poverty group, divorced women and children. Why are these women and children cast aside and made to be economic and psychological victims? Moral arguments based on rights and abstract reasoning, and decisions based on higher-order principles might claim that fathers have an obligation to support dependent minors. But what is rarely questioned is the extent to which bonds of caring, relationship, and response have been loosened in the private domain. Parents often do not possess responsive and caring dimensions with which to embrace their own children. The "habits of the heart" of a segment of society are heartless habits that concentrate on personal success, materialism, personal fulfillment, and newer forms of individualism.

For many years, there has been extensive criticism of life in the public domain and more recently even in the private domain. Increased concern with equality, fairness, freedom, justice, and rights has not substantially improved the climate of the workplace, schools, and other institutions. Women who have achieved success in the public domain are now questioning the quality of their private and public lives. Instead of advocating increased dosages of Kantian and Rawlsean categories, a rather different remedy must be sought. Even in those places, in intimate family life and friendship where caring and altruistic responses once dominated relationships, human life has taken on shallower, less feeling relationships. By being able to choose anything, many people are left with nothing. Gilligan, Blum, Noddings, and others highlight portions of moral life that too often have been forgotten.

The question here is how we should look at morality, the moral domain, moral personhood, and moral life in general. Previously it was argued that character and moral excellences should form a moral foundation. Such character develops in some sort of community life. By being nurtured within a responsive community, maturing young people form affectionate ties and become part of a caring moral universe. It was also argued that morality is not limited to dilemmas of conflict and alternative claims or interests, that morality can be found in the simple, common, everyday acts that we often take for granted. In the first part of this chapter, we recognized the present condition of moral cognitive development theories and moral theories advocating abstract, higher-order moral principles. Even though these moral theories are still advocated for the wider public domain, especially when decisions influence many people, we found that these theories have flaws. On the other side, a policy maker or moral agent most probably cannot rely solely on the moral character and virtues developed in primary communal life. This is expecially true if the agent must justify a public moral or policy decision to others.[89] Finally, we investigated why the ideas presented by Gilligan, Noddings, and Blum have now entered so forcefully into the intellectual arena. Some additive process by which all these diverse components are included in a jigsaw puzzle hardly seems possible. At the same time, a trichotomy that includes care at one corner, abstract, formal principles at another corner, and character at a third corner seems difficult to sustain. The question to be answered is how to include all the diverse characteristics of human morality in some coherent pattern.

7

Teachers and Moral Education: Moral Character and Roles

Moral education does not just refer to students, but must encompass all other aspects of the educational environment.[1] In an important way, teacher morality and the moral character of teachers influence the moral education that students receive. Teachers are not just facilitators or leaders of moral discussions or Socratic midwives, but serve as models for students. Socrates himself was not just a midwife but, as Alcibiades recognized, a model. Teachers influence student morality by the persons they are, how they act, how they relate to a student, what they say, how and what they teach, and what student behavior and achievement they expect.

In recent years, studies of teacher morality have been added to the field of practical ethics. These practical teacher ethics studies have primarily recommended the improvement of abstract and formal reasoning. In making recommendations for practical teacher ethics, writers concentrate on the moral requirements of a role, teaching. There has been no consideration of the moral character of the teacher or the relationship between character and role. The issues discussed in this chapter do not move in a radically different direction from the previous chapter's concern with abstract principled ethics and ethics of altruistic emotions. In this chapter, there is clarification of some of the problems raised in previous chapters. The topic of teacher ethics, the character, and the role of the teacher serve as examples to bring together some of the ideas discussed earlier in the book.

Among many other recent policies and developments, two policies have increased the distance between the public and private lives of teachers.[2] First, there have been moves to professionalize teaching,[3] and second, there have been considerable efforts to increase the testing and requirements of teacher candidates. Both efforts at professionalization and increased requirements for entrance presently mold the role of the teacher. The role of the teacher seems to be structured in such a way as to separate the moral dimensions of the role from the person behind it. Thus, some would argue that teacher practical ethics is dependent on the moral requirements of the role. However, the character of the person who is the teacher influences a teacher's moral decisions, and actions thus cannot be studied without reference to questions about the relationship between the role and the person behind that role. This statement can be justified only by examining a number of topics in greater detail.

The Moral Dimensions of Roles and Moral Character

Before examining the relationship between teacher character and the role of the teacher, we need to investigate broader issues. These issues include the moral constraints and dimensions of the various roles an agent acquires and the relationship between the moral dimensions of roles and moral character. In addition, there must be consideration of one question that can be raised about the morality of roles and moral character. Some might argue that a new form of moral education might be based on the differential moral constraints of different roles and how schools can teach students to become morally acceptable and successful players of roles. Since everyone acquires a variety of roles, students should recognize the moral dimensions of each role. The question is not whether students should study the moral dimensions of roles, but whether such studies would undercut their moral character, whether moral character would be undercut by the morality of roles.

In contemporary Western society, each individual accepts and plays many roles. The many roles any single person lives can be described in a number of ways. During face-to-face interaction between two or more people, each person expects certain types of behavior from the other person. Behavioral characteristics like demeanor and deference are connected with role and status. Behavior in face-to-face interactions is dependent not only on each role, but also on the context in which the role is performed. Spectators have expectations about the moral judgments and moral actions of colleagues, professionals, acquaintances, and service workers. These expectations also mean that spectators possess and expect some ordered and regularized structures that suggest which range of actions is morally permissible for a situation for a person in the role. Spectators are upset when moral action strays from these expected norms.[4]

A person's behavior and moral action, some sociologists argue, are dependent on the characteristics of some role.[5] By vividly portraying radical role changes, movies highlight the roles human beings play every day of their lives. How movies over the past five decades have changed their portrayals of roles and how they have depicted role transformations parallel changes in society and changes in role expectations. These various changes can be described in the following way: During earlier periods, individuals dominated roles, and at present, roles dominate individuals.

Through the forties, movies depicted radical role reversal in a number of ways. For example, in a situational comedy, a wealthy playboy first impersonates a hobo and then a butler. In a spy thriller, Ingrid Bergman became the wife of a German businessman in order to spy on his activities for American intelligence. However, neither situation comedies nor spy thrillers depicted continual, radical role changes and reversals as natural and commonplace. In these earlier movies, role changes depend either on extraordinary conditions like spying or on comedy. The deception of the moral agent could not be considered morally reprehensible. In each situation, deception was excusable. Bergman's disloyalty to her husband would normally be judged disapprobatory, but since she risked her life to "defend" her country, her behavior deserved approbation. Some might even claim her moral behavior and radical role transformation was supererogatory. Actually, this film and its role changes can be interpreted in a very different way. The movie never allows the viewer to believe that Bergman truly fit the spy role or the German wife role. Simultaneously, the playboy in the role of a hobo and then butler was actually neither a hobo nor a butler.

Movies now portray rather different protagonists and themes that indicate the role behavior expected during this new period. Some would argue that movies accurately depict present society's expectation that any actor can acquire radically different roles. Woody Allen's films often reveal the multiple roles of each person's life. For example, Zelig, the protagonist in the movie of the same name, takes on the ideal characteristics of every role with such accuracy and persuasiveness that he even acquires the physical attributes of some representative person in that role. Zelig's exceptional accuracy of role portrayal is symbolic of how an actual agent should play diverse roles. At present, it is tacitly assumed that whatever values and moral standards are necessary for that role portrayal should temporarily be accepted by anyone playing that given role.[6]

Movies are in some way representative of the values of contemporary society. They now reveal that anyone should accurately be able to play many different roles, each of which often possesses rather different moral expectations and dimensions. According to this view, the one lone human being takes on a wide variety of roles and behaves in rather different ways in each role. Since someone is always in some role, that individual behaves only in a way that accords with the moral dimensions of the role. This interpretation does not accurately describe the relationship between a moral agent and a role or between person and personae.[7] Someone may dream of playing many diverse roles, wonder what it would be like to be kissed by the spider woman, wonder how he would have lived as Achilles returning to his home, wonder what it would be like to be Madame Bovary's lover or Madame Bovary herself, have nightmares about being confronted with Sophie's choice, and imagine himself being Truman before and after Hiroshima.[8] Imagination and dreams are a secret garden, a hidden, private reality. Dreams and imagination may enrich our actual lives and may even motivate us to question our moral being, but some of these dreams are not transformed into the reality of our actual moral lives.

No one can play all roles, not just because human life is lived within time constrictions and because of attitudinal and intellectual limitations and preferences. What moral universe someone lives in, a person's values, moral commitments, moral sentiments and interests, what the person is as a moral being control which roles can be accepted. Because of their values and moral commitments, moral agents cannot play all roles. Even when two people play the same role, their role performances are not identical. Why are there differences in the moral actions of different people in the same role and in similar situations? Though the moral dimensions of some professional role, for example, may include a variety of role expectations, the actual moral decisions and actions of different people in these roles will depend on these agents' moral commitments. Moral commitments in the form of moral character influence how any role is actually lived. One person playing many different roles should still be the same recognizable person with a distinct moral character.

The individual's character as well as personality and cognitive structure influence how any role is interpreted and manifested in actual life. Thus, the person controls and dominates how the role is performed. The characteristics of a theatrical actor playing a role is different. An actor in a movie or a theatrical or television production performs a part that should not affect who the person actu-

ally is or the actor's moral being.[9] We do not believe some
actual person should continue to live the role performed in
a theatrical or television production. We might question
whether certain television shows should be aired. We might
argue about a protagonist's morality, but we do not question the morality of the actor in a television role because of
the protagonist's morality.

Someone might still argue that there is a tight fit between the idea of an actor playing a television role and the
actor playing some actual role in life. If such a close relationship were accepted, moral education would foster expertise in playing roles. Schools would become acting stu-
dios. Such a position is untenable. Though there may be
many similarities between theatrical roles and life roles, at
crucial points they diverge. As Wilshire states:

> Even when he [a person] can be called a "performer,"
> every "performance" is a reality which will charac-
> terize him in his individuality until the instant of his
> death, and, in a sense, beyond. It is forever true that
> he did it and not just a performer performed it.[10]

> We are morally responsible for actions done in our
> own person in a way that is different from those done
> as an artist. The self can deceive itself and believe that
> it is always "performing" and that its "performances"
> are more like performances than they really are. But
> it cannot escape itself, for the self *is* that being which
> deceives itself and suffers the effects for so doing.[11]

The moral actor's past, present, and future lives are judged
in a way the theatrical actor is not judged. Emphasis on
how moral character affects role performance is very different from how the actor's ability, skill, and style affect a
theatrical performance. We judge how well theatrical actors play their parts and whether they convince us they are
the protagonists. With a moral actor, we question and assess the person's moral being and not whether the actor can
lose that being in the performance. The moral actor is held
responsible for action in a very different way than the the-

atrical actor. Throughout life, the person qua actor qua moral agent brings a moral character to all the roles accepted. All roles are played and lived dependent on the moral actor's moral commitments and character.

The assertion that moral character affects and at times even controls the moral dimensions of role performance does not imply that there is always a harmonious relationship between character and role. Sometimes, moral character and the performance of certain roles do not conflict. At other times, there can be various sorts of moral conflicts. For example, the moral dimensions of a role and an agent's moral character may not be identical. The intuitive realization that the moral dimensions of a role conflict with the firmly held moral excellences of character may be one reason why an agent seeks certain work or professional roles and avoids others. People do not accept all roles because some of these require moral behavior that is unacceptable or even abhorrent to the moral agent or that excessively conflict with that person's character. A conscientious objector, for instance, will not accept roles in which killing is expected of an agent. In this case, the role of a soldier or police officer would have ethical dimensions that are at odds with the moral character and beliefs of the conscientious objector.

Other serious conflicts between certain moral dimensions of a role and a moral agent's character are not as clear-cut or resolved as easily. An agent may be faced with the problem of deciding which takes priority, the moral requirements of the role or the moral excellences of character. These conflicts are not easily resolved. Many alternative decisions are possible. The agent may discover that the cherished moral excellences are tainted and thus have previously undetected flaws. Changes in character may be necessary. Some changes may be minor and incremental changes by which a moral excellence now applies to a new range of cases. Other changes of character may seem quite drastic. But even here, we must question whether there generally is a wholesale overthrow and change of character. At various times, uncontrollable forces connected with a role create conditions in which the person compromises laudatory moral excellences. When someone chooses to enter the armed forces or become a scientist or enter political life, that person possibly flirts with uncontrollable, darker forces. The scientists who worked on the atomic bomb fulfilled the purposes and virtues of various professional roles and simultaneously unleashed the potential means of totally destroying human life. Did the role of scientist compromise moral character? A scientist such as Dyson was originally a pacifist who sought to improve human life, but eventually was drawn into situations that compromised this cherished moral excellence. Was this the inevitable fate of someone who acquired certain roles of the scientist? Or would this be an example of the conflicts that confront every human being?

For a number of reasons, those who enter public life and accept certain professional and public roles might have to compromise sincerely held moral excellences. First, the moral dilemmas of certain public roles involve large numbers of unknown people. There may be the temptation to resolve these problems in the most efficient, cost-conscious manner possible. Resolutions may inevitably involve losses or wrongs to some parties to further the welfare of many or maintain a professional commitment. Second, success in public and professional life often involves personal aggrandizement and the desire for power in a manner and to a degree that is not present in private life. Humility has rarely been a commendable quality for those in public positions of power. One thus might wonder whether desires for continuing success, authority, and power may interfere with the ability to make public decisions. Third, certain public and professional roles inherently include moral dilemmas that are not merely complex and difficult, but inevitably include unsavory elements and "evil" forces. One can think of those scientists who work on highly destructive weapons, the people who become secret agents for governmental agencies, and members of the armed forces. Yet these extreme cases are not the only instances in which there may be moral conflict between role and character. On a smaller scale, the average moral agent also experiences such conflicts.

There is another set of relationships between the moral dimensions of roles and the moral agent's character. Some moral dilemmas arising within the role's domain include features that cannot be settled by means of the agent's moral character. These moral dilemmas relating to role performance are not inconsistent with or antagonistic to the agent's moral character. These dilemmas may extend into areas that are neither consistent nor inconsistent with the accepted moral character. These problems and their tentative resolutions can be seen as incommensurable with the moral excellences of character. A number of different courses may be taken here. Moral character and excellences may be enlarged. The agent may also use other sorts of moral instruments to resolve such moral dilemmas. In the long run, however, the use of these other moral instruments to resolve these moral dilemmas of a role affect an agent's moral character. What began as a unique moral dilemma in the role's domain influences the moral character of the person making the decision. This implies that actually there can be no rigid separation between the public and private or between role and character. The moral character of an agent influences which roles are accepted and how those roles are lived. The roles someone accepts and the moral dilemmas of those roles then influence the moral character of the agent.

Moral Education: Roles and Character

What forms should education take if both moral character and the moral dimensions of roles are important? Should moral education even be concerned with the roles moral agents might accept? Or instead, should moral education concentrate on nurturing moral character and expect that character will provide the means to resolve the moral dilemmas of various roles? Schools cannot concentrate on either moral character or the practical ethics of different roles. Both these aspects of moral life must be educational concerns. However, there will be different emphases and different orientations depending on the educational levels of the students, the various contexts in which moral education occurs, and the roles for which students aspire. For example, during elementary school, there should be concentration on moral character, with the morality attached to roles having a subsidiary place. But even in elementary school, the notion of roles exists. In elementary school, roles might enter moral education by way of the roles of teachers and students. Reference to the roles of teachers and students is not the recommendation of any one view of how these roles should be played. Students are taught that in social institutions roles are structured and played out in certain ways. For example, with an authoritarian model of teacher and student roles, students acquire something more than a picture of what it means to be a teacher or a student. The demeanor and deference of the authoritarian model roles require unquestioning acceptance of those in positions of power and authority. Discipline in this case would depend on the will of an external authority. On the other hand, a democratic model of teacher-student roles would aim to have students become self-disciplined. Deference and demeanor would not be based on power or depend on those in authority, but would depend on the respect due equal human beings. One could extend these examples to examine how other models would influence how students evaluate roles and what students learn about institutional and social roles. For example, there could be attention to how a model (e.g., a bureaucratic model) affects how students believe roles should be played. These diverse models would not only influence student and teacher roles, but would extend to other aspects of education such as curriculum, evaluation and grading techniques, teaching methods, and extracurricular activities. What the structural model implies for these other dimensions of education affects how the roles of teachers and students are perceived and performed. In summary, then, the articulation of roles in elementary school education provides a pattern for how students later view other roles and relationships between individuals in different roles.

In high schools and universities, moral education takes on a different face with students questioning which roles they can accept, what the moral expectations of different roles are, and understanding how their moral character relates to various roles. Whereas professional schools primarily emphasize the moral dimensions of respective roles, character excellences are rarely examined in the context of the role.

One troublesome problem can only be noted at this juncture. This is the question of whether moral education should provide the means to criticize the moral dimensions of professional and public roles. The roles and moral actions of agents in professions, work, and public life often require change. The moral decisions of actors in certain public and professional roles have at times had unfortunate moral consequences. Agents in various roles reject personal moral responsibility and claim that they only followed orders or acted according to the "requirements" of the roles. The rare whistle-blowers with the personal integrity to reject unacceptable demands of roles have not been heralded as heroes, but have been shunned. In other cases, the moral dimensions of roles have begun to change and the new role configuration needs to be structured and assessed. Schools have not provided students with the skills to question and assess the moral dimensions of roles. The critical dimensions schools need to transmit cannot be couched in the form of negative evaluations or rabid attacks on particular individuals or temporary interest in celebrated cases of misconduct. The critique schools need to make possible is far more complex. It includes understanding the possible configurations of various roles, what their moral dimensions might be, and what dynamics of change are operating to modify those roles. At the same time, schools need to provide students with the inner strength, integrity, and courage to reject unacceptable aspects of roles. Education not only has to provide an environment in which character can flourish but also the means by which agents can question the moral dimensions of roles.

The question here is how formal education can interrelate moral character and the moral dimensions of roles. With moral character, there are questions of moral personhood and thus consideration of what theory of human nature underlies educational efforts. On the other side, the moral dimensions of diverse roles require sociological understanding of the nature of roles and recognition of the knowledge, skills, attitudes, interests, and reasoning required by these roles. Courses and studies of professional ethics now recognize the latter dimensions of roles, but professional ethics courses rarely examine moral personhood and moral character.[12] The problem here is not how the study of professional ethics can develop an agent's primary moral character but how professional ethics can relate the moral dimensions of a role to the character excellences of a professional qua moral person.

Moral Education: Teacher Character and Teacher Roles

To understand the relationship between moral character and the moral dimensions of a role, we turn to a specific example. This example refers to teachers' moral lives, moral character, and judgments. In addition, this example extends our understanding of moral education by indicating that teacher morality and moral decisions influence the moral education students receive. This examination of the moral character of a teacher and the moral dimensions of a teacher's professional role begins by looking at one instance in which character relates to the teacher's moral life. At the same time, this example questions the merits of some current proposals for practical teacher ethics.

When confronted by a moral dilemma in the classroom situation, teachers often know which alternative action is morally permissible and preferable but still do not carry it out in action. They can discuss and justify a preferred alternative, but simultaneously, in a flourish of intellectual showmanship they criticize and give reasons and excuses for rejecting the same judgment. Some might argue that this is a problem of moral apathy, weakness of will (*akrasia*), or a lack of sufficient moral courage or personal responsibility. Those positing practical ethics for teachers rarely address the issues relating to why these professional moral agents may make approbative moral judgments but never carry them out in moral action.

The problem of the teacher not carrying out approbative moral decisions can be related to what sort of moral person the teacher is. When speaking about the moral self or moral person of teachers, we refer to the inner moral being or character that affects moral practice in teachers' private, public, and professional lives. Though the responsibilities and requirements of the private and public domains, of different stations and places, do not necessarily wholly overlap for the teacher or anyone else, there cannot be a total schism between these arenas. The different domains from which moral dilemmas emerge can best be pictured as a set of Venn diagrams with varying degrees of overlap, depending on many dimensions (e.g., on the character of the moral agent, the virtues of a practice, the moral dimensions of some role, the institution within which the practice occurs, the ethos and life within respective associations). To understand teacher morality, we have to examine categories that are usually ignored in discussions of moral education and the practical ethics of teaching, these being virtues, ideals, and the good.[13] We need to pay attention to the teacher's moral self or character.

If he were examining a teacher's morality and the problem of professional ethics in teaching, MacIntyre, for instance, would view teaching as a practice that requires its practitioners to possess a certain set of virtues. Initiation into the practice of teaching would imply that teachers had also acquired the appropriate set of virtues. Only with the possession of these virtues can teachers achieve the goods inherent to teaching.[14] Though some sets of virtues underlie and are necessary conditions of the practice of teaching, they are not sufficient conditions for constructing the practical ethics of teachers. Other thinkers would argue that teachers should study how to resolve the practical moral problems of teaching. Through the development of abstract reasoning, problem-solving techniques, and the use of more adequate moral principles, teacher morality would improve. Training in problem-solving methods and reasoning ignores the moral being and moral commitments of the teacher. Courses and training refer only to practical moral dilemmas and their resolution, to moral principles and abstract reasoning. There is the assumption that the teacher is some sort of input-output device that can be programmed to resolve practical ethical teaching dilemmas in a wholly logical and correct form and then manifest the appropriate moral output. This ignores one basic feature of the situation. What is the moral being of the teacher? What is the teacher's moral character? What moral commitments does the teacher possess? Teachers qua moral agents should have unified moral selves and thus possess virtues and be committed to the moral ideals of their imperfect moral excellences.

Two sets of virtues define the moral life of teachers. There are virtues that describe the person as a moral agent and those that are intrinsically a part of teaching as a practice. These two sets of virtues at times may conflict with each other. The types of conflict that may occur highlight the relationship between the teacher's inherent moral virtues and the problems of practical teaching ethics. At times, there may be moral conflicts that cannot be resolved by the teacher's moral excellence and character. School or state policy creates an ethical problem for a teacher. An elementary student has failed a state required achievement test. Since the student had immigrated to the United States within the past year, the teacher does not believe that the achievement test is an accurate means of evaluating this student's achievement. The principal has said that because of the lower than acceptable test score the student must repeat the grade. The teacher who has expended considerable effort during the school year to help the child argues with the principal that the child should not repeat the grade. The teacher cites the student's improvement, the difference between how the child barely spoke English at the beginning of the semester and now is a rather fluent speaker of the language, the motivation of the child, the support of the family, and how this is not simply a matter of passing or failing. The teacher argues that something else is involved. For the teacher, the student's passing is both a matter of the satisfactory completion of academic work even if this is not supported by state examination and the teacher's personal integrity. The relationship between teacher and student was based on mutual trust. The student's trust, the teacher believes, will be shattered if the student in this case is failed. The principal disagrees and after again citing state and school policy, insists that the student must be retained in the same grade.[15] The principal also tells the teacher not to be so concerned. The student will not be on her fall roster, and thus the teacher will not have any unnecessary discomfort or embarrassment.

This rather trivial incident on the surface does not seem to be covered by the virtues required for teaching. Someone might naïvely comment that good teaching aims to have students pass state achievement tests. In addition, teaching virtues, some may assume, should be consistent with state and federal educational policy. Finally, teaching virtues include good communication skills. In this case, the teacher should be able to convince the parents that retention is in the best interest of the student. Yet it might also be pointed out that teaching requires some level of trust between teachers and students. What happens when school, state, and federal policy compromise that trust? Even if these issues can be settled in some manner, the problem posed here is not resolved. The issue is not just external policy, but the relationship between such policy and the teacher's character and moral excellences.

At times, prospective teachers decide not to enter the teaching profession. Some of these prospective teachers find that the chasm between their moral character and the behavior expected of teachers, between their moral excellences and governmental mandates of educational policy, is too great. Schools and teaching virtues may not necessarily be at fault in this case. The prospective teacher may not accept certain present dimensions and virtues of teaching even if these do not seem disapprobative to others. This conflict may not occur because of the moral failing of the teacher, but because that person's firmly held moral beliefs are incompatible with the virtues of the present practices of teaching. The problem here is that the conflict is not between the teacher's moral excellences and some objective set of teaching virtues. Other variables affect the actual features of teaching. These are derived from the ideological

and political orientation and structure controlling the
school. For example, the prospective teacher may completely reject state examination requirements and argue
that these are not tools for the objective assessment of student achievement. These examinations compromise and
denigrate teacher-student relationships and limit the type
of material the teacher can present. These examinations,
the prospective teacher may argue, only seek to continue
the socioeconomic class structure of society. In no way can
this prospective teacher accept this aspect of the teaching-
learning situation. Perhaps in this case the person should
not become a teacher. Or perhaps the person should seek a
different teaching situation and decide to teach in a private
school or eventually start an alternative school.

However, any decision to bar someone from teaching
because of such disagreements or differences in moral excellences may be disquieting, not because prospective
teachers have a right to possess distinctly different moral
virtues. Rights have little to do with this issue. Instead, the
requirements pluralism imposes on teacher selection has
some plausibility here. There has been the tacit belief that
pluralism strengthens American education and the American character. This pluralism is fostered not just because of
student pluralistic values and moral character, but because
of the advantages of pluralism in teacher moral excellences. One problem facing teacher selection is which sets
of personal virtues a teacher qua person can possess. Since
a teacher does not shed the person to become a persona,
some might wonder whether every moral excellence the
person may possess is acceptable in the persona. Though
this does not imply that all teachers possess identical virtues, there may be some sets of virtues that while being
acceptable in other contexts are unacceptable for a teacher.

Now let's return to the problem of the teacher who
cites personal integrity and matters of trust between student and teacher as well as other appropriate evidence for
questioning a principal's decision to retain a student. This
problem can be seen from a different perspective. Even if
the person's virtue system is compatible with the virtues intrinsic to the practice of teaching, the structure and char-

acter of educational institutions may not allow the fulfillment of such personal and teaching virtues. In other
words, though the teacher's virtues are compatible with the
virtues of the practice of teaching, the institution of school
has strayed so far from the practice's virtues that the teacher's virtues cannot be of use and are irrelevant. With this
new condition, what decision might the teacher take whose
request the principal has rejected? The teacher might
eventually begrudgingly accept the principal's decision, not
because of agreement, but because no other course of action can be taken. In this case, the teacher suffers the pain
of personal failure and feels the agony the child may also
experience. Some teachers may believe that trust and integrity have been compromised. Tragically, these may not
be uncommon experiences. However, one must ask, how
many such compromises and frustrations can occur before
the teacher must question whether personally accepted
moral excellences are no longer governing moral judgments and actions? At what point must a teacher resign
from a professional position to safeguard moral excellences?

Someone may ask us to turn back to another matter
and justify why two sets of virtues are stressed. Teachers,
like other human beings, are educated within families and
communities that cultivate certain virtues. If the person is
sufficiently fortunate, these virtues are humane and flexi-
ble and do not mandate mechanistic moral action. These
virtues continue to be nourished and grow deeper and
more complex. They become the basis for mature morality
and inform sensitive professional ethics. The example
given above referred to a teacher whose personal moral
character informed practical moral decisions in teaching.
What of the person who does not possess the virtues necessary for humane, sensitive, caring, and just life? Should we
assume that education in moral reasoning and courses in
professional ethics will provide the tools for morality in the
classroom? Should we assume that there will be a schism
between the virtues that inform moral action in private life
and those that guide moral action in the public domain of
the classroom? All adults at some time in their youthful

student days have had elementary or high school teachers who might have excelled in our practical ethics courses and could resolve all sorts of professional ethics problems with intellectual dispatch. However, as students, these adults intuitively knew that these teachers no matter what their intellectual and logical versatility did not possess humane and commendable moral qualities. Should these teachers be required to take a course in practical ethics for teachers? A teacher in an inner-city elementary school, for example, describes her class as a zoo and her school children as animals. Her behavior would not even be considered moral if she were an animal trainer, for she pinches, pulls, insults, and degrades students. This teacher does not see herself or anyone else in the school in a particularly positive light.[16] Would a course in practical ethics alone help this teacher? I doubt it. This was the thrust of Socrates' gadfly technique. How can the teacher who does not possess admirable, adequate, or valid moral qualities recognize this failing? Only by realizing there is a personal problem and recognizing that firmly held moral beliefs are not adequate may the person begin a process of self-examination that may lead the teacher to change her moral character. Changing the moral person also will then change the persona.

What of the virtues inherent in the practice of teaching? First, we must note that the above teacher in an urban school did not possess any qualities that might be considered the virtues of teaching as a practice. Thus, her failure was twofold, the failure of the personal moral self and the failure of the public, professional person. About the virtues required for the practice of teaching, another question arises, this being whether we even know what these virtues are. Though many of us could probably justify some virtues, there has been no sustained effort to develop a set of virtues necessary for teaching. Is it possible to construct such sets of virtues? Or the problem might be that such virtues are not just dependent on the practice of teaching as the activity of a given person, but also on a wider context, for example, the age level being taught, the student population, the subject matter, the structure and climate of the school, and wider political and social controls. One agenda for a future study would be to examine sets of virtues for the practice of teaching. Such a study could take a number of directions, for example, positing a set of the virtues of teaching practice for one context and test whether this set is valid for other situations; examining sets of teaching practice virtues that were accepted during other historical periods and questioning whether any of them have stood the test of time; investigating whether diverse philosophic assumptions may influence any set of teaching virtues posited or would philosophic assumptions change the conceptualization of a single set of teaching virtues.

Some philosophers would argue that teachers need some idea of the good. John Rawls, for example, asserts that happiness and the good(s) human beings desire are achieved through the "successful execution (more or less) of a rational plan of life,"[17] with lesser goods related within the larger plan. According to this view, teachers would have constructed a rational life plan with teaching as a central good of that life. This good would not be achieved merely if the person becomes a teacher, is certified, and works in the field. Rather, the teacher should be a successful, respected member of the teaching community and should acknowledge that teaching has a central role in the fulfillment of a satisfying, good life. In the first place, the person would have applied rational techniques to deciding to become a teacher and throughout the formative years of becoming a teacher would continue to evaluate other goods in terms of this rational life plan. This good as exemplified by the rational life plan of teaching would be governed by another moral standard, that for Rawls being justice as fairness.

This view of the good does not accurately depict how and why teachers become teachers, the good they cherish, and how this relates to their moral lives. Instead of accepting the Rawlsean position, another orientation is possible. The person recognizes some moral excellences even if these are only dim reflections of moral ideals, and then constructs or plans a life in teaching consistent with these excellences and ideals. In this case, teaching becomes one means of manifesting excellences and ideals in a personal life and the ideals become the defining moral standards for the teacher's private and public life.

Though many questions remain, only one problem can be examined. This is the relationship between the ideals accepted by the teacher qua private and public person and what might be required in an actual classroom or school. Unquestionably, practical and professional issues arise that never enter the private life of the teacher. Can moral excellences or the ideals envisaged by the teacher apply to these practical problems? Yes and no! On one side, the problems have special configurations, depending on specialized knowledge, practices, and conditions. Other moral standards may enter the picture. But this in no way implies that the teacher abandons commitment to primary moral excellences, but that educational moral judgments and practices become subsumed under and are compatible with those excellences.

How does this commitment to excellence or ideals relate to teachers' practical ethics? Instead of assuming that two moral agent-teachers will conditionally agree to accept that consequent X or Y is morally permissible if one set of reasons is true, personal moral commitments require the painting of a radically different picture. No matter what the assumed truth of either sets of reasons, a teacher will not accept X or Y if it is inconsistent with an unequivocal commitment to some good. Is this merely a type of stubbornness? No! Such commitments are not necessarily irrational, but can be justified when required. In the actual lives of teachers, as noted above, two forms of virtue may often be sufficient. But at times, when a situation occurs akin to the one the scientist Dyson or Oppenheimer faced, the teacher recoils and does not search for a rationalization to justify an action. Rationalizations, as Dyson discovered, often mean the abandonment of some moral commitment. Instead, the teacher realizes, beyond this point I cannot go.

In delineating these alternative ways of looking at the practical ethics of teachers, I am also saying a number of other things. First, though the ability to reason may be a necessary condition for moral judgments and moral life, proficiency at reasoning alone does not provide sufficient conditions for permissible, approbative, or correct moral action. Second, before anyone claims to have answers to the problem of what makes people moral in private and professional lives, we need to look at many more categories than usually have been suggested. Furthermore, we must look at these categories from different perspectives. We need to take off the glasses we have been wearing for quite a few years and see whether there are other ways of exploring the problems.

8

Epilogue: All Rising to Great Place Is by a Winding Stair

The way to a theory of moral education is not through a scenically pleasant green field. As Whitehead noted, "the broad primrose path leads to nasty places."[1] The search for a theory of moral education and a practical moral education program require the climbing of a steep and winding stair. There are many detours, many tiring steps, and unknown crevices. Our climb so far has led through a preliminary aspect of moral education, the fostering of character and moral excellences that then should provide the strength for a moral agent to continue the steep climb up the "winding stair." There was then another challenge to overcome, questions about whether what is often accepted as the end of the moral education road is really the end. In an earlier chapter, we examined whether the theories posited by Kohlberg or Gilligan, whether an abstract principle ethics or an ethic of caring and response, could add other dimensions to moral education theory. Though these ways of looking at moral development and moral education provided another perspective, we found that they did not provide the final answer for this present theory. In Chapter 7, we studied the problem of teacher morality and realized that practical teaching ethics is inimitably tied to the moral character of the teacher. The role of the teacher does not negate the moral character of the person. We recognized that current directions in practical ethics only concentrate on problem-solving techniques and abstract principles and do not investigate the relationship between person and role or between character and role. Thus, we discovered that instead of already completing the journey by "rising to great place," our journey had to be continued. Again we have to surmount another "winding stair" before reaching the great place. This is the journey of this chapter.

The issues of this chapter's journey are these. While moral character was posited as a necessary aspect of moral life and fundamental for the moral self, it cannot in its original form be the sole basis for mature moral judgments and actions. The moral character of a child is not the character of the fully mature moral agent. The formation of a more complex, mature form of character requires ways of changing, modifying, and enlarging character. Second, the chapter on ethics of principle and ethics of altruistic emotions seemed to create an impasse. On one hand, principled ethics and the two-gender moral language thesis were rejected. Yet neither view was totally rejected. It was argued that these positions contribute something to moral education, but have not taken us to the great place. If these two moral languages, for example, are not the final answer for moral education, we must continue the steep and winding climb through its final and perhaps most difficult segment.

Character Revisited: Character and Moral Development

Earlier, we examined why certain theories of character can no longer serve as the basis for a theory of moral education and we then proposed a new conceptualization of character. Moral education theory and practice was then discussed in the context of this conceptualization of character. In the main, these earlier chapters concentrated on how a child's character develops in a primary community and in school. We must now ask whether the view of character already presented is acceptable as a basis for the moral choices and action of adulthood. In other words, does this conceptualization of character include dimensions necessary to explain more mature moral judgments and moral action?

In the first place, certain views that would posit a sharp break between the two forms of character, the character of the child and the character of the adult, are denied. Instead of accepting the structuralist view of the discontinuity of developmental stages, development is viewed as a continuous process. Yet continuity does not provide a completely satisfactory answer. Most certainly, there are instances when a person confronts a moral or life crisis and questions whether present character can satisfactorily resolve the crisis. Some unexpected event and the way that event is experienced motivates people to question who they are and wonder about the dimensions of their character. In all these situations, there may be discontinuity and unexpected change in character. But such unexpected change can occur at any time in one's life. This discontinuity is not dependent on the sequential, universal development through stages. The possibility, but not necessarily the probability, of discontinuity needs to be explored in this section. Some may question whether such discontinuity is actually discontinuity or whether what at first seems to be an instance of discontinuity can actually be collapsed into a continuity model. In addition, there are other problems to be addressed in this section, in particular, an understanding of other dimensions of more mature moral character and how many of these dimensions relate to questions of discontinuity and continuity.

The question of whether development is discontinuous or continuous has continually bothered developmental psychologists and philosophers. According to Heinz Werner, discontinuity can have both qualitative and quantitative aspects. Philosophers accepting discontinuity refer to the qualitative aspects of discontinuity that can imply "'emergence,' i.e., the irreducibility of a later stage to an earlier; and 'gappiness,' i.e., the lack of intermediate stages between earlier and later forms."[2] These are the characteristics of the discontinuity Piaget and Kohlberg posit in their hierarchical, sequential stage theories.[3] The development of character cannot be described in these ways. We cannot speak of stages or the irreducibility of different structures of moral excellences. What then are we to make of the discontinuity versus continuity thesis as it applies to character development? Loren Eiseley had a more fitting way of describing change and growth: "To grow is a gain, an enlargement of life; is not this what they tell us? Yet it is also a departure. There is something lost that will not return."[4] As Robert Coles so eloquently presents in his case studies of the moral and political lives of children, the character of children possesses a certain wholeness, coherence, charm, at times sensitivity and sweetness, at other times ferocity, savagery, and courage. When reading Coles, we are not intent on understanding a scientific or intellectual issue, but are drawn into the moral worlds of children. Their character and ways of resolving moral dilemmas fascinate us. We suspect the truth of what Eiseley weeps about, that with adulthood "something lost . . . will not return." Yet we also know that with adulthood there must be a gain, an enlargement and increasing depth of moral character.

But the issue still remains, whether the maturing and developing of character implies some sort of discontinuity even if it is not the discontinuity understood by cognitive stage theorists. Or is character development a continuous process whereby step by step, the person slowly develops an enlarged, broader, and deeper set of moral excellences? Lester Hunt, for example, seems to side with a continuity position when stating, "Traits of character . . . are very hard to bend, and experience cannot destroy them in such a simple way; . . . this would be so because experience alone cannot contradict beliefs about what is right and good."[5] Do moral agents merely become what they already are? Is this the irreversible march of character in which virtues and vices follow the beat of some basic theme? The point here is different. Character change is not simply a matter of having certain experiences or of continual change on the basis of the quantity of diverse experience.

The modification and enlargement of character and moral excellences does not occur in such an offhand, simple manner, but requires an intermingling of thought and experience, of moral reasoning and moral action, of having beliefs and principles and testing what those principles and beliefs mean in moral dilemmas and imply for new situations. Continuity rather than discontinuity can be seen in the enlargement and increasing complexity of the moral excellences an agent possesses. Continuity refers to the quality of experiences and changes. Moral excellences cannot be understood through habits or dispositions alone. Moral excellences cannot be equated solely with principles or beliefs or with the acts these generate.[6] Rather, moral excellences are complex psychological and philosophical phenomena, but each moral excellence often does not have the same formal structural dimensions, does not include the same principles or require similar emotions.[7]

What does the enlargement, development, or increasing complexity of moral excellences mean? One example allows us to see how in a life lacking in self-consciousness, a moral excellence can remain a fairly simple quality, while for the fully self-conscious person the same virtue can take on additional dimensions and meanings. In Plato's early dialogue, *Laches,* Socrates asks the respected general Laches to define the virtue "courage." Readers believe that Laches must know the meaning of courage because he is a general and has demonstrated courage in his life. Laches has often lived the courageous life and thus seems to have beliefs about courage, but "he is not necessarily aware"[8] of his courageous state or his beliefs about courage. Socrates on the other hand requires word and deed to demonstrate that an interlocutor understands and possesses the virtue "courage." As the dialogue progresses, we the readers begin to recognize the complex dimensions of this virtue. We are certain that Socrates is courageous and that his instantiation of this virtue has considerable complexity. Yet he never defines the term "courage." At times we sympathize with Laches and still remain certain that he possesses courage. However, we also know that the courage Laches possesses is far less complex than that of Socrates.

Apparently, additional experience in battles and in the Agora, both of which required courage, did not insure that Laches would achieve the complex structure of courage that Socrates possesses. Laches never was self-conscious and never questioned the dimensions of courage. The enlargement of character can occur through an integration of many types of experience, thought, events, problem solving, and relationships. There is no one single road to take the person to this golden end.

But still the question about discontinuity remains. At the beginning of this selection on the enlargement and deepening of moral excellences it was suggested that discontinuity as well as continuity has a role. Discontinuity as used here does not refer to "gappiness" since this inelegant term refers to stage theory. Rather, the discontinuity referred to here occurs when a moral agent for some reason questions and rejects some aspect of present character and makes fairly major changes in character. The term "reason" here does not imply that such major changes are usually motivated by rational thought processes. Feelings about a situation, desires, and interests regarding some case, caring, and compassion may provide the reasons for someone's questioning character. This questioning can occur in two ways. First, there can be the agent who through some unexpected event or experience begins to see the world in a rather different way. One newspaper editor speaks of his deepest insight into the world and thus into himself as occurring when he began to garden. What a ridiculous example, someone may claim! What could one possibly learn about morality from gardening? Why might the discontinuous growth of a moral excellence occur with gardening? The only point made here is that moral character and the increased depth of moral excellences can come from unexpected sources. Those who recommend moral education practice at present usually constrain moral education to a narrow set of practices and experiences, to a limited environment and set of problems. If character, moral excellence, and a greater understanding of the moral world can be deepened and might flourish in rather different environments and with a wide range of practices, then educational policy makers might have to consider how to provide experiences in these situations. Second, discontinuity can occur when someone is faced with a major life crisis and decides that present moral character is no longer acceptable. During such crises, people may search deeply into their character and notice vices as well as virtues. How can vices be changed or controlled?

Character in Conflict: Resolving Moral Dilemmas

As psychological and philosophical phenomena that can attain complex structural dimensions, moral excellences can be the basis for a considerable portion of moral life. However, this does not imply that the agent does not make moral judgments regarding alternative courses of action or that there will be few difficult moral dilemmas or that character is never assessed and changed. Sometimes, moral excellences will suffice to resolve moral dilemmas, but even in these cases there must be thought and problem solving. In other words, moral excellences in themselves do not provide a pattern of necessary actions, but form the tools for making moral judgments and insuring intelligent moral action. In many instances, moral excellences do not suffice and the moral agent is puzzled about which moral judgment and moral action is good or right. These diverse dilemmas can include the following. (a) A moral dilemma that one single moral excellence can resolve. (b) Dilemmas in which more than one moral excellence could recommend a moral judgment and action or dilemmas for which a moral excellence might recommend more than one moral judgment or a moral dilemma in which a moral excellence is pitted against a vice or a dilemma in which some unexpected interest or emotion is pitted against a moral excellence. To separate these dilemmas from another rather different set of moral dilemmas, these moral dilemmas are called moral dilemmas involving diverse moral excellences. These dilemmas may also involve questions of the adequacy of character, whether the problem is not one of conflict, but the inadequacy of the structure of moral excellences. The moral dilemma in this case can be resolved through an expansion or growth of the agent's character and moral excellences. Yet the moral judgment and action are not obvious. There is conflict of alternative decisions and these conflicts depend not just on resolving the conflict but on the growth of the agent's moral excellences. How are these judgments made? (c) There are dilemmas that seem to move outside the agent's character. These dilemmas involve conflicts between sincerely held moral excellences and the claims, interests, and rights of other people or groups in the public domain. These dilemmas may involve questions of which alternative judgment in the public domain is right or good. On the surface, these dilemmas seem to have little to do with the agent's character in that the possessed moral excellences perhaps cannot resolve these public dilemmas. However, there is another way to understand these dilemmas. Perhaps the moral agent cannot resolve this dilemma with moral excellences and firmly held moral beliefs, not because logically they are inappropriate for the dilemma but because the agent's moral character does not possess sufficient complexity and depth. These moral dilemmas are called moral dilemmas of roles and of public life. (d) Another type of problem is the question of conflicts between two evils. In this case, one alternative judgment among many seems necessary. Each of the possible judgments when evaluated according to one's character or in the cool light of another day would be wholly unacceptable. Yet in this situation one must choose. How does one make this choice? What happens when someone must decide between two public policies neither of which the agent would accept as consistent with character excellences? (e) There must be a few additional words about how the resolution of these complex dilemmas relate to moral education.

One Single Spectrum of Moral Excellences and a Moral Dilemma

In this section, I speak of a single spectrum of moral excellences and not a single moral excellence. In actuality, it seems impossible to cite a single moral excellence that does not require other subordinate and superordinate moral excellences and phenomena for the making of moral judgments and carrying out moral actions. The question of how a moral dilemma is resolved with a single spectrum of moral excellences can best be understood by beginning with an example. A student's term paper is due. This student does not have particularly onerous nonacademic responsibilities, but has not devoted the time and effort necessary to write the paper. One might say the student lacks the self-discipline to complete the necessary research. One might also say that the student has been more interested in enjoying university social life than concentrating on academic studies. Many would thus say that the student does not have good reasons for not submitting the required paper. The night before the paper is due, just as the student was beginning to write it, a friend exclaims, "Why write the paper? The fraternity (or sorority) has a large collection of appropriate papers. Just submit one of them. If you must, make a few changes to bring it up to date."

The issue here is not what judgment the student should make, but the process by which the judgment might be made and how moral excellences affect this process. What dimensions of this situation might influence the student's decision? Does the student possess the character excellence "honesty" in that past actions have demonstrated consistency between the excellence and action? Does the student also possess the courage and fortitude, the ability to withstand peer pressure and contrary desires to act on the moral excellence? As the student demurs from accepting the offer of a paper, the friend may again begin to argue: "I know what you are thinking. You think that this is a case of dishonesty and cheating. But it really should not be seen in this light. First, fraternities and sororities build up libraries to help members. Just as one might use a book for ideas, you can use one or more of these papers for ideas. Second, every practice has its virtues. Isn't it possible that using such techniques has always been part of the practice of being a student? Why not just take the paper and let's go to that party in the next dorm?" Instead of arguing whether this additional rationalization is farfetched, let's look at how the student might make the necessary judgment.

The important points here regarding the student's decision and the moral excellence are as follows: (i) Does the student actually possess the moral excellence or has the student merely verbally stated a position without any concomitant action? (ii) Does the student possess a sufficiently complex, mature structure of the moral excellence for it to inform moral decisions and actions? (iii) Does the student possess the intellectual virtues to assess the situation? If in this case as well as many other situations the student cannot withstand the pull of desires, emotions, and interests that override the moral excellence, then it is doubtful that he possesses that moral excellence.

If the student possesses the necessary spectrum of moral excellences, the following points summarize some of the ways this single spectrum of moral excellences may enter into the resolution of a moral dilemma.

i. First, in some situations the moral agent may immediately and clearly see what course of action should be taken, what action is right or good. This heightened intuitive awareness is the instantaneous interconnecting of all the dimensions of the dilemma, the relevant moral excellences, and the proposed action. In these cases, which are similar to Poincaré's solution of a complicated mathematics problem, even if there is eventually extensive intellectual clarification and examination of the moral problem, the intuitive solution proves correct.

ii. A moral dilemma is seen as a moral dilemma not merely because of disharmony, confusion, or difficulty, but also because it falls within the range of general situations covered by a person's moral excellences.

iii. The parameters of the moral dilemma are examined in various ways: ideas and data sought, questions asked, thoughts sorted out, possible consequences of imagined actions assessed, and intuitions occur about which course of action should be taken. These and other matters in part make up the intellectual virtues. There may be reasoning and questioning, analysis and imagination, research and hypothesizing.

iv. In all of this, the spectrum of moral excellences is not left aside. In other words, there is no sharp boundary between the use of moral and intellectual virtues when resolving moral dilemmas. How did the agent know which moral excellence(s) were relevant for the dilemma in question? Recognition of the moral dilemma and a sketch of its parameters implies reference to the appropriate moral excellence(s). In other words, to know what the dilemma is requires the agent to assign certain moral categories including moral beliefs or excellences to that dilemma. It may be that in the course of further reasoning and investigation, the moral agent may realize that the moral excellences first connected to the dilemma are inadequate to resolve the problem. Additional moral excellences may have to be added to the problem-solving situation or the dilemma may be redefined, enlarged, or contracted to include a different set of moral excellences, or the moral excellences the agent possesses may prove insufficient or too limited to resolve the problem. In this last case, the moral agent may be faced with a new problem, how to enlarge and modify present moral excellences to meet the needs of more complex and different types of moral dilemmas. In any case, the relevant and interconnected moral excellences continually come into play at every stage of resolving the moral dilemma. Resolving a moral dilemma is not a cool, detached, logical exercise, but instead the agent takes different stances that involve both embedding and detaching oneself from the situation. It involves a play of emotions and feelings, intelligence and reasoning.

v. Once the agent makes a judgment and decides on moral action, the moral action must follow. This is not just because moral dilemmas require some sort of action for their solution, but also because the eventual moral action demonstrates whether the moral agent actually possesses the moral excellences used to resolve the moral dilemma. The agent may possess such strong emotions, desires, feelings, and interests in a direction contrary to the moral action that the moral action may never occur. If such cases are frequent and there is little consistency between moral excellences and moral action, it is doubtful whether the agent possesses those moral excellences no matter how sophisticated the agent's word play.

vi. Now there must be a redoubling back to comment on how moral action affects moral excellences. Moral action both strengthens already possessed moral excellences and simultaneously may enlarge and deepen their complexity. In various ways, moral agents may discover that any moral excellence reaches out to connect with other moral excellences and that emotions may have new relationships with moral excellences. Thus, we find that moral action precedes moral excellences, and simultaneously, moral excellences and intellectual virtues become means of insuring moral action.

Moral Dilemmas and Diverse Moral Excellences

Many moral dilemmas in the average person's daily life can be resolved with the moral excellences of character. But even in these cases, there must also be intellectual virtues for the agent to judge which moral excellences apply to the dilemma and how these govern the moral judgment and action. In some situations, however, alternative possible judgments for resolving a moral conflict each involve different spectra of moral excellences. Let's slightly change the moral dilemma noted above in a way that highlights this type of conflict. A graduate student is overwhelmed with the responsibilities of work and family. The student is taking a required course in a sequence that leads to a necessary advanced professional certificate. The student has demonstrated knowledge of the subject matter through satisfactory grades on the required examinations, but finds it impossible to complete a term paper. Someone tells the graduate student about a library of term papers on the assigned topic. In desperation, the graduate student submits a "library file" paper. The professor grades the paper and the graduate student completes the course with a favorable grade.

One spectrum of moral excellences in this situation relates to the student's family responsibilities. The student possesses beneficence, compassion, and sympathy and cares for the needs of a family. This caring might have gone beyond the normal responsibilities of parenting or being a spouse and might have taken the form of caring for a sick parent, child, or spouse. At the same time, this caring for family necessitated employment and thus the maintenance of a professional license. The graduate student qua moral agent also subscribed to moral excellences that related to morality in an academic community. This agent believed in the importance of such moral excellences as honesty, trustworthiness, and fairness. Yet in the confusion of the situation, after considerable effort to comfort a family member, and with the emotional pain of caring for a sick family member, this moral agent submitted the spurious paper. There had been little or no thought about sincerely held moral excellences or beliefs. The moral agent followed desires and emotions that were inconsistent with firmly held moral beliefs and moral excellences. Though primarily about courage, Lester Hunt's comment may help us understand this example and then move further to posit ways that moral dilemmas that involve conflicts among moral excellences might be resolved: "Having such a character-trait (e.g., as courage) means acting on the principle consistently, and sooner or later in the course of one's life—perhaps very often—passion and desire will conflict with principle; in such cases we need the ability to disregard them."[9] We can again ask whether the moral agent of the above example usually manifested actions consistent with the moral excellence in question or was there very frequent slippage. Did the moral agent frequently cite the moral excellence, but rarely manifest it in action? If this were the case, then the student would not possess this moral excellence. The action of submitting a spurious paper would then be consistent with the moral agent's character, even if that action and character were disapprobative.

Let's give this story another twist. A few weeks after the end of the semester the graduate student called the chairperson of the department and blurted out the truth, that the paper had been copied. The student remorsefully continued that since submitting the paper there had been continual concern about this action. The student had thought about the action, had lost considerable sleep, had been bothered by conscience, and had thought about which moral beliefs were actually sincerely held. Let's ignore the choices the professor now has to make and briefly continue to concentrate on the student and how this new twist relates to moral excellences. The moral excellence and the connecting belief apparently was sufficiently important and basic to the moral person that the student was willing to take a considerable risk. In addition, the student's confession indicates that one single moral excellence often is not sufficient to insure consistent moral action. In revealing the truth, other moral excellences were revealed, for example, concern for truth, courage to confess the truth and accept the consequences of the action, and personal integrity. Also, intellectual virtues were demonstrated, for example, the ability to reason about how the consequences of the agent's original action related to firmly held moral beliefs and cherished moral excellences. Finally, there were suitable emotions, desires, and interests consistent with the moral excellences.

Still, there needs to be some attention to how moral dilemmas that seem to involve conflicts between moral excellences could be resolved. Only a few points are made here. Some of these overlap and extend the points made in the last section about moral problem solving.

i. Moral excellences in themselves cannot provide the means of resolving moral dilemmas. Suitable intellectual virtues must exist, for example, the ability to discern what the problem is; analytical abilities to discern what moral excellences are involved with the various dimensions of the problem and with alternative solutions of the problem; experimental and data-collecting skills to choose which information and data relate to the problem and also how these data relate to the agent's moral excellences; imagination and creativity to envisage the problem in a different way, to think of novel solutions to the problem, and to foresee the success or failure of various solutions to the problem and how these solutions might affect the agent's moral excellences; reasoning ability to discern and evaluate the dimensions of presently held moral excellences and then possible implications for moral judgments and action.

ii. As noted in an earlier chapter, moral excellences must possess suitable emotions and the agent must have the ability to withstand emotional pulls that designate unacceptable directions and diminish moral excellences. In this latter case, the moral agent through the use of intellectual and moral virtues must evaluate the worth of emotions, desires, and interests. This implies that emotions, desires, and interests can be cultivated, changed, and developed. Rather than speaking of emotions, desires, and interests, it seems more advisable to refer to these changes as the development of rational emotions, rational desires, and rational interests. In saying this, it is asserted that various affective qualities are not wholly separated from the cognitive and from intelligence except perhaps in the most savage of beasts. In place of such separation, the emotional provides brakes for and nourishes the rational and the rational provides a means of changing the emotional.

iii. At times, character or the structure of moral excellences needs to be enlarged. Dimensions need to be added to already possessed moral excellences. The moral agent may discover that a moral dilemma actually does not involve a conflict between various moral excellences. Rather, the problem may involve an inadequate structure and understanding of moral excellences. The problem may point to inadequacy in intellectual virtues or the relationship of intellectual virtues to moral virtues.

Moral Dilemmas of Professional Roles and of Public Life

Certain moral dilemmas are much more difficult and complicated than the ones already mentioned. These dilemmas involve clashes between moral excellences and the morality suitable for professional roles and public life. A state official in a department of education may be faced with such a dilemma. This official possesses personally accepted moral excellences and moral beliefs that have consistently governed private life. Often, these moral excellences are also suitable for interpersonal decisions in the workplace. In an official capacity, however, the person is a representative of the state government and is expected to make and carry out educational policy consistent with state mandates concerning education, state laws, the state and federal constitutions, and legal precedents. Other factors and constraints may also enter into any policy decision. These include various types of evidence (e.g., if the official were to recommend the purchasing of computer hardware and software, there would have to be knowledge of the adequacy of the various components); cost effectiveness and economic constraints (e.g., the comparative costs of educational programs in relation to the number of students included in these programs and the state budgetary allocations); the knowledge base in various areas (e.g., as this might apply to proposed curriculum mandates). All this diverse evidence the official might seek and include in the decision-making process. There may also be a need to consider various value and philosophic assumptions. For example, in deciding about curriculum mandates, does the official posit separate disciplines, fragmented knowledge, or curriculum unity in which subjects are interrelated with one another.[10]

The official's policy decisions are not just based on various evidence and political and economic contraints. Even the inclusion of the philosophic assumptions of the evidence is not a sufficient warrant for the decision. How does the official make this policy decision when numerous unknown people will be affected by the decision and when character moral excellences do not seem to provide the necessary moral standards? Let's briefly sketch some of the directions this process might take.

i. In the first place, there is a preliminary question about whether the official should make the judgment. This does not mean that the official should suspend judgment or have some higher authority make the judgment. Rather, the idea of a centralized agency or an authority representing a state body making the judgment is at issue. It was noted that the official in question possesses moral excellences and moral beliefs, and for this argument, it can also be assumed that the official was raised in a community and still has communal ties. The official's identity as well as moral excellences were first molded in a community. The community forms one good in the life of the official. Should the official not also recognize that communities play a similar role in other people's lives? The question that the official might need to ask before prematurely making the policy decision is, how can communities be included in this policy-making decision?[11] The official might suggest that a pilot project be tried in which the educational issue would be addressed in a rather different way. A group of school districts would be told that some policy issue must be resolved, but that the school districts in conjunction with the communities of the district can propose alternative ways of resolving the issue. If school districts had not previously embarked in similar policy decision making in a form advocated here that would involve all communities, a state department of education might suggest a variety of ways that such decisions might be made and offer consultants to help with the process. However, a critic may fault this idea on two counts. First, the state official will finally have to decide whether to accept the diverse proposals. How, it is asked, will this decision be made? Second, perhaps there can be greater grassroots community involvement in policy making in some areas, but there are policy decisions that do not just concern individual school districts. These decisions relate to formal education in the whole state. Though both these problems might have to be examined, they do not negate the advantage of involving local communities in policy making.

ii. We found that even if the official broadens the base by which educational policy decisions are made, the official must still make them. Thus, we return to the original question of this section about conflicts between personally accepted moral excellences and moral dilemmas in the public realm. Without repeating the various evidential dimensions already mentioned, we must assume that the official examines the relevant evidence, data, and constraints. By emphasizing the need for a sufficient evidential base for policy making, the idea of abstract reasoning and formal moral principles in the absence of a concrete dilemma and its many evidential features is rejected. Two other aspects of policy making need to be noted here: first, differences between expert and novice moral problem solving, and second, the function of imagination, style, and creativity.

When relevant evidence or data are mentioned, this does not refer to unorganized, fragmented information. Studies of problem solving in the sciences have distinguished between the way novices and experts solve problems. The differences in how novices and experts play chess is often the starting point of such studies. The process by which experts see diverse, interrelated features of a problem in a variety of ways has been called "chunking." Novices on the other hand see fragmented features of the dilemma and cannot connect the separate parts of the problem. Maybe it would also be appropriate to say that the expert sees the many dimensions of a complex matrix, while the novice sees fragmented parts of a segment of the problem. In approaching the evidential base of the policy problem, the official would have to use the "chunking" method of the expert and would have to see the many dimensions of the complete matrix.

Second, there are questions about how imagination, style, and creativity function in policy making. The moral agent making policy decisions needs to have imagination and creativity to see evidence and constraints in a new

light, to be able to structure the diverse variables of the
dilemma in new ways, and to posit a policy decision that
will move in a new direction and provide a novel means of
solving the dilemma. At the same time, however, imagination and creativity must be held in check. There cannot be
wild, irrational decisions that have no relationship with actual evidence or what is possible in the given situation.[12]
Again, style comes into play. Style provides the integrating
dimensions for the many diverse dimensions of decision
making noted here.

iii. There are at least three moral criteria that need to
enter the official's policy decision: the official's moral excellences and moral beliefs, abstract moral principles, and
moral ideals. Though these are discussed separately here,
they are not necessarily applied sequentially. They are integrally related within the decision-making process. An official is not just a place mark that makes a policy according to
some prearranged formula. Instead, the official is a moral
person who possesses moral beliefs and self-consciously
subscribes to a set of moral excellences. This moral agent
will thus have intuitive and not fully articulated beliefs
about what a policy should be. At some time, however, the
official must escape these moral excellences that may just
be exemplars of a particular community, of some place and
time. The moral agent turns to more abstract forms of justification, questions whether the policy will be just, whether
justice for all segments of the population is being upheld,
whether the decision will provide the greatest good for the
greatest number, whether the decision will maximize welfare, whether the policy is fair. The official may not only
justify alternative policies with the moral principles of one
theory, but might assess whether different ethical theories
would recommend different courses of action or different
policy. While continuing all these more abstract forms of
assessment of alternative policy proposals, the official may
continually refer to sincerely held moral excellences and
thus reflexively assess alternatives according to different
justificatory criteria. The official may find that some policy
and the abstract principles used to justify it are not incon-

sistent with personally held moral excellences. The policy decision and abstract principles may provide another way of understanding and structuring moral excellences.

There is a final recourse the official may have in a particularly difficult policy decision that seems to have little to do with personal moral excellences. The official may ask how the moral excellence in its present form relates to some moral ideal. Are a set of moral excellences so shallow that the proposed policy cannot be evaluated through this means? There are two ways to see this problem. In one case, the policy may have very little to do with personally held moral excellences. But then one should question the moral excellences. After all, one possible moral excellence of character is justice. If the official has no moral belief about justice, then there may be some failure of character structure. In this case, the moral reasoning and principles relating to the policy judgment may also eventually affect how the official evaluates personal moral beliefs and character. Second, there is the other situation in which the official looks outward to the moral ideal of which the moral excellence is an imperfect form. In this case, the official seeks to understand the moral excellence in its ideal dimensions in the belief that this ideal can inform both the moral excellence and the more abstract moral criteria used. At this point, someone may argue that there may be times when a policy justified by an abstract moral principle conflicts with a moral excellence, a case in which the agent finds the policy morally repugnant. Why even bother with moral excellences? Why not just use abstract moral criteria in the form of principles to justify policy decisions? These questions in a way are at the heart of the problem here, how moral excellences relate to moral judgments and policies made in the larger public forum. Moral excellences can act as a brake for the problems that might arise from abstract reasoning. Moral excellences interject concern for concrete persons and foster more humane and sensitive feelings, compassion and sympathy, concern for moral ideals and qualities that abstract principles often seem to ignore. If an official finds a policy morally repugnant, it could very well be that the policy is wrong.

Conflicts Between Two Evils or Wrongs and Moral Character

Other types of moral dilemmas are much more difficult to analyze. These are moral dilemmas that only seem to involve alternatives that the moral agent believes are wrong. At the outset, let's leave aside moral dilemmas in education of this type. In the public domain, however, moral agents may at times be confronted with such dilemmas and thus moral education has to take such possibilities into consideration. For example, since the dropping of atomic bombs on Hiroshima and Nagasaki, people have asked whether this decision was necessary. Wasn't there another way? On one side Truman had seen the continuation of the war with considerable loss of life. On the other side, there was the dropping of the bomb and the considerable number of civilians who would die. Certain consequences might not have been fully recognized, the numbers who would suffer during their entire life and the yet unknown effects on future generations. Some critics of Truman's decision have said that all possible alternatives were not considered. Instead of having two alternative wrong or evil decisions, these critics would argue, another course was possible. Truman could have invited Japanese leaders to a test of the atomic bomb on an uninhabited island. But in the emotional climate and practical realities of the moment, there were too many reasons for not making this choice. In the end, the choice was between the two alternatives we now recoil at. Other repulsive or unpleasant choices continue to present themselves to moral agents. How should moral agents make these choices? Again, alternative decisions that consider multidimensional concerns, claims, interests, and evidence need to be weighed against the various moral standards already mentioned. In the end, a decision may be made to minimize harm and/or not to compromise one's moral ideals. There may be no choice that will eliminate evil or wrong or injustice. What of the moral agent in this situation? These decisions cannot just involve some rationalization to insure political power or personal aggrandizement. Even if the moral agent judges and acts with the purest motives, the most comprehensive reasoning and evidence possible, and the most sensitive consideration of moral excellences, moral principles, and moral ideals, evil may still remain. The decision is the better alternative of two evils. And some would argue that this better decision must be considered right or just. The moral agent cannot be faulted. There can be no moral tarnish. Yet the moral agent feels that cherished moral ideals have been compromised and experiences the anguish and pain of the tragedy. These feelings and experiences are often the consequences of public decision making. Here we have Odysseus, who is described thus when making his choice of a future life:

> And it fell out that the soul of Odysseus drew the last lot of all and came to make its choice, and, from memory of its former toils having flung away ambition, went about for a long time in quest of the life of an ordinary citizen who minded his own business, and with difficulty found it lying in some corner disregarded by the others, and upon seeing it said that it would have done the same had it drawn the first lot, and chose it gladly.[13]

The toils of Odysseus' earlier life, like the life of the political and public person, involve the choices of a Machiavellian Prince. The question one must ask, however, is whether this public and political person remains sensitive and alive to moral possibilities, whether compassion and sympathy are retained, whether the person feels the pain and suffering of moral tragedies, or whether the person becomes callous to the moral suffering and tragedies of decisions. Yet there is a point at which the moral person must say, "No."[14] Beyond a point no human being can go and retain moral personhood and moral excellences. There are decisions that must be, "Rather death than this."

How the Resolution of These Complex Dilemmas Relates to Moral Education

An earlier chapter on moral education did not mention problem solving or the resolution of more complex moral dilemmas, but concentrated on character development. Moral education must also include attention to the improvement of how students resolve moral dilemmas. The nurturing of character and moral excellences is not opposed to moral problem solving or reasoning. Moral excellences include moral beliefs, standards that would be used to resolve moral dilemmas. However, a practical moral education program must include dimensions that extend beyond student moral excellences. This is as it should be. Moral education must involve the growth and enlargement of moral character and moral excellences. Through solving moral dilemmas, such growth can occur. Thus, the moral problems that may be a part of a moral education program may seem to move beyond the agent's moral beliefs and character. There are moral problems all of whose diverse, incompatible solutions seem to be consistent with rather different moral excellences and moral standards. In actuality, however, these various moral dilemmas are meant to foster thought and the expansion of moral excellences.

What can educators do to foster student thinking skills and the practical reasoning necessary for resolving moral problems? How might such reasoning also enlarge, correct, and clarify the moral excellences of character? The vast majority of writings and practical recommendations on moral education concentrate on the improvement of problem solving and reasoning. One might wonder, why not just use that material here? There is no need to add to this vast literature and develop yet another way. However, even though these writings do provide some clues, they are not wholly suitable for this present theory of moral education. At this juncture, only a few ideas to redirect present efforts to improve moral reasoning are noted. (i) Instead of concentrating on artificial moral dilemmas, students need to work on a different type of moral problem, those that relate to their own lives, those that are raised from questions about sympathy and benevolence. Students must not only make moral judgments but also must follow moral judgments with moral action. Moral excellences and character are not extended, corrected, and sustained through making judgments. Only through a continuing interaction among desires, emotions, reasoning, judgments, actions, and subsequent evaluation can character and moral excellences develop. (ii) Practical reasoning to resolve moral dilemmas needs to be enlarged to include many dimensions no longer a part of moral education. (iii) Practical reasoning needs to foster student questioning about their moral selves and their character, and what judgments their moral excellences would suggest and how their judgments and actions would affect their character. (iv) There might also be recourse to how other moral agents in different times and places resolved analogous moral problems. Through literature, biographies, and historical examples, students may see another way and recognize the ideals that guided other moral agents' lives. By understanding the moral character, judgments, and actions of others, students may begin to understand their own moral excellences. (v) Moral standards must enter moral reasoning in a different manner than now advocated. Students must be able to draw from the wide stock of moral excellences, moral ideals, and view of the right and the good to be able to understand the complexity and variety of actual moral life.

Moral Ideals

Before discussing moral ideals, reasons must be given for including the notion "moral ideals" as well as the more common "*the* Good" in this theory of moral education. Many would question including moral ideals or the Good and would argue that these notions have too many unacceptable conceptual features and historical connotations. For example, some would say that such notions have supported elitism. Others cite the difficulties of using such a notion as the standard for making moral judgments. Both moral ideals and the Good thus seem to be some sort of ambiguous, intuitive, hierarchical notion that few if any people could ultimately know.

Certain metaphors of moral qualities, "the beautiful," "the true," "the good," and others, are invaluable for expressing moral ideas that sometimes elude the confines language imposes on us. Even during the present skeptical age, the notion of moral ideals and the Good continually intrude into many aspects of practical life. This occurs even when these terms are not used. In this last section we look at these two notions, first moral ideals and then the Good.

First, there is the problem of whether a moral education theory that includes moral ideals also implies some form of elitism and is an advocacy of elitist education. It would be easy enough to claim as other theorists have that a moral development theory does not evaluate persons, but only their moral reasoning. But this response does not solve the problem. The elitism and untenable ontological divisions of some earlier hierarchical theories can be avoided by seeing moral excellences and ideals in a different way. Elitism, some might argue, is connected in some way to ontological hierarchical divisions and only a small class of human beings can attain knowledge at the highest ontological levels. Ontological divisions into lower and higher levels of moral excellences and ideals is not the position taken here. This statement, however, is not made to sidestep the real problem of theories that imply that only a small elite can attain objective knowledge of moral ideals and thus the "purest" sort of moral character. Instead of being known by some small elite, moral ideals can be found within the moral lives of average human beings who struggle to live the moral and good life.

But still the problem remains of why moral ideals should be a vital component of morality and moral education. Alfred North Whitehead refers to this issue as a paradox. Whitehead states: "Moral consists in the aim at the ideal, and at its lowest it concerns the prevention of relapse to lower levels. Thus stagnation is the deadly foe of morality. Yet in human society the champions of morality are on the whole the fierce opponents of new ideals."[15] Whitehead asserts that aiming at ideals does not imply a conservative morality or the stagnation of morality. Aiming at ideals requires "the vigour to adventure beyond the safeties of the past."[16] Moral education theories and ethical theories that aim at ideals have often been seen as conservative in that it is assumed that once some knowable and absolute end is known, no further moral growth and change is necessary or possible.[17] How can moral ideals contribute to growth, change, and moral vigor? Moral vigor, it would be argued, requires an open-ended moral universe in which individuals seek diverse and changing ends and temporary ideals. These criticisms are misplaced. Finite human beings living during a particular time and place can never fully articulate the nature of moral ideals. During each historical period and in different societies, human beings understand moral ideals in different ways and stress a rather different spectrum of ideals. As a first answer to why one particular spectrum of moral ideals intrudes at some historical moment, we can turn Edel's interpretation of ideals as related "to the needs and conditions of [the] life in which they operate."[18] Moral ideals then derive meaning within "the conceptual apparatus of morality" and become the "ideals of character"[19] that are "objects of aspiration." Widespread concern during a given historical period with some spectrum of moral ideals occurs within the context of that age, its aspirations, needs, and conditions. These ideals can be assessed and characterized in a number of ways, according to the breadth of the ideal's foundation, its intensity, motor power or dynamism, attainability, and effectiveness.[20] With the breadth of an ideal's foundation, we refer to how widespread the craving is for the spectrum of ideals, whether they have import for an entire society or a large number of people. Ideals, for example, may have either low or high intensity in a person's life. If the intensity of an ideal were too low, then we would have to question whether it was an ideal for the moral agent. On the other side, an excessive intensity may be a form of fanaticism.[21] Though this search for a mean between two extremes may accord with Aristotle, we are left with a number of questions. For example, how do we interpret the moral ideals of a Gandhi or Martin Luther King? Is it possible that some forms of excessive intensity (or fanaticism) may be acceptable, while others are not? Do the other dimensions given to ideals provide the evaluative tools necessary to assess whether an excessive intensity is morally acceptable?

This way of interpreting moral ideals places them firmly within human life and a given historical period. It naturalizes and socializes ideals but does not dilute them into short-term or fragmented ends-in-view. Important in this view of moral ideals is their historical development. The history of an ideal does not only map its wandering road and clarify why during certain periods the ideal gains prominence. Through an historical study, we may begin to discern core features, the unit idea, of a moral ideal. Philosophic analysis can also contribute to our understanding of a spectrum of moral ideals. At the same time that moral ideals have naturalized and social attributes and functions, their characteristics extend beyond their meaning for any single historic period. When Edel speaks of the "receding horizon" of moral ideals,[22] he implicitly accepts that any conceptualization of moral ideals implies an external standard toward which all progressive approximations of some specific moral ideal or spectrum of related moral ideals must then aim. Rather than solely referring to moral ideals, Sidgwick's distinction between excellences and ideals is helpful. This is the distinction that has been used throughout this book. A moral excellence is the present configuration of a moral ideal, how the moral ideal is actually instantiated in moral character, how some given historical period views a moral ideal. The moral excellence is the actuality, the moral ideal the receding horizon.

Moral ideals exist both within and beyond human life. We recognize them in the lives of ideal types. Some of these ideal types are portrayed in literature and myths. If moral excellences were wholly time constrained and understood only by those living at some particular time and place, these ideal types and their lives and moral struggles would be wholly inaccessible to future generations. But this is not the case. Throughout history, we continually return to literature, myth, and religious writings for moral nourishment.

The moral lives of these ideal types, their successes and failures, their grandeur and tragedy tell us not just what moral life is but also what moral life can be. Other exemplars of ideal types are found in actual human life. We admire people who have sacrificed, been compassionate, performed the supererogatory, been courageous, overcome incredible handicaps and pain to live the good life. In the lives of these average people who have attained moral grandeur, we recognize moral ideals. Moral education in part occurs through the recognition of, identification with, and modeling of these ideal types. In one sense then, this is one reason why the various people who educate young people and who are respected and idealized by children and adolescents must recognize their moral responsibilities. The lives of these adults influence the moral education and character of children and adolescents. These adults should be living personifications of moral excellences.

In moral philosophy, there has been continual concern about whether there is some overarching moral standard that serves as a way of adjudicating problems of conflicting moral excellences or ideals. One standard has been to seek some overarching good whether in the form of pleasure, happiness, or the maximization of welfare. Some philosophers have recently conceptualized the good in other ways, in the execution of a life plan or in the construction of a coherent life narrative or in the retrospective evaluation of a life narrative. In this case, the spectrum of moral excellences or ideals chosen would be those that are necessary to achieve the chosen life plan. Perhaps in their own lives, some academicians actually follow their own conceptualizations of the good life. For the many people who live the life that Odysseus of the *Republic* would choose, the situation is quite different. Sometimes, during the course of their lives, people have to abandon life plans. Economic conditions, natural disasters, revolutions and wars, an absence of some degree of luck, unfavorable health conditions, family crises and needs, limited intellectual ability and a lack of certain attitudes, or psychological crises might cause people to change life plans. However, whether they retain or abandon rational life plans, people often have explicitly or implicitly sworn allegiance to particular moral ideals that are not changed no matter whether these agents' life plans change.[23] These moral ideals and moral commitments are so basic to what the person is that to give them up would do serious damage to the most fundamental part of the person.

When someone's moral judgment and moral action are inconsistent with these irrevocable commitments, the results can only be described as one of the tragedies of human life. People feel pain and sorrow when these moral ideals are compromised. For example, Freeman Dyson records such a tragedy. Dyson had firmly believed in pacifism. He had decided that it was impossible to fight in the Second World War because of this pacifism. Thus, in both word and deed he demonstrated consistency. He rejected any judgment or action that would take human life. Eventually, however, he chose to help his country by doing some scientific work for the military. His reason for this was not a change of moral beliefs, but the idea that such assistance and research could save human lives. After taking this first step, there is one compromise, then another, and another. He finally loses sight of his original commitment to pacifism. No one can read Dyson's honest and soul-searching account of how the commitment to pacifism was negated by continual compromises without recognizing the personal anguish and tragedy Dyson experienced. Someone may recuperate from a changed life plan, but the rejection or compromise of a moral commitment causes scars that no plastic surgery can eliminate.

Moral ideals are not just temporary ends desired by an agent, but are general moral criteria on which moral agents base their lives. Moral excellences change and develop, become more complex, and acquire greater depth depending on people being able to see a moral ideal with greater clarity and acquire greater understanding of what the moral ideal means and requires. The term "require" might cause intellectual pain for those who claim that people create their own moral world and are autonomous moral agents. What can the term "require" mean here and how does it relate to moral ideals? People subscribe to moral excellences like justice, question how to insure a world without pain and suffering, believe in compassion and sympathy, benevolence and altruism. Moral excellences and their ideals are standards that describe character and people's moral actions. If the continual striving to reach these standards ceases, then moral character withers. The moral excellence is no longer a part of the person's life. Acceptance of a moral excellence means that the moral person continues to search for a more adequate instantiation of the moral ideal. Through reasoning and feeling, through judgments and actions, a moral agent develops a more complex form of the moral excellences and more closely approximates the moral ideal. However, this is not the search for a perfection that is wholly outside of cultural life and society. The moral ideal is both within and outside, internal and external to a culture, society, and historical period. Moral ideals are internal to a society and historical period in that they are seen through a new light and conceptualized in new ways at different times and in different places. At the same time, moral ideals reach beyond any limited society or period. On one side, a moral excellence reaches back into the past to discover its roots in human history. The virtues of ancient Athens, it has been said many times, are exceptionally different from the virtues of the late twentieth century. Yet we view Socrates as an ideal type, as possessing moral excellences in their ideal dimensions. He escapes the constraints of time and place. Similarly, during any historical period, we look to the future and imagine what moral excellences might be. Imagining other dimensions for a moral excellence and envisioning a more perfect instantiation or picture of a moral excellence means that the ideal is seen in another way. We also view a more perfect picture of the moral ideal through the moral excellences portrayed in our literature and philosophy.

Often moral beliefs and moral excellences are pale shadows of moral ideals that possess complex dimensions and are interrelated with other moral ideals. Even if people try to make judgments and act in accordance with their moral excellences, these moral excellences are not perfect instantiations of moral ideals. The impossibility and hope-lessness of fully achieving the demands of moral ideals is well recognized by most people. At times, this hopelessness and the shortcomings of moral life, as Dostoevsky noted in another context, are the secrets "which a man is even afraid to tell himself, and every decent man has a consider-able number of such things stored away. That is, one can even say that the more decent he is, the greater the number of such things in his mind."[24] In the context of this book, these secrets are not raging, unconscious desires, but the knowledge that often moral excellences do not fulfill their ideal dimensions and moral judgments and actions fall short of the moral ideal. A moral agent is generous, but generosity for the average human being extends to a few favored causes and people. We sometimes know that the elimination of certain pain and suffering, gains in sympa-thy and benevolence cannot be the responsibility of a few people in public or political life. We look to the few ideal types—to a Jesus and a Socrates and a Buddha—as in-stantiations of the ideals we cherish. We see those moral ideals in Alcibiades' tribute to Socrates, the "godlike and extraordinary," who has "little figures of the gods inside."

Yet there must be some way of measuring the limits of some moral excellence, or how to adjudicate the conflicts that may exist between moral ideals? And for this we need yet another standard. In the story told to Socrates by Di-otima, in the Allegory of the Cave, and in the celestial pa-rade of the gods and goddesses, we receive a hint of this other standard. More recently, Iris Murdoch reconstructs this journey to the Good.[25] In this last section, there must again be a "rising to great place . . . by winding stair."

One does not need a higher education or philosophic analysis to know there is some good beyond and yet within the mundane: the fields of buttercups, the perfect sun-flowers in the heat of a summer day, the birds flying above the tilled fields, the mountains gently rising in the back-ground. We garden and struggle with the reality of nature. We garden and see what Blake sung about "a world in a grain of sand and a Heaven in a wild flower." We garden and the daffodils and tulips that braved the winter frost give us hope and make us believe that there is another way. These "fields of daffodils and buttercups, the birds and fields of brown and green all seem so perfect and so much more ideal than anything that can be described." Any analysis or explanation falls short of what these scenes are. As Eliot recognized, "Words break." But it is ordinary words that break. They cannot convey the perfection of this scene. But then this scene is pictured in another form, in the words of the poet or the painting of the artist. It is no longer the scene, but another view of reality that gives us yet greater meaning and provides nature with a depth it never seemed to have. These new perfections are even more complex, have deeper meanings, and they move into other dimensions. They submerge us in another reality.

There are other experiences besides these: the intensity of creative writing, concentrating on resolving a mathematics problem, trying to understand possible causes of an historical event, reading a novel or a poem, and working intensely on a scientific experiment. Murdoch describes the relation of the self to these experiences:

> In intellectual disciplines and in the enjoyment of art and nature we discover value in our ability to forget self, to be realistic, to perceive justly. We use our imagination not to escape the world but to join it, and this exhilarates us because of the distance between our ordinary dulled consciousness and an apprehension of the real.[26]

How do we come to know of the good? The way is not simple. As with the newspaper editor who learned his finest lessons of the world from gardening, we too can learn about morality from many experiences and relationships. Art and music take us out of our selves for us to learn about our selves. We do not just understand art and music but come to understand the world and ourselves. This was what Swann found in music,

> that was no longer pure music, but rather design, architecture, thought, and which allowed the actual mu-

sic to be recalled. . . . [The music] had at once suggested to him a world of inexpressible delights, of
whose existence, before hearing it, he had never
dreamed, into which he felt that nothing else could
initiate him; and he had been filled with a love for
it.[27]

This is a strange and foreign road to moral knowledge and
understanding of the good. Yet in Coles's case studies of
the moral and political lives of children, we find that their
moral understanding does not derive from the forms of
moral education recommended by philosophers and psychologists. These children's moral understanding comes
from unexpected sources. In a more direct way, there are
times when we too have these moral experiences and relationships, when we realize that there is something more, an
understanding that heightens and enlarges the way we see
moral ideals and the Good. As Odysseus at the end of the
Republic and Murdoch recognize, it is not necessarily some
intellectual elite that achieves this knowledge. Very often, it
is the humble person who "is not by definition the good
man [but] perhaps he is the kind of man who is most likely
of all to become good."[28]

Notes

Chapter 1

The chapter title is from H. G. Wells, *The Outline of History*.

1. The "race" theme occurs in many early twentieth-century European novels. The race between education and catastrophe has also been an explicit theme in recent national reports and studies that call for educational reform, for example, the *Nation at Risk* report.

2. James's continual description of idyllic natural scenes is not just a narrative frame, but vital symbols to heighten the contrasting meanings of the novel.

3. Of all the young people, only Clifford Wentworth briefly strays from the correct, prescribed path. His wayward conduct begins when he leaves his familial intimate surroundings and ventures into the larger world of foreign ideas, more specifically student life at Harvard College.

4. Actually, Felix's dilettantism is consistent with James's vision of the harmonious *gemeinschaft*. Any professional specialization or commitment to a cause would require allegiance to its values and thus separate someone from the dominant values of the original community. Only concentration on communal values or dilettantism would guarantee the maintenance of the original *gemeinschaft*.

5. By the time James wrote *The Europeans,* the idyllic picture of American family and extended familial and communal life had already undergone radical changes. James was writing about a dream world and the title of the book thus has an

ironic connotation. For a discussion of changes in American family life, see Alexis de Tocqueville, *Democracy in America*, trans. George Lawrence (Garden City, N.Y.: Doubleday/Anchor, 1969), pp. 585–586.

6. Ironically, James's first description of American city life is uttered by the Baroness Münster. As a formidable protagonist, the Wentworth European cousin, the Baroness Münster, represents the struggle between the values of the *gemeinschaft* and the *gesellschaft*, and then the forthcoming demise of the moral foundation of the *gemeinschaft*. Not only does the Baroness intimate an influx of foreign influences into the idyllic Wentworth society, but her entire lifestyle symbolizes the dissolution of the moral foundation of the *gemeinschaft*. Even though the Baroness expresses repugnance for Boston city life, her feelings viewed within the context of her values and behavior seem a perfect example of Freudian reaction formation, by which she scorns the very traits she accepts. Though she disdains the "indifference" of the city, she proves indifferent to the cherished values and interests of the Wentworth family. What proclaimed the new social and moral age was that the Baroness played different roles, whatever part was expected of her and suitable for diverse social surroundings. When it seemed appropriate to flirt, she flirted; when flattery would win her case, she flattered; when she needed to lie, she lied. The Baroness saw her untruths as instances of tact, what would amuse and fascinate her audience. Whereas the Wentworths were real and natural since their behavior wholly conformed with their unchanging, internalized values, the Baroness's behavior and values varied depending on what people and society found pleasing. The Baroness Münster represented a new social and moral order and thus implicitly an ominous threat to traditional moral education.

7. James also stresses the moral struggles of the average human being who in unique situations either rises to meet the moral challenge or continues to live out a moral life that cannot make room for the grandeur of the situation. James depicts how moral agents question who they are, revise their characters, and are significantly touched by moral intuitions. James examines the character of both the unique and the ordinary protagonists to understand how they meet the moral challenges of their lives.

8. John Wilson, *Discipline and Moral Education* (Windsor, Eng.: NFER-Nelson, 1981), pp. 67–68.

9. Christopher Lasch, *Haven in a Heartless World* (New York: Basic Books, 1977); Uri Bronfenbrenner, "Disturbing Changes in the American Family," *Search* 2 (1976): 4–10; Kenneth Keniston et al., *All Our Children* (New York: Harcourt, Brace,

Jovanovich, 1977), e.g., pp. 3–23. One survey, however, suggests that a decade ago one sample of educators had a rather different view; see Kevin Ryan and Michael G. Thompson, "Moral Education's Muddled Mandate: Comments on a Survey of Phi Delta Kappans," *Phi Delta Kappa* 56 (1975): 663–666.

10. The current moral climate can be analyzed in various ways. I claim only that no matter what data are cited, a writer can begin with a predominantly pessimistic or optimistic bias. Lasch, for example, takes a pessimistic stance and does nothing to soften his view; he provides no solutions to the problems he posits: for example, Christopher Lasch, *The Minimal Self* (New York: W. W. Norton, 1984). Mosher, on the other hand, begins with a negative picture, for example, Watergate and the American public's distrust of political leadership, corporations, military establishment, police. Ralph Mosher, "An Uncommon Cause," in Ralph Mosher, ed., *Moral Education* (New York: Praeger, 1980), p. 7. However, Mosher offers moral education programs to ameliorate the gloomy social and political data. Similar, antithetical interpretations can be found in philosophical writings. Frankena, for instance, posits a negative view of present moral life. William Frankena, "Philosophy and Moral Standards," in Peter Caws, ed., *Two Centuries of Philosophy in America* (Totowa, N.J.: Rowman & Littlefield, 1980), pp. 311–313. Edel, in response to Frankena, interprets the current moral climate very differently and asks how to discover valid moral responses to meet the needs and recognize the new dimensions of this present moral period. Abraham Edel, "Comments on Frankena's 'Philosophy and Moral Standards,'" in Caws, ed., *Two Centuries of Philosophy in America,* pp. 329–339.

11. W. T. Jones, "Public Rules, Private Roles, and Differential Moral Assessments of Role Performance," *Ethics* 14 (1984): 603–620.

12. Kohlberg for one has continually criticized traditional forms of moral education. For example, see Lawrence Kohlberg, "Indoctrination versus Relativity in Value Education," *Zygon: Journal of Religion and Science* 6 (1971): 285–291. See also Lawrence Kohlberg, "Moral Education in the Schools: A Developmental View," *School Review,* 74 (1966): 14.

13. Regarding this radical transformation of present society and its values, see Lasch, *Haven in a Heartless World;* Christopher Lasch, *The Culture of Narcissism* (New York: W. W. Norton, 1979); Lasch, *Minimal Self.* During earlier periods, sociologists and other writers uncovered society's underlying contradictions and problems. For example, a reviewer of Robert S. Lynd and Helen Merrell Lynd, *Middletown in*

Transition (New York: Harcourt, Brace, 1937) states that the town's "inhabitants are almost as regimented as those of a South Sea Islander under the taboo system." R. L. Duffus, "Getting at the Truth About an Average American Town," in Garry Wills, ed., *Values Americans Live By* (New York: Arno Press, 1974), p. 58. Throughout human history, literary writers and poets have been particularly sensitive to a loss of confidence in traditional morality and to an ostensible "degeneration" of traditional values. During the present era, a number of European and American novels stress this theme (e.g., in the novels of Broch, Mann, Musil, Lewis, and Dreiser).

14. *Meno* 70a, Guthrie trans.

15. For example, how can parents provide moral education for a young child when the very basis of morality, caring, compassion, concern for the interests of others, seems undermined? Children of this generation, it can be argued, must be wary not only of strangers, but even of friends and family members. Child abuse in families and daycare centers, the kidnapping and exploitation of children, suggest that children must remain cautious and ready to protest any unwarranted intrusion by others. Children thus must learn the realities and cruelties of actual life instead of developing compassion, empathy, and trust for other human beings. Must unfortunate social conditions have a negative effect on moral education? Will children become distrustful and fearful of other people instead of being open and understanding human feelings, needs, and interests? Must we reject an optimistic account of this present historical period and instead side with pessimists who bemoan the difficulty of transmitting an objective and compassionate form of morality?

    The pessimistic view need not be accepted. Evidence in various cases can lead us in a more optimistic direction. Child abuse, the exploitation of and violence against children, are not new phenomena. Tommy Morgan, for instance, notes that when he was an infant during the Edwardian age, his mother hurled him at his father. Thea Thompson, *Edwardian Childhoods* (London: Routledge & Kegan Paul, 1981), p. 10, cf., p. 24. Tommy was crippled for life. Charles Dickens in *Dombey and Son* describes the kidnapping of two children and how terrified the young girl felt. In some societies, infanticide was practiced, especially when the infant was female, deformed, or a weakling. These and numerous other similar examples in no way excuse present crimes against children. However, the late twentieth-century phenomena are different from those of earlier periods. People are outraged about the kidnapping and abuse of children. Society's mores and legal system severely punish those who commit these crimes. For like any other human beings, children, it is now recognized, should have basic rights. Thus, though these offenses still exist, there is considerable repugnance toward them. Unlike earlier periods, the public and children alike are now educated to stem child abuse.

16. Among the many books on moral education, a few of the recent publications include Marvin W. Berkowitz and Fritz Oser, *Moral Education: Theory and Application* (Hillsdale, N.J.: Lawrence Erlbaum Associates, 1985); Barry Chazan, *Contemporary Approaches to Moral Education* (New York: Teachers College Press, 1985); R. S. Peters, *Moral Development and Moral Education* (London: George Allen & Unwin, 1985); Jack Braeden Arbuthnot and David Faust, *Teaching Moral Reasoning: Theory and Practice* (New York: Harper & Row, 1981); Mosher, ed., *Moral Education;* Richard H. Hersh, John P. Miller, and Glen D. Fielding, *Models of Moral Education* (New York: Longman, 1980); Richard H. Hersh, *Promoting Moral Growth* (New York: Longman, 1979); Thomas C. Hennessy, *Value/Moral Education: Schools and Teachers* (New York: Paulist Press, 1979); Robert T. Hall and John U. Davis, *Moral Education in Theory and Practice* (Buffalo, N.Y.: Prometheus Books, 1975); Paul H. Hirst, *Moral Education in a Secular Society* (London: University of London Press, 1974); Barry I. Chazan and Jonas F. Soltis, eds., *Moral Education* (New York: Teachers College Press, 1973); Peter McPhail, J. R. Ungoed-Thomas, and Hilary Chapman, *Moral Education in the Secondary School* (London: Longman, 1972); John Wilson, *Practical Methods of Moral Education* (London: Heinemann Educational Books, 1972); Norman J. Bull, *Moral Education* (London: Routledge & Kegan Paul, 1969); John Wilson, Norman Williams, and Barry Sugarman, *Introduction to Moral Education* (Baltimore: Penguin Books, 1967); W. R. Niblett, ed., *Moral Education in a Changing Society* (London: Faber & Faber, 1963).

17. Regarding this view in relation to normal science, see Thomas S. Kuhn, *The Structure of Scientific Revolutions* (Chicago: Phoenix Books, 1962).

18. For another criticism of the centrality of rights theories, see Brian Barry, "Courts and Constitutions," *TLS* 1,308 (1985): 1195–1196.

19. Gerald Grant, "The Character of Education and the Education of Character," *Daedalus* 110 (1981): 145–146.

20. For example, Kenneth Strike, *Educational Policy and the Just Society* (Urbana: University of Illinois Press, 1983). For a criticism of this resurrection of older theories, see Betty A. Sichel, "Review of Kenneth Strike's *Educational Policy and the*

Just Society," Journal of Research and Development in Education 17 (1984): 78–83.

21. Similarly, questions have been raised about Kuhn's revolutionary paradigmatic changes. Are scientific revolutions totally disconnected from the past? For these questions, see Imre Lakatos and Alan Musgrave, eds., *Criticism and the Growth of Knowledge* (Cambridge, Eng.: Cambridge University Press, 1970).

22. C. G. Jung, *Memories, Dreams, Reflections,* trans. Richard and Clara Winston (New York: Pantheon Books, 1961), p. 236.

23. For example, Lawrence Kohlberg and Rochelle Mayer, "Development as the Aim of Education," *Harvard Educational Review* 42 (1972): 449–496.

24. Henry Giroux and David Purpel, eds., *The Hidden Curriculum and Moral Education* (Berkeley, Calif.: McCutchan, 1983).

25. Albert Bandura, *Social Learning Theory* (Englewood Cliffs, N.J.: Prentice-Hall, 1977).

26. Robert Hogan, John A. Johnson, and Nicholas P. Emler, "A Socioanalytic Theory of Moral Development," in William Damson, ed., *Moral Development* (San Francisco: Jossey-Bass, 1978), pp. 1–18.

27. The winter 1984 issue of the *Review of Educational Research* is devoted to "the teaching and learning of reasoning skills," including not only literacy but civicism as well. Though the aim of the eight papers is summary and synthesis, each separate paper attacks the problem from within each writer's own discipline: for example, Geraldine Joncich Clifford, "Buch and Lesen: Historical Perspectives on Literacy and Schooling," *Review of Educational Research* 54 (1984): 472–500, the historical perspective; Lee S. Shulman and Neil B. Carey, "Psychology and the Limitations of Individual Rationality: Implications for the Study of Reasoning and Civility," *Review of Educational Research* 54 (1984): 501–524, the psychological perspective; Frederick Erickson, "School Literacy, Reasoning, and Civility: An Anthropologist's Perspective," *Review of Educational Research* 54 (1984): 525–546, anthropological perspective; Maxine Greene, "Philosophy, Reason, and Literacy," *Review of Educational Research* 54 (1984): 547–559, philosophical perspective. Similarly, recent works in philosophy have incorporated ideas and material from various other disciplines. Alisdair MacIntyre, in *After Virtue* (Notre Dame, Ind.: Notre Dame University Press, 1981), has examined how current sociological role theory relates to moral philosophy. Michael Walzer, in *Spheres of Justice* (New York: Basic Books, 1983), enriched his theory of justice with ideas from sociology, anthropology, and other diverse sources. Cf., Lee S. Shulman, "The Practical and the Eclectic: A Deliberation on Teaching and

Educational Research," *Curriculum Inquiry* 14 (1984): 183–200.

28. Abraham Edel and Elizabeth Flower compare the first (1908) and second (1932) editions of Dewey and Tufts's *Ethics* and note that the drastic changes between the two editions were in part dependent on Dewey's study of new material in newly emerging disciplines, for example, anthropology. Abraham Edel and Elizabeth Flower, "Introduction," in Jo Ann Boydston, ed., *John Dewey: The Later Works, 1925–1953* (Carbondale: Southern Illinois University Press, 1985), pp. vii–xxxv. Thus, without citing these courses, Dewey was greatly influenced by findings in the social and behavioral sciences.

29. Richard Rorty, *Philosophy and the Mirror of Nature* (Princeton, N.J.: Princeton University Press, 1979), p. 5. At present, one might argue that television and movies have taken the place of poets and novelists.

30. Lawrence A. Cremin, *The Genius of American Education* (New York: Vintage Books, 1965), especially chap. 1, "The Commitment to Popular Education."

31. John I. Goodlad, *A Place Called School* (New York: McGraw-Hill, 1984), for example, pp. 39–43.

32. For an interesting treatment of the relationship between psychological and sociological abstractions in morality, see Dorothy Emmet, *Rules, Roles, and Relations* (Boston: Beacon Press, 1966), pp. 138f.

33. D. D. Raphael, "The Standard of Morals," *Proceedings of the Aristotelian Society* 75 (1975): 1–12.

34. Character and moral excellences are now beginning to have avid philosophical supporters. For example, see Gregory E. Pence, "Recent Work on Virtues," *American Philosophical Quarterly* 21 (1984): 281–297, for an extended study of "recent work on virtues." This renewed interest does not exist in psychology or education.

Chapter 2

1. In light of the emergence of a renewed interest in philosophic notions that were ignored up to the present decade, any statement that character and virtue are not now advocated seems anachronistic and wrong-headed. For recent important, influential theories and studies on these subjects, see Alasdair MacIntyre, *After Virtue* (Notre Dame, Ind.: Notre Dame University Press, 1981); Philippa Foot, *Virtues and Vices* (Berkeley: University of California Press, 1978); Gregory E. Pence, "Recent Work on Virtues," *American Philosophical Quarterly* 21 (1984): 281–297. The claim here is

quite different, but equally important. Philosophy of moral education and educational theory and practice have not been affected by the various new ways moral philosophers are conceptualizing moral phenomena and moral personhood.

Those few educational theorists who explicitly propose a central role for character and virtue in moral education are generally traditionalists or conservatives, and thus their images of character education rely on traditional, sometimes unexamined moral traits, rules, and ideas; for example, Edward A. Wynne, "The Declining Character of American Youth," *American Educator* 3 (1979): 29–32. A few other thinkers cite the importance of character, but then do not refer to this concept again. For instance, while Mosher states his "personal belief that character is absolutely central in human beings and to the quality of their social life," he then treats moral education from a Kohlbergean cognitive developmental framework and totally ignores character. Ralph Mosher, "An Uncommon Cause," in Ralph Mosher, ed., *Moral Education* (New York: Praeger, 1980), p. 6.

2. Kohlberg questions "common" and theoretical notions of moral character. Lawrence Kohlberg, "Development of Moral Character and Moral Ideology," in Martin L. Hoffman and Lois Hoffmann, *Review of Child Development Research* (New York: Russell Sage Foundation, 1964), pp. 383–431. He faults "character as superego strength," "character as good habits," and "character as ego strength." Ibid., pp. 387–388, 388–389, 389–392. By not doing justice to these different views of character, Kohlberg has little difficulty locating "fatal" flaws. Kohlberg's terse exposition of "character as good habits," for example, does not recognize the complexity of either the concept "habit" or "character." By referring to "Boy Scouts" and "Sunday school" character traits and only noting imitation, reinforcement, and direct training, Kohlberg tacitly fits character into a narrow box. As Peters points out, Kohlberg does not explore other vital aspects and functions of either habits or character. R. S. Peters, "Moral Development: A Plea for Pluralism," in Theodore Mischel, ed., *Cognitive Development and Epistemology* (New York: Academic Press, 1971).

3. For one contemporary use of *arete*, see William K. Frankena, "The Ethics of Love Conceived as an Ethics of Virtue," *Journal of Religious Ethics* 1 (1973): 21–36.

4. For the sake of brevity, this section on Homeric character and education does not examine substantive questions about (1) challenges to traditional Homeric views of manly virtues and (2) whether the Homeric epics depict some actual society. However, the Homeric epics as well as other stories fur-

nished standards for morality and moral education during the Classical period. For discussions of heroic, manly virtues and character and moral education, see Arthur W. H. Adkins, *Merit and Responsibility* (Oxford: Clarendon Press, 1960), pp. 30–60; H. I. Marrou, *A History of Education in Antiquity*, trans. George Lamb (New York: Sheed & Ward, 1956), pp. 6, 10–12.

5. For a neo-Marxist interpretation of the ideological nature of Homeric society, see Ellen Meiksins Wood and Neal Wood, *Class Ideology and Ancient Political Theory* (Oxford: Basil Blackwell, 1978). For a different interpretation of Homeric ideology, see Betty A. Sichel, "Correspondence and Contradiction in Ancient Greek Society and Education: Homer's Epic Poetry and Plato's Early Dialogues," *Educational Theory* 33 (1983): 49–59.

6. On the implications of hierarchical moral theory, Aurel Kolnai, *Ethics, Value, and Reality* (Indianapolis: Hackett, 1978), ch. 8, "The Concept of Hierarchy," pp. 165–186.

7. MacIntyre, *After Virtue*.

8. For additional comments on *oikos*, see M. I. Finley, *Economy and Society in Ancient Greece* (New York: Viking Press, 1981), p. 98; M. M. Austin and P. Vidal-Naquet, *Economy and Social History of Ancient Greece*, trans. M. M. Austin (Berkeley: University of California Press, 1977), pp. 40–45.

9. Historical setting is not used as modern thinkers would use the term "history." Rather, the historic setting of the *oikos* refers to its transtemporal continuity and mythic meanings.

10. This worship of rationality and assumption that a particular form of reasoning can surmount all difficulties has flawed not only moral theory, but also a considerable portion of policymaking and public expectations about the extent to which such reasoning can solve problems. More recent attacks on this form of ethical theory have taken a number of directions. For a most interesting interpretation of "luck and ethics in Greek tragedy and philosophy" that escapes the confines of narrow rationalism, see Martha C. Nussbaum, *The Fragility of Goodness* (Cambridge, Eng.: Cambridge University Press, 1986), especially chap. 1, "Luck and Ethics," for the underpinnings of Nussbaum's study.

11. Adkins, *Merit and Responsibility*.

12. Irwin notes that "the conflict between the Homeric outlook and the law-conception [of post-Homeric ethics] should not be exaggerated." Terence Irwin, *Plato's Moral Theory* (Oxford: Clarendon Press, 1977), p. 17. However, Irwin's arguments do not aim to discover similarities between the earlier and later ages.

13. G. E. L. Owen, "The Platonism of Aristotle," in P. F. Strawson,

ed., *Studies in the Philosophy of Thought and Action* (London: Oxford University Press, 1968), p. 171.

14. Alfred North Whitehead, *Adventures of Ideas* (New York: Macmillan, 1935), p. 330.

15. Greater discussion of this way of looking at the moral domain and moral dilemmas cannot be included here. A few words will suffice to indicate that these wide-sweeping claims are not rash. Though some theorists still analyze utilitarian concepts and theories with their emphasis on achieving the greatest good for the greatest number, the larger number of theorists concentrate on neo-Kantian formalism. For example, perusal of extant philosophical studies of moral education demonstrate only a few studies in the last two decades devoted to utilitarianism. The vast majority of studies subscribe to Kantian deontology.

16. This aspect of Kohlberg's moral dilemmas is discussed at greater length in Chapter 6.

17. In a discussion of the results of a survey of public opinion and teacher attitudes about moral education, John Wilson posits a number of conclusions that are relevant here. For example, teachers/educators felt frustrated and hostile about moral education for a number of reasons. Even if they believed that moral education should be educators' responsibility, they tacitly articulated a number of concerns about what needed to be done to facilitate such moral education. For example, educators were concerned about "bridging the gulf between academic and practical." John Wilson, *Discipline and Moral Education* (Windsor, Eng.: NFER-Nelson, 1981), p. 119. While many were aware of scholarly work by experts, for example, Kohlberg, they note "it's hard to get hold of" experts' ideas. Teachers spoke of themselves as amateurs. Their solution was for someone "to bridge the gulf between proper philosophers and psychologists and so on, and hard-working teachers like me." Ibid. When reading Wilson's survey and conclusions, one becomes aware of other problems (e.g., in particular, teachers not being certain about what the moral domain includes or where its boundaries should be drawn). Even though they do not state this explicitly, their concern about social control vis-à-vis moral reasoning and moral principles, about authoritarian versus permissive attitudes, and about moral creeds implies concern over what should be considered moral and the moral domain. Interestingly, in this book as in other works, Wilson himself recognizes this need to enlarge the moral domain. For example, by connecting discipline and moral education, Wilson realizes not only that many people mistake adherence to an authority as moral

education, but that there is a very close relationship between certain types of discipline, (e.g., self-discipline) and morality.

18. Concerning the difficulty of discerning alternatives and their respective consequences, see Lars Bergstrom, *The Alternatives and Consequences of Actions* (Stockholm: Almqvist & Wiksell, 1966).

19. On the other hand, people may also have lacked self-consciousness about unacceptable interactions.

20. Noted in Edward T. Hall, *The Silent Language* (Garden City, N.Y.: Doubleday/Anchor, 1959/1973), p. 187.

21. At times, moral evaluation is withheld but there is annoyance or embarrassment.

22. Schutz and Bollnow are exceptions, philosophers who have been intrigued by the ordinary and taken-for-granted.

23. Thuc.II.37.

24. Even John Dewey, *Democracy and Education* (New York: Macmillan, 1916), p. 21, refers to manners as "minor" morals. Foot's argument about the relationship between etiquette and morality extends in a different direction from Dewey's. Foot seeks to justify "morality as a system of hypothetical imperatives," which is a radical departure from neo-Kantian theories based on categorical imperatives. Though Foot at first recognizes that "moral rules are often enforced much more strictly than the rules of etiquette" (p. 162), she concludes "that moral judgments have no better claim to be categorical imperatives than do statements about etiquette" (p. 164). Philippa Foot, "Morality as a System of Hypothetical Imperatives," in Foot, *Virtues and Vices*. This article was seen by critics as an attempt to "reconstruct morality or replace it with something else." For one such criticism of Foot's position, see William K. Frankena, "The Philosopher's Attack on Morality," *Philosophy* 49 (1974): 345–356. For Foot's reply to this criticism, "A Reply to Professor Frankena," in Foot, *Virtues and Vices*, pp. 174–180.

25. For this, see G. E. M. Anscombe, "Modern Moral Philosophies," in Judith J. Thomson and Gerald Dworkin, eds., *Ethics* (New York: Harper & Row, 1968).

26. Hersey quoted in Foot, *Virtues and Vices*, pp. 4–5.

27. Leonard Gross, *The Last Jews in Berlin* (New York: Simon & Schuster, 1982), p. 46.

28. Whitehead, *Adventures of Ideas*, passim.

29. Rawls's theory of justice is an exception since it also recognizes the importance of the family, the school, and the workplace for fostering moral education and thus contributing to the just society. But Rawls understandably does not stress the contents or form of early moral education (i.e., from infan-

cy). John Rawls, *A Theory of Justice* (Cambridge, Mass.: Harvard University Press, 1971).

30. The Stanley and Azrak articles on moral education by families are primarily concerned with the preadolescent and adolescent. Sheila Stanley, "The Family and Moral Education," in Mosher, ed., *Moral Education,* pp. 341–355; Robert Azrak, "Parents as Moral Educators," in Mosher, ed., *Moral Education,* pp. 356–365.

31. Interestingly, neither of two recent books on gender and science mention John Dewey's theory. Sandra Harding, *The Science Question in Feminism* (Ithaca: Cornell University Press, 1986), and Evelyn Fox Keller, *Reflections on Gender and Science* (New Haven: Yale University Press, 1985).

32. Throughout *The Moral Life of Children,* Coles describes children who lead sensitive, compassionate, thoughtful, caring, meritorious moral lives in the face of painful, difficult moral situations. Robert Coles, *The Moral Life of Children* (Boston: Atlantic Monthly Press, 1986). How should these children's moral lives be interpreted? Should one say that their morality cannot be judged or that we should wait to see what sort of adults they become? In some ways, we suspect that their adult moral lives may not mirror the commendatory quality of their childhood moral lives. But Coles is not saying that we should compare these children's moral lives with that of adults. He is making two other points that are rarely considered by theoreticans investigating moral education. First, scholars also have to look at children in themselves and not compare them with what might or might not be. We have to look at the manifold variables, the complexities of their social and personal lives, their dreams and realities, the external pressures and the internal motivations, the moral self that is already formed. Yes, as educators, there is the need to look at the future and to have moral ideals and standards as bases for moral growth. But maybe educators too often forget the strengths of children and concentrate on what needs to be changed. Second, Coles is suggesting that morality and moral development are far more complex than moral development theorists and educators picture. What happens then to adults who no longer possess the hopes, ideals, intuitive sensitivity, enthusiasm and anger, and compassion and feeling of these children? Perhaps the educational system and society have destroyed what was invaluable in children's morality.

33. Though the term "predict" is used, there is little evidence that Piagetean moral judgment theory "predicts" what an agent views as a moral problem or what her moral judgment or behavior will be. Regarding the predictive nature of Piaget's

cognitive, logical theory, see Charles J. Brainerd, "The Stage Question in Cognitive-Development Theory," *Behavioral and Brain Sciences* 2 (1978): 173–182.

34. For example, ibid.; Owen J. Flanagan, Jr., *The Science of the Mind* (Cambridge, Mass.: MIT Press, 1984), pp. 137–149.

35. Henry George Liddell and Robert Scott, *Greek-English Lexicon*, rev. Henry Stuart Jones, 8th ed. (Oxford: Clarendon Press, 1897, repr. 1968).

36. James Hastings, ed., *Encyclopaedia of Religion* (New York: Charles Scribner's Sons, 1958).

37. Similarly, Flew does not mention character. Antony Flew, *A Dictionary of Philosophy* (New York: St. Martin's Press, 1979).

38. Even Nelson B. Henry, ed., *Modern Philosophies and Education: The Fifty-fourth Yearbook of the National Society for the Study of Education,* pt. I (Chicago: NSSE, 1955), still continued to reflect this concern with the relationship between the metaphysical and education.

39. These three thinkers complemented each other to transform radically the behavioral sciences and human philosophy. Darwin pried under organic life to understand how all species evolved. Marx pried under human society and culture to understand how societies and culture evolve. Freud pried within human beings to understand how the human psyche is formed and evolves.

40. MacIntyre, *After Virtue,* pp. 6–21, argues that emotivism still dominates moral philosophy and moral arguments.

41. Of course, there was criticism of emotivism: for example, John Dewey, *Theory of Valuation* (Chicago: University of Chicago Press, 1939), pp. 6–13.

42. Shaming and humiliation are still advocated by some: for example, George Sher and William J. Bennett, "Moral Education and Indoctrination," *Journal of Philosophy* 79 (1982): 676.

43. For one reading of seven films "made in Hollywood between 1934–1949," see Stanley Cavell, *Pursuits of Happiness: The Hollywood Comedy of Remarriage* (Cambridge, Mass.: Harvard University Press, 1981).

44. David I. Macleod, *Building Character in the American Boy* (Madison: University of Wisconsin Press, 1983).

45. Unquestionably, moral character could be instilled (or nurtured) through all the methods discussed here, through youth organizations, stories, children's magazines, and movies. However, it is expected that the moral excellences of character can be justified by some external standards and warrant. Emotivism denied this and assumed that moral beliefs could not be justified by any objective means.

46. For one emotivist's attempt to sanitize moralizing, exhorta-

tion, and propagandizing, see Charles Stevenson, *Ethics and Language* (New Haven, Conn.: Yale University Press, 1944), e.g., pp. 242–252, 332–335.

47. August B. Hollingshead, *Elmstown's Youth* (New York: John Wiley & Sons, 1949).

48. Such conceptual analysis was ahistorical, representing language usage during one period and often by one group; its purported descriptive analyses were never neutral, but had implicit, hidden assumptions and normative agendas. For this criticism, see Abraham Edel, "Analytic Philosophy of Education at the Crossroads," in James F. Doyle, ed., *Educational Judgments* (London: Routledge & Kegan Paul, 1973).

49. The agenda and consequence of linguistic analysis for ethical theories are more complicated than indicated here. By not accepting the intrusion of facts or evidence, the linguistic analysis formalists also touted the autonomy of ethics. Whether such complete autonomy can be sustained is only now being questioned. For example, one might ask what the relationship is between moral philosophy and a philosophy of mind or moral philosophy and epistemology, between moral theory and psychological evidence, and between moral theory and commonsense morality.

50. In retrospect, some would argue that linguistic analysis was not neutral, that it did support a certain moral stance and implied certain moral practice. The linguistic analysis of moral concepts inevitably ended with one way of seeing morality.

51. Henry Giroux and David Purpel, eds., *The Hidden Curriculum and Moral Education* (Berkeley, Calif.: McCutchan, 1983).

52. For example, Christopher Lasch, *Haven in a Heartless World* (New York: Basic Books, 1977); Elizabeth Hardwick, "Domestic Manners," *Daedalus* 107 (1978): 10–11.

53. Someone may claim, as MacIntyre has in *After Virtue* regarding moral judgments, that such classroom discussions and their diverse, conflicting moral judgments are examples of emotivism. However, what distinguishes these discussions from emotivism was the assumption that, with sufficient analysis and discussion, there would be greater understanding and consensus. With increased rational abilities, there would be agreement about abstract principles and judgments.

54. For a criticism of shielding children from "the normal run of distress experiences," see Martin L. Hoffman, "Empathy, Role-Taking, Guilt, and Development of Altruistic Motives," in Thomas Lickona, ed., *Moral Development and Behavior* (New York: Holt, Rinehart, & Winston, 1976), p. 142.

55. Robert V. Burton, "Honesty and Dishonesty, in Lickona, ed., *Moral Development and Behavior,* p. 175.

56. Many critics of psychological and educational research claim that this empirical research still has logical positivistic underpinnings.

57. John Stuart Mill, *On Liberty* (Indianapolis: Bobbs-Merrill, 1956), p. 73.

58. Hirsch decries such multitudinous and pluralistic cultural stimuli and argues that formal education should provide a uniformed cultural base. E. D. Hirsch, Jr., "Cultural Literacy," *American Scholar* 52 (1983): 159–169.

59. Bronfenbrenner sounded an ominous warning about child-rearing practices and television when he begins chapter 4, "The Unmaking of the American Child," by claiming, *"Children used to be brought up by their parents"* (p. 95). Bronfenbrenner then analyzes and criticizes the two major influences on American children, the peer group and television. For Bronfenbrenner on children and television, see pp. 109–115. Urie Bronfenbrenner, *Two Worlds of Childhood: U.S. and U.S.S.R.* (New York: Russel Sage Foundation, 1970). For a summary of studies on "television as a moral teacher," see Robert M. Liebert and Rita Wicks Poulis, "Television as a Moral Teacher," in Lickona, ed., *Moral Development and Behavior,* pp. 284–298.

60. Albert Bandura, for example, indicates how television behavior is imitated by children through identification with admirable models (admirable for the child) and anticipatory control dependent on the consequences of the model's behavior. The following citations are only a few of Bandura's numerous studies: Albert Bandura and R. H. Walters, *Social Learning and Personality Development* (New York: Holt, Rinehart & Winston, 1963); Albert Bandura, "Influence of Models' Reinforcement Contingencies on the Acquisition of Imitative Responses," *Journal of Personality and Social Psychology* 1 (1965): 589–595; Albert Bandura, Dorothea Ross, and Sheila Ross, "Imitation of Film-Mediated Aggressive Models," *Journal of Abnormal and Social Psychology* 66 (1963): 3–11. For an analysis of social learning theory, see J. Philippe Rushton, "Altruism and Society: A Social Learning Perspective," *Ethics* 92 (1982): 425–446. Liebert and Poulis delineate "a schematic presentation of the stages of observational learning" that has no explicit reference to reasoning. Liebert and Poulis, "Television as a Moral Teacher," p. 286.

61. Noel Annan, *Leslie Stephen: The Godless Victorian* (New York: Random House, 1984), p. 106.

62. For the educational implications of this view of character, see Ralph H. Turner, "Sponsored and Contest Mobility and the School System," in Ronald M. Pavalko, ed., *Sociology of Education* (Itasca, Ill.: F. E. Peacock, 1976), pp. 48–66. Turner likens the American educational system to a race that any-

one can enter or leave at any time. Rules govern the fairness of the race, but the cunning participant can stretch these rules beyond their normal interpretive limits and thus win the race. English education, for Turner, follows a different model. It is a form of initiation. Prospective members of an elite group are invited into the educational club because they already possess the requisite personal qualities for membership. Most certainly, this contrast in its most exaggerated form existed during Mill's era. But at present, we must question whether any Western society can maintain such a system and whether Turner is speaking about bygone days instead of the present period.

63. Though Bellah, Madsen, Sullivan, Swidler, and Tipton see certain sets of virtues or traits undergirding late twentieth-century American character, we must wonder whether educators *should* foster the development of these qualities. Robert N. Bellah, Richard Madsen, William M. Sullivan, Ann Swidler, and Steven M. Tipton, *Habits of the Heart* (Berkeley: University of California Press, 1985).

64. John Dewey, *Human Nature and Conduct* (New York: Modern Library, 1922/1957), p. 37; cf., John Dewey and James H. Tufts, *Ethics,* rev. ed. (New York: Holt, Rinehart, & Winston, 1932), p. 183. The Dewey and Tufts 1932 book revises what was said about character in the earlier 1908 edition. Elsewhere, Dewey defines character as "attitudes of participative response in social affairs." Dewey, *Democracy and Education,* p. 370.

65. For example, Dewey and Tufts, *Ethics,* rev. ed., pp. 178–188.

66. With his conceptualization of habits, as well as with other concepts, Dewey follows in Aristotle's footsteps and advocates a mean between two extremes.

67. R. S. Peters, "Moral Education and the Psychology of Character," *Philosophy* 30 (1962): 40.

68. Ibid., pp. 38–39.

69. Ibid., p. 39.

70. For a criticism of Peters's view, see Dale Kennedy, "R. S. Peters' Concept of Character and the Criterion of Consistency of Actions," *Educational Theory* 25 (1975): 54–64.

71. Peters, "Moral Education," p. 39.

72. Ibid., p. 46.

73. Peters notes these, ibid., p. 38.

74. R. S. Peters, "Reason and Habit: The Paradox of Moral Education," in Israel Scheffler, ed., *Philosophy and Education* (Boston: Allyn & Bacon, 1966); cf. Peters, "Moral Development."

75. *Protagoras* 325C, Lamb trans.

76. Dewey, *Democracy and Education,* p. 383.

77. There is considerable disagreement about how to conceptualize education; for example, see Jane Roland Martin,
"The Ideal of the Educated Person," in *Philosophy of Education, 1981* (Normal, Ill.: Philosophy of Education Society,
1982), for a criticism of Peters.
78. Martin Buber, "The Education of Character," in Martin
Buber, *Between Man and Man,* trans. Ronald G. Smith (New
York: Macmillan, 1965), p. 106.
79. Regarding this criticism of Dewey, see Martin Hollis, "The
Self in Action," in R. S. Peters, ed., *John Dewey Reconsidered*
(London: Routledge & Kegan Paul, 1977), pp. 56–75. Dewey himself recognizes this problem when he states, "I am
obliged to admit what he [Allport] says about the absence of
an adequate theory of personality. . . . I failed to show how
natural conditions provide support for integrated and potentially equilibrated personality-patterns." John Dewey,
"Experience, Knowledge, and Value: A Rejoinder," in Paul
A. Schilpp, ed., *The Philosophy of John Dewey* (New York:
Tudor, 1939), pp. 555–556.

Chapter 3

1. In very recent years, there have been a few tenuous attempts to
study friendship, for example, Robert L. Armstrong,
"Friendship," *Journal of Value Inquiry* 19 (1985): 211–216.
Perhaps Sidgwick's frustration with the concept "fidelity"
should cause us to wonder whether this was a signal to philosophers that this notion could not be accommodated by
certain ethical theories and thus should not be subject to
philosophical analysis. Or maybe, fidelity and friendship
were such dominant, important notions with substantive
meaning in human life that their characteristics did not
seem to require analysis. For Sidgwick's comments on
fidelity, see Henry Sidgwick, *The Methods of Ethics,* 7th ed.
(London: Macmillan, 1962), pp. 258–259.
2. This is an interesting problem that deserves further comment.
Some might say that the school should not be concerned
with such personal and private matters. Of course, schools
should not give a course called Friendship I or Seminar in
Fidelity, but schools do possess other ways of nurturing
friendship and fidelity. Other personal matters, from con-
traception to venereal disease to marriage, are now considered the purview of schools. These most certainly are as
private and personal as friendship and fidelity. Others
might argue that children of all ages form friendships and

the problem, especially with adolescents, is not their lack of friendships, but the power and influence of their friendships. Two points indicate that these claims have little merit. First, many of these relationships are not friendships but peer or group relationships. Second, many of the basic features of fidelity never flower from these relationships.

3. See Bernard Williams, "A Critique of Utilitarianism," *Utilitarianism: For and Against* (Cambridge, Eng.: Cambridge University Press, 1973), on integrity and utilitarianism.

4. Anscombe notes that "it is not profitable for us at present to do moral philosophy . . . until we have an adequate philosophy of psychology, in which we are conspicuously lacking." G. E. M. Anscombe, "Modern Moral Philosophies," in Judith J. Thomson and Gerald Dworkin, eds., *Ethics* (New York: Harper & Row, 1968), p. 186.

5. Two points should be stressed here. First, it is doubtful, no matter the categorical imperatives, whether Kant was actually as severe as he is now interpreted. It might be that the underlying, taken-for-granted moral world was simpler and more harmonious than during the late twentieth century. Second, even in more recent neo-Kantian philosophers, there are hints of not wholly following the logical implications of their theories. For example, when he states that to understand why a moral agent makes a particular moral judgment, one would have to ask the agent to explain his life, Hare goes beyond the parameters of a neo-Kantian formalism.

6. On calculative reasoning, see Stuart Hampshire, "Public and Private Morality," in Stuart Hampshire, ed., *Public and Private Morality* (Cambridge, Eng.: Cambridge University Press, 1978), pp. 23–53.

7. Sidgwick, *Methods of Ethics*, p. 258.

8. Ibid., p. 259.

9. Ewin, for example, analyzes friendship through a different moral theory. He questions whether friendship has unjust consequences because it cannot neatly be squeezed into a morality of sociobiological cooperative justice. He concludes that friendship in certain ways remains outside the pale of his theory. R. E. Ewin, *Co-operation and Human Values* (New York: St. Martin's Press, 1981).

10. David Hume, *An Enquiry Concerning Human Understanding*, 2d ed. (Oxford: Clarendon Press, 1962), sec. VIII, pt. 1, par. 68.

11. Michael Straight, *After Long Silence* (New York: W. W. Norton, 1983), e.g., p. 100–103.

12. As a matter of fact, Oppenheimer's moral dilemma would have to be described as possessing all the elements of a trag-

edy. No matter the course Oppenheimer had taken, there would have been failure, tragedy, and sorrow.

13. With Achilles, there was a different form of moral slippage. Achilles was so overly concerned about the insult against him that he did not recognize the implications of Patrocles' wearing another's armor. This example is important for any treatment of character excellences, not merely because of historical interest or because it relates to one character excellence, "fidelity." In this case, Achilles' emotion, "anger," so overwhelmed his thoughts that it had a negative effect. He did not recognize the implications of lending his armor to Patrocles.

14. For example, one could hardly imagine other moral issues challenging the fidelity the members of the Bloomsbury Circle possessed for one another. Perhaps one reason this group has remained so fascinating for readers and scholars is that fidelity was a primary moral excellence of its members.

15. *Republic* VII, 515C, Shorey trans.

16. For a version of "turning-around," see Abigail L. Rosenthal, *A Good Look at Evil* (Philadelphia: Temple University Press, 1987), p. 152.

17. These speculations have some merit in that Oppenheimer was frequently pictured as naïve and lackadaisical in relation to certain matters that others felt were important.

18. We will have to return to this issue at a later point in this investigation.

19. *NE* VI, 1139a, Ross trans.

Chapter 4

1. G. E. M. Anscombe, "Modern Moral Philosophies," in Judith J. Thomson and Gerald Dworkin, eds., *Ethics* (New York: Harper & Row, 1968), p. 186.

2. There are a number of diverse places where such a study could begin. These might include a study of a few philosophers— for example, Dewey—to see how far their theories take us in the direction of finding a self; examination of novels that portray a coherent, continuing self; and investigation of scientific findings, for example, those of neuroscience.

3. In this statement and elsewhere, I refer only to the moral use of the term "character." Other uses of the concept, for example, acting or playing a stage character such as Hamlet or slang expressions such as "she's a character," are not consid-

ered here. Bruce Wilshire, *Role Playing and Identity* (Bloomington: Indiana University Press, 1982). Yet it would be valid to compare these uses and see how far each concept overlaps other usages. Whereas Peters analyzes each use of the concept "character," he stresses differences and does not sufficiently recognize or investigate their common features or the "unit ideas" underlying the term itself. R. S. Peters, "Moral Education and the Psychology of Character," *Philosophy* 37 (1962): 37–56.

4. Ibid., p. 38.

5. Regarding ways of life, see Stuart Hampshire, *Morality and Conflict* (Cambridge, Mass.: Harvard University Press, 1983). This ideal of ways of life is explored later in this section and in a later chapter.

6. Henry Sidgwick, *The Methods of Ethics*, 7th ed. (London: Macmillan, 1962), p. 10, n. 4.

7. Ibid.

8. Martha Nussbaum, "Consequences and Character in Sophocles' *Philoctetes*," *Philosophy and Literature* 1 (1976): 29.

9. Ibid.

10. For Nussbaum's assertion that the *Philoctetes* examines a struggle between integrity and the common good, see ibid.

11. Present studies of practical ethics of teaching do not consider certain aspects of this problem and the moral situation of teachers. It is not sufficient to use a model of the autonomous moral agent to examine a teacher's ethics and how a teacher's ethics can be changed. Other questions need to be asked. For example, studies have indicated that teacher behavior and decision making most often is dependent on the institutional setting, the school environment, and the type of authority in the school. Though the issue of the individual teacher's behavior and decision making may be important, as important (and maybe more important) is the institutional climate and environment and how that environment contributes to teacher ethics.

12. J. J. C. Smart, "An Outline of a System of Utilitarian Ethics," *Utilitarianism: For and Against* (Cambridge, Eng.: Cambridge University Press, 1973), pp. 3–74.

13. Richard B. Brandt, *A Theory of the Good and the Right* (Oxford: Clarendon Press, 1979), part II.

14. At the same time, one can disagree with Brandt concerning how rules should be devised.

15. John Rawls, "Two Concepts of Rules," *Philosophical Review* 64 (1955): 3–32.

16. The subjects of the studies in question (e.g., Hartshorne and Mays) were children. Children's character and virtues cannot be used as the "ideal" standard for character or virtue development.

17. For one of these studies, see Gordon W. Allport, *Pattern and Growth in Personality* (New York: Holt, Rinehart, & Winston, 1937), pp. 353–354.

18. Ludwig Wittgenstein, *Philosophical Investigations,* trans. G. E. M. Anscombe (Oxford: Basil Blackwell, 1958), I. 67, 108, 111.

19. There have been numerous psychological studies of the problem of family resemblances: for example, Eleanor Rosch and Carolyn B. Mervis, "Family Resemblances: Studies in the Internal Structure of Categories," *Cognitive Psychology* 7 (1975): 573–605.

20. For this problem, see Sissela Bok, *Lying: Moral Choice in Public and Private Life* (New York: Pantheon, 1978), p. 10.

21. Sidgwick, *Methods of Ethics,* p. 223.

22. For example, Dewey speaks of "arrested and encrusted habits" and "strict conformity." In such cases, the agent will not recognize the wider dimensions of a moral situation and will not accept data and alternatives that would conflict with encrusted habits. John Dewey, *Human Nature and Conduct* (New York: Modern Library, 1922/1957), p. 99.

23. The term "importance" is used here to indicate an external criterion for deciding such prioritization. Whitehead recognizes how vital the concept "importance" should be in discussions of morality, art, and the like. Alfred North Whitehead, *Modes of Thought* (Cambridge, Eng.: Cambridge University Press, 1938), for example, lect. 1.

24. Hampshire, *Morality and Conflict,* p. 13. Given Hampshire's advocacy of a morality consistent with a way of life, one can also say that a person's moral conclusions pertain to that agent's moral character and its relationship to moral dilemmas.

25. The role of dispositions is not analyzed here since it already has undergone considerable analysis in recent philosophical writings.

26. For a criticism of this aspect of Kohlberg's thought, see R. S. Peters, "Moral Development: A Plea for Pluralism," in Theodore Mischel, ed., *Cognitive Development and Epistemology* (New York: Academic Press, 1971), pp. 245–262; Betty A. Sichel, "Can Kohlberg Respond to Critics?" *Educational Theory* 26 (1976): 338–342.

27. It is worth noting how widespread this rejection of habits is. In her book, Gilligan does not explicitly attack the concept "habit" but totally ignores it. Carol Gilligan, *In a Different Voice: Psychological Theory and Women's Development* (Cambridge, Mass.: Harvard University Press, 1982). For a similar omission, see Nel Noddings, *Caring: A Feminine Approach to Ethics and Moral Education* (Berkeley: University of California Press, 1984).

28. Stewart Paton, *Human Behavior* (New York: Charles Scribner's Sons, 1922), p. 278.

29. For example, B. F. Skinner, *Beyond Freedom and Dignity* (New York: Bantam/Vintage, 1971).

30. For Kohlberg's earlier rejection of indoctrination, see Lawrence Kohlberg, "Indoctrination versus Relativity in Value Education," *Zygon: Journal of Religion and Science* 6 (1971): 235–310. Though Kohlberg states that he examines "arbitrary indoctrination" (p. 286), he does not actually fulfill this promise. Instead, Kohlberg attacks only a select spectrum of moral education approaches (e.g., including "a bag of virtues" (p. 288). There is no consideration in this article of the complex features of the concept "indoctrination." For this complexity, see I. A. Snook, ed. *Concepts of Indoctrination* (London: Routledge & Kegan Paul, 1972). For the relationship between indoctrination and education, see I. A. Snook, *Indoctrination and Education* (London: Routledge & Kegan Paul, 1972). For Kohlberg's later acceptance of indoctrination, see Lawrence Kohlberg, "Revisions in the Theory and Practice of Moral Development," in William Damon, ed., *Moral Development* (San Francisco: Jossey-Bass, 1978), pp. 84–85.

31. Nowell-Smith describes habits as "the most lowly type of dispositional explanation." P. H. Nowell-Smith, *Ethics* (Baltimore: Penguin Books, 1954), p. 122, only telling us that the moral action was expected. Action explained in terms of habit is action that a person did not choose. But Nowell-Smith adds a caveat that sustains the position I take. Speaking of whether someone "choose[s] to do what he does," Nowell-Smith states, "He may have deliberately acquired the habit; but that is another matter." Ibid., pp. 122–123. Though this other matter is not discussed by Nowell-Smith, the door is left open for the view that habits can be based on intelligent choice.

32. Jean Piaget, *The Moral Judgment of the Child*, trans. Marjorie Gabain (New York: Free Press, 1932/1965), p. 51.

33. My emphasis.

34. Piaget, *Moral Judgment*, p. 47.

35. Ibid., p. 163.

36. Jean Piaget, *Play, Dreams, and Initiation in Childhood*, trans. C. Gattegno and F. M. Hodgson (New York: W. W. Norton, 1962), p. 85; cf., pp. 75, 83.

37. P. F. Strawson, "Freedom and Resentment," in P. F. Strawson, ed., *Studies in the Philosophy of Thought and Action* (London: Oxford University Press, 1968), pp. 71–96; Piaget, *Play, Dreams, and Initiation*, p. 78.

38. This position requires more analysis than can be given in this short section. An additional brief comment can provide fur-

ther justification for these ideas. Piaget questions whether sensory-motor intelligence is "entirely transformed into conceptual thought under the influence of language and social intercourse, or does it persist independently, still having something of its original form, on a lower level of behaviour, like the reflexes, perceptions and *habits,* all of which appeared long before verbal intelligence and which persist throughout life at the base of the hierarchy of activities?" Ibid., p. 75, my emphasis. In the end, Piaget finds that sensory-motor intelligence and thus the habits of this period are not the lowest level of a hierarchical development. Rather, habits, imitation, assimilation, and schemas that are part of the sensory-motor period are reintegrated within the structures of higher-level stages. What function thus do habits have? Habits, according to this view, are not rigid, fragmented phenomena that determine specific behavior, but rather means by which intelligent structures are formed.

39. Piaget, *Plays, Dreams, and Initiation,* p. 78.
40. Piaget, *Moral Judgment,* p. 136.
41. Conquering great fear may be one instance of courage, but it certainly is not the only circumstance in which courage is exhibited. As Taylor and Wolfram point out, courage is also dependent on the person assessing the risk of the proposed action. Gabriele Taylor and Sybil Wolfram, "Virtues and Passions," *Analysis* 31–32 (1971): 79–80.
42. Michael J. Sandel, *Liberalism and the Limits of Justice* (Cambridge, Eng.: Cambridge University Press, 1982), pp. 147–154.
43. Sandel's interpretation of Rawls.
44. John Rawls, *A Theory of Justice* (Cambridge, Mass.: Harvard University Press, 1971), p. 418.
45. Ibid., pp. 416–417.
46. Unquestionably, communities vary and some communities, as is apparent from any historical investigation, have brainwashed and manipulated their members. But this is not the form of community being advocated here.
47. Fried, for example, makes a similar but weaker point when criticizing utilitarianism. "The integrity of the person as the center of moral choice and judgment requires that we find room for the inescapably particular in personality that we avoid disintegrating universality." Charles Fried, *Right and Wrong* (Cambridge, Mass.: Harvard University Press, 1978), p. 34, cf., p. 104.
48. Sandel, *Liberalism,* p. 149.
49. Rawls, *Theory of Justice,* p. 467–472.
50. Ibid., pp. 467–468.
51. Ibid., p. 471.
52. Ibid., p. 468.

53. Erikson for one notes that children change families as much as families nurture children. However, such changes in families are very different from children intentionally changing game rules. Erik H. Erikson, *Identity: Youth and Crisis* (New York: W. W. Norton, 1968), p. 96.
54. Sandel, *Liberalism*, p. 150.
55. At present, philosophers designate way of life by a number of different expressions, for example, life-styles, life narratives, and the like. Though these various expressions are usually connected with different philosophic ideas, in this book I will use them interchangeably unless otherwise noted.
56. Edel believes that the present emphasis on life plans is misplaced and that this expression can only be used in a much more limited sense than current philosophic usage. Abraham Edel, *Interpreting Education* (New Brunswick, N.J.: Transaction Books, 1985).
57. Michael Walzer, *Spheres of Justice* (New York: Basic Books, 1983), pp. 7–8.
58. For a nineteenth-century view of these, Alexis de Tocqueville, *Democracy in America*, trans. George Lawrence (Garden City, N.Y.: Doubleday/Anchor, 1848/1969). For a recent though flawed view, see Robert N. Bellah, Richard Madsen, William M. Sullivan, Ann Swidler, and Steven M. Tipton, *Habits of the Heart* (Berkeley: University of California Press, 1985). Also, cf., Michel Crozier, *The Trouble with America*, trans. Peter Heinegg (Berkeley: University of California Press, 1984).
59. For example, Crozier, *Trouble*.
60. Though not discussed here, the present relationship among community, society, and culture often reveals excessive tension. How is this to be explained? Is this merely a matter of normal stress in these relationships or are there unique reasons for strain at the present time? Persuasive reasons can be given for present strains; among these are the technological transformation and excessive changes in societal values.
61. Sidgwick, *Methods of Ethics*, p. 10, n. 4.
62. See P. F. Strawson, "Social Morality and Individual Ideal," *Philosophy* 36 (1961): 1–17.

Chapter 5

1. John I. Goodlad, *A Place Called School* (New York: McGraw-Hill, 1984); Lawrence A. Cremin, *The Genius of American Education* (New York: Vintage, 1965).

2. For example, Oser describes moral education as referring to justice, formal principles, and abstract reasoning. Fritz K. Oser, "Moral Education and Values: The Discourse Perspective," in M. C. Wittrock, ed., *Handbook of Research on Teaching,* 3d ed. (New York: Macmillan, 1986). Cf., Marvin W. Berkowitz, "Four Perspectives on Moral Argumentation," in Carol Gibb Harding, ed., *Moral Dilemmas* (Chicago: Precedent, 1985).

3. In this quest to maintain the integrity and strength of communities, it should be stressed that not all communities have been politically visible. At times, those that have remained comparatively invisible in political terms have suffered the most. Political silence has meant that some communities have become fair game in political battlefields.

4. Erik H. Erikson, *Identity: Youth and Crisis* (New York: W. W. Norton, 1968), p. 82.

5. Ibid., p. 96.

6. Ibid., p. 82.

7. Ibid., p. 96.

8. Ibid., p. 97.

9. Ibid., p. 104.

10. Ibid., p. 106.

11. In one short, infrequently cited article, Erikson briefly examines "the roots of virtue." Erik H. Erikson, "The Roots of Virtue," in Julian Huxley, ed., *Humanist Frame* (New York: Harper & Brothers, 1961), pp. 145–165.

12. Ronald D. Milo, *Immorality* (Princeton, N.J.: Princeton University Press, 1984), p. 77.

13. Erikson, *Identity,* p. 103.

14. In any human society optimum conditions rarely exist and thus there usually is not the attainment of absolute trust or "unambivalent attachment." Robert Hogan, John A. Johnson, and Nicholas P. Emler, "A Socioanalytic Theory of Moral Development," in William Damon, ed., *Moral Development* (San Francisco: Jossey-Bass, 1978), p. 9.

15. John Dewey, *Human Nature and Conduct* (New York: Modern Library, 1922/1957), p. 85.

16. Ibid., p. 86.

17. The distinction made here is between social conventions and morality. Communities, it might be argued, teach social conventions, customs, and mores. Public schools, however, must be concerned with a different framework, with the development of a fully self-conscious form of moral reasoning and the use of higher-order abstract moral principles. Moral dilemmas, it is argued, are very different from dilemmas involving social conventions. Nucci, for example, argues this position. Larry P. Nucci, "Conceptual Development in the Moral and Conventional Domains: Implications for Val-

ues Education," *Review of Educational Research* 52 (1982):
93–122. It was argued earlier in this book that this rigid
boundary cannot be sustained, and thus the rigid boundary
between moral education in communities and schools also
should not be sustained. It should not be a matter of
whether the social or moral have priority or whether each
should be assigned to a different institution. Rather, the social and moral domains overlie each other and are nurtured
within all sorts of educational institutions.

18. Thomas Green raised many provocative issues about moral
education inside and outside the wall in a paper presented
at the fall 1986 Middle Atlantic States Philosophy of Education Society.

19. It is difficult to delineate the development of moral character
and excellences not just because of the general difficulty
and complexity of moral education, but because of certain
present trends in formal education. For example, one such
problem is the current emphasis on a single form of empirical research, testing, and on the evaluation of results. In
all formal school subjects, testing is now seen as the only
way to judge what a student has achieved, whether a student has succeeded or failed in the course of study. While
there are many discussions of the shortcomings of such testing, there has been little attention to how this testing agenda has affected moral education recomendations. Kohlberg
for one has argued that perceptible changes in the moral
agent's form of making moral judgments occur with appropriate moral education programs. The argument here is
not whether Kohlberg's claim is valid, but that his moral
education recommendations and theoretical notions are
consistent with this present concern of educational policy
makers. Students can be tested and can display whether
moral cognitive development has occurred. What about
character education? A similar means to that presently used
for Kohlbergean theory cannot (and should not) be used to
test character development. Thus, critics would ask, how
would one *know* whether character education had been successful? The response would probably be, the only real
proof is the quality of the long-term moral life of the community and society or the quality of life within the school.
In the present climate of educational policy, however, this
would hardly be a sufficient response. Such a response
would not satisfy those who demand hard evidence. But as
Mannheim noted during an earlier period, the most important phenomena are possibly those that cannot be caught
with our present statistical, scientific tools. And this is as
true today of present attempts to quantify moral development as it was of science in general during Mannheim's
time.

20. Hacker, for example, in a review of a number of national educational reports speaks of this problem, that if there are no general educational aims then programs flounder because they wander in every possible direction. Andrew Hacker, "A Nation at Risk: The Imperative for Educational Reform," *New York Review of Books* 31 (1984): 35–36.

21. In relation to this, Hawkins, for example, notes that "public education is in a moral quandary." Robert B. Hawkins, Jr., "Strategy for Revitalizing Public Education," in J. H. Bunzel, ed., *Challenge to American Schools* (New York: Oxford University Press, 1985), p. 46.

22. Alfred North Whitehead, *The Aims of Education* (New York: Free Press, 1929/1967), p. 13.

23. Ibid., p. 23.

24. Ibid. To understand Whitehead's aims of education, we would have to dig deeper and search in his writings on culture, history, aesthetics, science, and symbolism.

25. Whitehead does not use the expression "desirable ends," but the use of criteria to evaluate ends is implied by his discussion of eternal objects and perfection(s).

26. However, it should be noted that these recommendations have rarely been translated into the structural actuality of the school. When Grant among other writers stresses how the ethos of private schools in particular contributes to student moral character, he actually is implicitly speaking about more than the ethos of the school. He tacitly refers to whether the school is a community and what the features of that community are.

27. In the recent past, certain moral education programs (e.g., values clarification) concentrate on the values a student already possesses. There is little or no exploration or consideration in this program of how one can evaluate already possessed values. The program emphasizes the internal components and almost ignores the external dimensions.

28. There is no question that discipline, class management, and student behavior are important matters as well as moral education programs that refer specifically to moral issues. Some of the methods that have been recommended by others could be reworked or restructured to conform with the moral education theory proposed here. But such an endeavor will have to wait until another time.

29. Edith Cobb, *The Ecology of Imagination in Childhood* (New York: Columbia University Press, 1977), p. 28. In a rather different way, Bell studies the various aspects of imagination in moral education. Gordon H. Bell, "Imagining and Moral Education," *Journal of Moral Education* 8 (1979): 99–109.

30. For Whitehead's discussion of these stages, Whitehead, *Aims,* pp. 26–38.

31. Ibid., p. 38.

32. Ibid., pp. 28–29.
33. R. S. Peters, "John Dewey's Philosophy of Education," in R. S. Peters, ed., *John Dewey Reconsidered* (London: Routledge & Kegan Paul, 1977), p. 119.
34. Whitehead, *Aims*, p. 29.
35. Ibid., p. 30.
36. Other examples can be found in studies of teaching excellence; for example, without mentioning Whitehead's rhythmic method, Macrorie's description of Sam Bush's teaching of carpentry and woodworking. The following is a very brief suggestion of how Bush's teaching can be used as an example of Whitehead's rhythmic method: Romance is found in the classroom itself, "a high-windowed great English-Gothic room," and the pieces of furniture at different stages of completion "all around the edges of the room." Ken Macrorie, *Twenty Teachers* (New York: Oxford University Press, 1984), p. 3. Some of this furniture had been completed by students and some by Bush and another teacher-craftsman. One can imagine the wonder students experience when entering this room and seeing the tools and equipment, inspecting the various pieces of furniture, and seeing peers working on these pieces. The next stage, the precision stage, begins when the student makes specific decisions about the exact features of the furniture that he will make. But precision comes to the fore with the next two aspects of the process. First, Bush insists on "lots of drawing," a very exacting endeavor. Ibid., pp. 4–5. Second, the actual carpentry is an exercise in precision. What of generalization? Generalization and thus the beginning of a new cycle occur many times in this process. There is generalization when the student has clearly articulated which piece of furniture will be made. Again there is generalization when the drawing is completed and when various parts of the furniture are completed. What of moral education? Bush sees woodworking as extending into the moral domain, as including courage and decisiveness. Ibid., p. 5. Lies about work are not accepted. In such a case Bush states, "I couldn't let him lie like that about the craft that was our concern. . . . [The] school is the training ground for developing the personal qualities requisite to . . . larger undertakings." Ibid., p. 7.
37. Whitehead, *Aims*, p. 49.

Chapter 6

The chapter title is from William Wordsworth, "Thoughts of a Briton on the Subjugation of Switzerland."

1. D. D. Raphael, "The Standard of Morals," *Proceedings of the Aristotelian Society* 75 (1975): 4.

2. Richard B. Brandt, *A Theory of the Right and the Good* (Oxford: Clarendon Press, 1979).

3. J. J. C. Smart, "An Outline of a System of Utilitarian Ethics," *Utilitarianism: For and Against* (Cambridge: Cambridge University Press, 1973), p. 42f.

4. During the last few decades, there have been many questions about why some of the brightest, most talented young people in public spheres make questionable moral judgments or do not even consider the moral component when making decisions. Is this a matter of not having been taught and not understanding moral discourse? Perhaps the problem is larger than this. These young people were not educated within a moral community where community policy decisions were dependent on moral standards, not solely on economic and political pressure.

5. Michael Rutter et al., *Fifteen Thousand Hours* (Cambridge, Mass.: Harvard University Press, 1979).

6. The issue here is not whether there is some other more appropriate standard than that proposed by utilitarianism but the problems with utilitarianism providing such a standard.

7. Lars Bergstrom, *The Alternatives and Consequences of Actions* (Stockholm: Almqvist & Wiksell, 1966).

8. A utilitarian might argue that even recent decisions about banning athletes from participating in sports can be justified according to the utilitarian principle. The utilitarian would argue that the good of strengthening college academic standards is greater than the enjoyment of sports by a large audience.

9. Whether one can do this is questionable.

10. An examination of the role of moral principles in moral education concentrates on Kohlberg's theory for many reasons. The number of studies investigating moral development and educational intervention from a Kohlbergean perspective is considerable. The extensive replication of Kohlberg's experiments in different cultures, with various socioeconomic and ethnic groups and different religions, has seemingly created a broad evidential base for the theory. Numerous scholarly references to Kohlberg have made his theory a frontrunner for explaining and describing the development of moral cognitive judgments. Kohlberg's own ability to analyze philosophical issues and interrelate the psycho-

logical, philosophical, and educational has also contributed to his theory's popularity. Finally, though important negative critical analyses challenged many aspects of his theory and empirical evidence, Kohlberg has valiantly battled to retain the main thrusts of his theory.

11. For an investigation of the shortcomings of the theoretical paradigm Kohlberg accepts, see D. C. Phillips and Jennie Nicolayev, "Kohlbergian Moral Development: A Progressing or Degenerating Research Program?" *Educational Theory* 28 (1978): 286–301.

12. This critical section does not aim to recapitulate readily available criticism of Kohlberg's theory: for example, William P. Alston, "Comments on Kohlberg's 'From Is to Ought'," in Theodore Mischel, ed., *Cognitive Development and Epistemology* (New York: Academic Press, 1971); R. S. Peters, "Moral Development: A Plea for Pluralism," in Mischel, ed., *Cognitive Development;* R. S. Peters, "The Place of Kohlberg's Theory in Moral Education," *Journal of Moral Education* 7 (1978): 147–157; William Kurtines and Esther Blank Greif, "The Development of Moral Thought: Review and Evaluation of Kohlberg's Approach," *Psychological Bulletin* 81 (1974): 453–470; E. L. Simpson, "Moral Development Research: A Case of Scientific Cultural Bias," *Human Development* 17 (1974): 81–106; Betty A. Sichel, "Can Kohlberg Respond to Critics?" *Educational Theory* 26 (1976): 331–347, 394; Israela Ettenberg Aron, "Moral Philosophy and Moral Education: A Critique of Kohlberg's Theory," *School Review* 85 (1977): 217–227; Cornel M. Hamm, "The Content of Moral Education, or In Defense of the 'Bag of Virtues,'" *School Review* 85 (1977): 218–228; F. E. Trainer, "A Critical Analysis of Kohlberg's Contribution to the Study of Moral Thought," *Journal for the Theory of Social Behavior* 7 (1977): 41–63; Phillips and Nicolayev, "Kohlbergian Moral Development"; Kenneth E. Goodpaster, "Kohlbergian Theory: A Philosophical Counterinvitation," *Ethics* 92 (1982): 491–498.

13. For an early form of this theory, see Lawrence Kohlberg, "The Development of Modes of Moral Thinking and Choice in the Years Ten to Sixteen," doctoral dissertation, University of Chicago, 1958.

14. Lawrence Kohlberg, "From Is to Ought: How to Commit the Naturalistic Fallacy and Get Away with It in the Study of Moral Development," in Mischel, ed., *Cognitive Development*, p. 166.

15. Samuel Bowles and Herbert Gintis, *Schooling in Capitalist America: Educational Reform and the Contradictions of Economic Life* (New York: Basic Books, 1976).

16. John Rawls, *A Theory of Justice* (Cambridge, Mass.: Harvard University Press, 1971), pp. 462–479. For an analysis of this aspect of Rawls's theory, see Betty A. Sichel, "John Rawls' Theory of Moral Development," in Ira S. Steinberg, ed., *Proceedings of the Thirty-third Annual Meeting of the Philosophy of Education Society* (1977): 247–256.

17. Rawls, *Theory of Justice*, pp. 461–462, n. 8.

18. It would be valuable to investigate more extensively why Kohlberg's theory retained its intellectual stranglehold on moral development in the face of considerable valid, important criticism of the theory. This investigation would not merely shed light on the politics or selling of Kohlberg's theory, but also the wider, similar phenomenon in the social and behavioral sciences. One would have to move beyond a Kuhnian analysis since the humanistic and/or behavioral sciences seem to change in ways and have dimensions other than the physical sciences as analyzed by Kuhn. This issue, however, remains outside the scope of the present investigation.

19. Lawrence Kohlberg, Charles Levine, and Alexandra Hewer, *Moral Stages: A Current Formulation and a Response to Critics* (Basel: S. Karger, 1983), pp. 30–31.

20. Coles demonstrates that children are much more sophisticated politically than most adults think. The issue here is not whether children are sophisticated politically now, but whether the historical context affects the type of political knowledge, awareness, and ability the children of Coles's study have. Robert Coles, *The Political Life of Children* (Boston: Atlantic Monthly Press, 1986).

21. This changed perspective can be found in the various moral issues recommended for student study, for example, Jack Braeden Arbuthnot and David Faust, *Teaching Moral Reasoning: Theory and Practice* (New York: Harper & Row, 1981), pp. 204–205.

22. The publication of Kohlberg's collected essays added to the confusion since earlier papers and studies were not edited, but rather include very different formulations of and evidence for the theory.

23. Kohlberg, Levine, and Hewer, *Moral Stages*.

24. Kohlberg's claim that a stage is a structurally whole way of thinking seems to diverge both from his own and from Piaget's comments. Regarding those who simultaneously reason at two different but contiguous stages, Piaget states, "We have ... two processes partially overlapping, but of which the second gradually succeeds in dominating the first." How long do these overlapping processes continue to inform the agent's decisions? If such overlapping stages ex-

ist for an extended period of time, is the agent using a holistic way of reasoning? Piaget also notes that there are actually "innumerable intermediate stages between . . . [the] two attitudes of obedience and collaboration, but it is useful for the purposes of analysis to emphasize the real opposition that exists between them." Jean Piaget, *The Moral Judgment of the Child*, trans. Marjorie Gabain (New York: Free Press, 1932/1965), pp. 133, 138. Piaget argues that logical cognitive stages are structural wholes, but he does not make similar assertions regarding moral judgment stages. If there are "innumerable intermediate stages," can this be considered a holistic way of reasoning? Kohlberg's claim that stages are structural wholes is puzzling since only 50 percent of an individual's answers must be at a given stage for those moral judgments to be scored at that stage. Would it be more accurate to say that agents selectively use different moral standards dependent on the nature of the problem, the available evidence, the consequences of the proposed action, and so on? If moral agents use different moral standards, would this be analogous to some of Dewey's thoughts on resolving moral dilemmas and not in accord with Kohlberg's theoretical claims?

25. This educational technique was recommended and developed by Blatt, see Lawrence Kohlberg, "The Just Community Approach to Moral Education in Theory and Practice," in Marvin W. Berkowitz and Fritz Oser, eds., *Moral Education: Theory and Application* (Hillsdale, N.J.: Lawrence Erlbaum Associates, 1985), p. 27.

26. Even though cognitive dissonance had already been widely discredited, Kohlberg during this earlier period turned to Festinger's ideas about cognitive dissonance.

27. Blatt and Kohlberg give various speculative reasons for stage regression. Moshe Blatt and Lawrence Kohlberg, "The Effects of Classroom Moral Discussion upon Children's Level of Moral Judgments," *Journal of Moral Education* 4 (1975): 140–141. However, the problems of stage regression and the relationship between moral judgment and moral action are more complicated and important than Kohlberg allows. For example, Kurtines and Greif question the temporal stability of "a given individual's stage of moral reasoning" and find "no reported estimates of temporal stability" in the Kohlberg studies (p. 457). These critics also note that "Kohlberg's framework does not require a relationship between moral reasoning and moral action. In relation to one study, Kurtines and Greif note that its results raise "questions about the discriminant and predictive validity of the stages" (p. 459, of. pp. 459–460). Kurtines and Greif, "The Development of Moral Thought."

Though Schlaefli, Rest, and Thoma present positive conclusions concerning moral education programs to improve moral judgments, some of their cautious comments must cause the reader to question whether there are also underlying difficulties with Kohlberg's theory or the educational proposals. In this 1985 study, the authors state, "To date, no studies have demonstrated directly that changes wrought by these moral education programs have brought about changes in behavior" (p. 348). Though there have been indirect presumptions, the problem of the relationship between moral judgment and behavior continues to vex Kohlbergean researchers (ibid.). It was also found that "exposure to Kohlberg's theory" affects the size of stage development. Does this indicate some form of contamination (p. 347)? Andre Schlaefli, James R. Rest, and Stephen J. Thoma, "Does Moral Education Improve Moral Judgment? A Meta-Analysis of Intervention Studies Using the Defining Issues Test," *Review of Educational Research*, 55 (1985): 319–352.

28. Even if theorists do not explicitly investigate these various theoretical components, these elements implicitly exist.

29. Kohlberg would have to provide longitudinal evidence that moral development and consistent moral action occur not only within the just community school, but also remain stable without regression after students leave this protected environment. If Kohlberg cannot furnish such evidence, he would have a similar problem to the one Skinner and many behaviorists have when conditioned behavior continues only as long as there is some schedule of positive reinforcement. Extinction of modified behavior often occurs when students are in different environments with very different schedules of reinforcement. There is an additional empirical problem: While Kohlberg might compare the just community school sample with the remainder of the school as a control group to assess differences in moral development, this control group is not necessarily a valid comparative measure. The comparative analysis might be very different if the control group were taken from one of the schools Rutter recommends or one of the excellent high schools noted by Lightfoot. Does the just community school make the difference or can other institutional configurations also improve morality and moral reasoning? The problem here for Kohlberg is whether the ostensible development and action are context-dependent or whether they remain unchanged no matter the context. Will student moral judgments eventually regress when the students are no longer members of a just community? Criticism could come from another direction, this relating to how the evidence

from the just community school is interpreted. Are reported student statements and reasoning complete or are they selective, reworded, or edited versions of what would support the just community school? Most reports issued thus far have been exceptionally impressionistic, and thus objective evaluation of these communities by a variety of scholars has not yet been possible.

30. In addition to those conducted in Taiwan, Turkey, Mexico, Israel, and other countries, studies include different religious, ethnic, and socioeconomic groups in this country.

31. Though the many ways of criticizing Kohlberg's theory cannot be fully addressed here, a few of these ways are briefly addressed. These problems include the following: (1) There are Kohlberg's method of experimental research and his contention that "normal" ways of assessing empirical research cannot challenge a stage theory. Lawrence Kohlberg, "Revisions in the Theory and Practice of Moral Development," in William Damon, ed., *Moral Development* (San Francisco: Jossey-Bass, 1978), pp. 85–86. (2) What is the relationship between empirical verification and theory building, between empirical verification and confirmation of "the normative validity of theories of justice as reversibility?" Kohlberg, Levine, and Hewer, *Moral Stages*, p. 16. (3) How valid is a theory that has been able at different times to ascribe to "a Platonic view" of justice and virtue, Dewey, Hare, and Rawls? (For this view, see Lawrence Kohlberg, "Education for Justice: A Modern Statement of the Platonic View," in Nancy F. Sizer and Theodore R. Sizer, eds., *Moral Education: Five Lectures* (Cambridge, Mass.: Harvard University Press, 1970), pp. 57–83.) Can all these diverse theories be amalgamated in the way Kohlberg suggests? Kohlberg, Levine, and Hewer, *Moral Stages*, pp. 30–31. (4) There are questions of whether Kohlberg's theory is tainted by assumptions of Western ethical philosophy and downgrades Eastern ethical views. (5) There are questions about why "higher" stages are better or philosophically more adequate than lower stages. (6) Kohlberg's recent advocacy of indoctrination, the omission or denigration of the concept "habit," and his overly narrow criticism of virtues have already been discussed. (7) Critics have also noted difficulties with Kohlberg's conceptualization of the moral domain, the theory's lack of moral content, and an excessively zealous view of one moral philosophy, "deontology."

32. Gibbs argued that the two highest stages, stages five and six, are not structural stages in the Piagetean sense, but refer to existential moral development and meta-ethical notions. John C. Gibbs, "Kohlberg's Stages of Moral Judgment: A Constructive Critique," *Harvard Educational Review* 47

(1977): 43–61; John C. Gibbs, "Kohlberg's Moral Stage Theory: A Piagetean Revision," *Human Development* 22 (1979): 89–112.

33. Kohlberg, Levine, and Hewer, *Moral Stages*, p. 61, cf., pp. 62–63.

34. Ibid., p. 6.

35. Ibid., p. 42.

36. Abraham Edel, *Interpreting Education* (New Brunswick, N.J.: Transaction Books, 1985), p. 228.

37. The only interest Kohlberg has shown in the problem of the relationship of reasoning and action has been in relation to what empirical evidence suggests. The theory itself has no place for this problem.

38. Kohlberg, "From Is to Ought," pp. 226–231.

39. Cf., R. Harre, "Some Remarks on 'Rule' as a Scientific Concept," in Theodore Mischel, ed., *Understanding Other Persons* (Totowa, N.J.: Rowman & Littlefield, 1974), e.g., p. 138.

40. For another study of this, see ibid., pp. 155–161.

41. This problem of the emergence of a moral problem from the multitude of experience, feelings, perceptions, events, relationships, and so forth is itself a topic in need of much more theoretical examination.

42. How emotions function in mathematical or logical problems and in moral dilemmas is more complex than noted here thus far. For example, as noted in a previous chapter, moral excellences are not without their emotional components. Courage does not exist without the desire to be courageous and the emotional components of courage. However, the intellectual excellences necessary for the solution of a mathematical or logical problem do not include an integrated emotional component in the same manner as with moral excellences.

43. These three steps are not necessarily linear, but often involve considerable crosshatching.

44. Carol Gilligan, *In a Different Voice: Psychological Theory and Women's Development* (Cambridge, Mass.: Harvard University Press, 1982).

45. One problem with Gilligan's position is which of three interpretations she accepts for the two moral languages. Does she posit (1) a theme interpretation with each moral langauge being a different moral theme, (2) a gender interpretation with men and women each speaking a different moral language, or (3) a dialectic reflexive tension language with all human beings eventually speaking both moral languages? This is an important issue since if Gilligan uses a theme interpretation, she is only saying that certain categories have been omitted from neo-Kantian moral theories. This is a rather common philosophic argument, crit-

ics differing only about the categorical limitations of deontology. If, on the other hand, she uses the gender language dichotomy, she creates numerous problems for her position. For example, feminists are already issuing cautionary warnings about her theory and wonder whether this dichotomy might be a reversion to traditional male-female role divisions. Furthermore, what justification might be given for such a gender dichotomization? For a longer analysis of this problem, see Carol B. Stack, "The Culture of Gender: Women and Men of Color," *Signs* 11 (1986): 321–324; Betty A. Sichel, "Women's Moral Development in Search of Philosophical Assumptions," *Journal of Moral Education* 14 (1985): 150–151.

Gilligan's recent response to critics does not ameliorate these dilemmas. She claims that these are not gender-related moral languages but identifies them by theme; yet at the same time she continually makes reference to the different voice of women and their different psychological life cycle. Carol Gilligan, "Reply by Gilligan," *Signs* 11 (1986): 327. Both in a recent reply to critics and in the earlier book, Gilligan constantly changes her interpretation of the two moral language thesis. In this chapter, I refer to these two languages or two themes as women's moral language of response and care and men's moral language of rights and justice and will not become embroiled here about which is the "real" interpretation.

46. For example, Nails questions Gilligan's presentation as the impressionistic strokes of a narrative, literary work, rather than the hard evidence and analytic reporting of a psychologist. Nails argues that the actual responses by the abortion sample should be interpreted in a rather different manner than Gilligan has. Debra Nails, "Social-Scientific Sexism: Gilligan's Mismeasure of Man," *Social Research* 50 (1983): 643–664.

47. Gilligan does not note that some earlier psychologists did recognize that men and women have different psychological life cycles, for example, Peter Blos, *The Young Adolescent* (New York: Free Press, 1970), p. 27. However, Gilligan would argue that Blos did not go far enough, that his unique comment was tainted since his analysis relied on a traditional Freudian model. The argument here, however, is not that Blos discerned a unique theme and posited a different theory, but that there were theorists other than Erikson and Freud who delineated another way of looking at psychological development. Some of these theorists (e.g., Karen Horney) should be cited. Their different psychological themes would contribute to a more rigorous psychological theory than Gilligan has proposed.

48. Kohlberg in his early studies discerned that women tested at lower stages than men, but this difference, he argued, was due to the type of education and social condition they received. He assumed that in time, with increased equality for men and women and a decrease in the inculcation of stereotypical roles, men and women would develop in an identical fashion. More recently, Stephen J. Thoma has surveyed research studies of moral development in men and women and reported that there is no difference in the development of moral cognitive judgments dependent on sex as a variable. Thoma, "Estimating Gender Differences in the Comprehension and Preference of Moral Issues," *Developmental Review* 6 (1986): 165–180. Gilligan would argue that Thoma's findings have little (or nothing) to do with the issue. The issue, for Gilligan, is not whether women can also use the form of reasoning advocated by Kohlberg, but whether this is their inherent way of making moral judgments.

49. Gilligan, *Different Voice,* p. 1, cf. p. 4.

50. Piaget, *Moral Judgments,* p. 77; cf. Janet Lever, "Sex Differences in the Complexity of Children's Play and Games," *American Sociological Review* 43 (1978): 471–483; Gilligan, *Different Voice,* p. 10. Lever concludes that girls play many fewer games than boys. Gilligan and Lever, however, disagree about how to interpret this evidence and the implications of such evidence. Lever notes that the playing of complex games is propaedeutic to taking multiple, complex roles in public and professional life. Lever argues that in order to be successful in careers, women as girls must play complex games with multiple roles. She also argues that with the mandates of Title IX and changes in child-rearing techniques, girls will be encouraged to play the complex games that have made boys so successful in careers. Gilligan would not side with Lever. Gilligan would say that Lever's evidence revealed differences in how boys and girls naturally play, interrelate with human beings, and resolve moral and social problems. Instead of advocating that girls play more complex games, Gilligan would want to continue to foster the games they now play. These reflect the way girls structure their social environment. Someone may wonder how Lever and Gilligan come to such different conclusions when looking at the same data. Gilligan argues that past psychological theories are based on a male bias, what some would call an ideology. Similarly, we can say that both Gilligan and Lever interpret the same data in different ways because they subscribe to very different ideologies.

51. Gilligan does not use the term "ideology," but this is the import of her comments.

52. Gilligan, *Different Voice,* p. 10.
53. I compare Gilligan with Kohlberg here and elsewhere not because of convenience, but because Gilligan herself refers to Kohlberg's theory of development as men's language of justice and rights. She continually compares her enlarged, two moral language thesis with Kohlberg's developmental theory. In a number of ways, however, this has unfortunate consequences. For example, one must wonder whether the two positions are comparable. Whereas Kohlberg accepts Piaget's structuralism, Gilligan's language of care and response does not yet seem to have a paradigmatic framework to understand how the various categories function. Unquestionably, it cannot follow Piagetean structuralism. What sort of developmental theory is it? (For a discussion of this, see Sichel, "Women's Moral Development" p. 153.) Is it what Kohlberg has called a soft stage theory? Kohlberg, Levine, and Hewer, *Moral Stages,* pp. 29–41.
54. Gilligan, *Different Voice,* p. 31.
55. For a most perceptive and important criticism of this study, see Nails, "Social-Scientific Sexism."
56. Robert T. Hall and John U. Davis, *Moral Education in Theory and Practice* (Buffalo, N.Y.: Prometheus Books, 1975), pp. 145–149.
57. Ibid., p. 145.
58. Martha Craven Nussbaum, "Flawed Crystals: James's *The Golden Bowl* and Literature as Moral Philosophy," *New Literary History* 15 (1983): 25–50.
59. The terms Gilligan uses are sometimes puzzling. For example, she speaks of a moral language of rights when referring to neo-Kantian theory. She uses the term "rights" interchangeably with "right," even though these two terms are not identical.
60. One of her studies in particular, the abortion study, uses only a sample of women. Though there is no way to know how men would interpret and judge this situation, Gilligan compares the moral language and standards used by the women of this study with the moral language she only assumes men would use. There is no reason this assumption would be validated.
61. Lawrence Kohlberg and Rochelle Mayer, "Development as the Aim of Education," *Harvard Educational Review* 42 (1972): 449–496.
62. R. S. Peters, "Reason and Passion," in R. F. Dearden, P. H. Hirst, and R. S. Peters, eds., *Education and the Development of Reason* (London: Routledge & Kegan Paul, 1972), pp. 208–229.
63. Gilligan cannot accept Peters's model since, according to her

thesis, each language is primary for either men or women. Neither language is fuel for the other. In any case, Peters's model is flawed in other ways. Does Peters stress sufficiently that the cognitive has affective components, while the affective has been evaluated and developed with cognitive tools?

64. William K. Frankena, "The Ethics of Love Conceived as an Ethics of Virtue," *Journal of Religious Ethics* 1 (1973): 24.

65. Ibid., p. 27.

66. Lawrence A. Blum, *Friendship, Altruism, and Morality* (London: Routledge & Kegan Paul, 1980).

67. In a footnote, Lyons accepts "Blum's philosophic argument" for "the work presented here." Nona Plessner Lyons, "Two Perspectives on Self, Relationship, and Morality," *Harvard Educational Review* 53 (1983): 135, n. 4. However, Lyons does not indicate the similarities between Blum and Gilligan or how Gilligan or Blum would apply any one moral language to the full range of moral dilemmas. There is another more serious problem with Lyons's references to Blum. In addition to Blum's altruistic emotions, Lyons also refers to Murdoch's idea of love. However, Lyons does not recognize that Murdoch and Blum are speaking about two very different phenomena. Murdoch speaks of an ideal and the concept of the Good, whereas Blum refers to emotions in the form of altruistic emotions.

68. Rawls, *Theory of Justice*, p. 43. However, the use of this form of serial or lexical ordering by Gilligan and others may not be in line with Rawls's intentions. Rawls speaks of justifying a rule or principle, while Gilligan and others are referring to justifying a practice under a rule or principle.

69. Other criticism of Gilligan can be classified according to the following problems: (1) Gilligan's view includes an incomplete conceptualization of justice. For example, Prakash notes that often the contrast between a male and female ethic rests on an impoverished conceptualization of justice. Mahdu Suri Prakash, "Review of Carol Gilligan, *In a Different Voice: Psychological Theory and Women's Development*," *Educational Studies* 15 (1984): 193–194. (2) Gilligan does not sufficiently emphasize the affective domain. Bush argues that the major implication of Gilligan's work "is the emphasis on affect . . . [but] Gilligan does not explicitly develop the affective component in the construction of separate, gendered worlds." Diane Mitsch Bush, "The Impact of Changing Gender Role Expectations Upon Socialization in Adolescence: Understanding the Interaction of Gender, Age, and Cohort Effects," *Research in Sociology of Education and Socialization* 5 (1985): 281. (3) Gilligan does not consider

how social, political, and economic factors affect morality and moral development. Prakash, "Review," pp. 198–200; Bush, "Impact," pp. 282–284.

70. Nel Noddings, *Caring: A Feminine Approach to Ethics and Moral Education* (Berkeley: University of California Press, 1984), p. 46.

71. Ibid., pp. 112–113.

72. Ibid.; cf., pp. 18, 21.

73. Ibid., p. 112.

74. Martin Buber, *I and Thou*, trans. Ronald G. Smith (New York: Charles Scribner's Sons, 1958).

75. Max Scheler, *The Nature of Sympathy*, trans. Peter Heath (New Haven, Conn.: Yale University Press, 1954).

76. Martin Buber, "Interrogations of Martin Buber," in Sydney Rome and Beatrice Rome, eds., *Philosophical Investigations* (New York: Holt, Rinehart, & Winston, 1964), p. 40.

77. Buber, *I and Thou*, p. 58.

78. Similarly, for Scheler, authentic sympathy occurs when interpersonal encounters are genuine and each person is unequivocally accepted and recognized.

79. Buber quoted in Jack Mendelsohn, "Between Man and Man," *Congress Weekly* 24 (1957): 9.

80. Noddings, *Caring*, p. 113.

81. See Blum, *Friendship*, pp. 2–3, for this Kantian view.

82. There are a few exceptions to this generalization.

83. For essays discussing the difficulty of drawing a sharp boundary between the private and public, see Stanley I. Benn and Gerald F. Gaus, eds., *Public and Private in Social Life* (London: Croom Helm, 1983). Also W. T. Jones, "Public Rules, Private Roles, and Differential Moral Assessments of Role Performance," *Ethics* 14 (1984): 603–620.

84. Gilligan, *Different Voice*, p. 147.

85. Noel Annan, *Leslie Stephen: The Godless Victorian* (New York: Random House, 1984), p. 142.

86. There is yet another direction that could be taken. One could also say that Hilary (and Gilligan) do not understand the two dimensions of the legal system. Even though the adversarial system is a powerful dimension, lawyers must balance the adversarial against a quest for truth. Attorneys have been cited for withholding the truth in their quest to push the adversarial role beyond its limits. Thus, even professional advancement might not require Hilary to withhold evidence.

87. Stuart Hampshire, *Morality and Conflict* (Cambridge, Mass.: Harvard University Press, 1983), pp. 84–85, cf. pp. 89, 101, 123.

88. Ibid., p. 123.

89. Ibid., p. 122.

Chapter 7

1. Empirical studies of student moral development examine only the improvement of their moral judgments in narrowly defined situations and do not consider the broader features of the educational environment. For example, Schlaefli, Rest, and Thoma note the various positive effects of different moral education intervention programs. Andre Schlaefli, James R. Rest, and Stephen J. Thoma, "Does Moral Education Improve Moral Judgment? A Meta-Analysis of Intervention Studies Using the Defining Issues Test," *Review of Educational Research* 55 (1985): 319–352. The authors also note that "academic courses in the humanities and social studies do not seem to have an impact on moral judgment development" (p. 346). The problems that can be noted with these (and other conclusions) include the following: (1) As the authors themselves note, there is no evidence thus far to demonstrate that changes in moral development stage also engender changes in moral behavior (p. 348). (2) This analysis does not mention whether other educational (school) variables influence moral growth in its broader sense. On the other hand, while not concentrating on moral behavior or moral judgments, Rutter argues that the school's ethos affects student behavior and life. Michael Rutter et al., *Fifteen Thousand Hours* (Cambridge, Mass.: Harvard University Press, 1979). An empirical study of the position taken in this book would require methodology, sample, variables, and tools other than those used so far.
2. Though many other conditions have changed the nature of teaching in both positive and negative ways, the policies mentioned here are two that directly relate to the argument of this chapter.
3. Whether teaching should be a profession or under present conditions can be a profession is not the issue. The only issue here is that both teacher and state organizations have argued for this professionalization.
4. Harold Garfinkel, "A Conception of, and Experiment with, 'Trust' as a Condition of Stable Concerned Action," in O. J. Harvey, ed., *Motivation and Social Interaction: Cognitive Determinants* (New York: Ronald Press, 1963); Erving Goffman, *The Presentation of Self in Everyday Life* (Garden City, N.Y.: Doubleday/Anchor, 1959); Erving Goffman, *Interaction Ritual* (Garden City, N.Y.: Doubleday/Anchor, 1967); Erving Goffman, *Strategic Interaction* (Philadelphia: University of Pennsylvania Press, 1969); Lewis White Beck, *The Actor and the Spectator* (New Haven, Conn.: Yale University Press, 1975). The intention here is not to discuss all the various

features or dimensions of successful role attribution but to question the relationship between roles and moral education and between roles and character.

5. Some thinkers argue against using the term "determined." Bernard Mayo, "The Moral Agent," *The Human Agent* (New York: St. Martin's Press, 1968), p. 58. Mayo argues that, with roles, behavior can be expected but not determined. Thus, the agent behind the role retains freedom to decide whether to manifest some role behavior.

6. Though increasing bureaucratization and other reasons have been given for the emphasis on playing multiple roles, this acceleration of multiple role playing can be seen in another way. Instead of still accepting the dour elements of a Protestant ethos, people have become more playful and their playfulness can often be found in the seriousness with which they play life's many roles.

7. Dorothy Emmet, *Rules, Roles, and Relations* (Boston: Beacon Press, 1966), e.g., chap. 8.

8. P. F. Strawson, "Social Morality and Individual Ideal," *Philosophy* 36 (1961): 1–17.

9. Woody Allen's Film (capital "F" refers to the Film we watch) *The Purple Rose of Cairo* raises important philosophical questions relating to this matter. In this Film, a woman escapes from her mundane life by attending movies and becoming absorbed within the movies' worlds. On a particularly unhappy occasion, she continues to sit through the film *The Purple Rose of Cairo* (small "f" refers to the film within the Film, the film the unhappy woman watches). After she had seen the film many times, Tom, one of the film's protagonists, steps out of the screen and exits outside the reality of the film to become part of the world of the film's viewers. Without repeating the ensuing story or the confusion created by Tom's entering a different reality, it must be stated here that the ontological confusion also creates moral dilemmas and changes in the moral universe. Whom should the distraught, lonely woman trust? Which person is real in the sense of being natural, in the sense of consistency between words and deeds? Who is the truly moral person? Is it the Tom of the film, the Tom who steps out of the film, the Tom of the Film, or the actual actor playing Tom in the film or in the Film? Are only appearances morally real? Is the actuality of human moral life only an appearance of what it could be?

10. Bruce Wilshire, *Role Playing and Identity* (Bloomington: Indiana University Press, 1982), p. 266.

11. Ibid.

12. The few articles that hint at such dimensions rarely come to grips with the complexity and breadth of these moral con-

cerns, for example, Gregory E. Pence, "Can Compassion Be Taught?" *Journal of Medical Ethics* 9 (1983): 189–191.
13. As indicative of present philosophic discussions of the practical ethics of teaching, a recent issue of the *Journal of Teacher Education* 37 (1986): 2–20 on this theme can be cited. None of the articles in this issue examines what this alternative way of looking at morality and the moral person would imply for practical ethics.
14. Alasdair MacIntyre, *After Virtue* (Notre Dame, Ind.: Notre Dame University Press, 1981), pp. 169–189, esp. p. 178.
15. Of course, there is another option here. The principal may have convincing reasons that the teacher eventually agrees with. The teacher may recognize, by seeing the problem through other eyes, that the original evaluation of the dilemma was incorrect.
16. G. Alexander Moore, Jr., *Realities of the Urban Classroom* (Garden City, N.Y.: Anchor Press, 1964).
17. Rawls, *Theory of Justice*, for example, p. 409.

Chapter 8

The chapter title is from Sir Francis Bacon, "Of Great Place."
1. Alfred North Whitehead, *The Aims of Education* (New York: Free Press, 1929/1967), p. 16.
2. Heinz Werner, "The Concept of Development from a Comparative and Organismic Point of View," in Dale B. Harris, ed., *The Concept of Development* (Minneapolis: University of Minnesota Press, 1957), p. 133.
3. Lawrence Kohlberg, Charles Levine, and Alexandra Hewer, *Moral Stages: A Current Formulation and a Response to Critics* (Basel: S. Karger, 1983), e.g., p. 31.
4. Loren Eiseley, *All the Strange Hours* (New York: Charles Scribner's Sons, 1975), p. 33.
5. Lester H. Hunt, "Character and Thought," *American Philosophical Quarterly* 15 (1978): 183.
6. Lester H. Hunt, "Courage and Principle," *Canadian Journal of Philosophy* (1980): 291.
7. For a similar view, see ibid., p. 293.
8. Hunt, "Character," p. 183.
9. Hunt, "Courage," pp. 291–292.
10. In this case, a history course would include the art and architecture of the period, the great literature and ideas, the scientific ideas and politics, and how art, architecture, religion, literature, politics, social life, and the sports of the period related to one another.

11. One way that has been taken is not at all consistent with what has been presented thus far in this book. According to this technique, the state department of education has hearings across the state to take evidence about how various pressure and social groups evaluate the proposed policy. This hearing technique is rarely effective. (1) Hearings on proposed mandates rarely end in major changes in the proposals. (2) Hearings assume a conflict model in which diverse groups present very different positions. (3) Communities have very little substantive input in the actual formation of the policy during its most formative stages.

12. In recent years, we have seen political decisions that might be described as imaginative and creative, but also were rash and uninformed. Therefore, the imaginary and creative thrust had no relationship with reality. This is what is rejected here.

13. *Republic* X, 620c–d, Shorey trans.

14. This Noddings recognizes in Nel Noddings, *Caring: A Feminine Approach to Ethics and Moral Education* (Berkeley: University of California Press, 1984).

15. Alfred North Whitehead, *Adventures of Ideas* (New York: Macmillan, 1933), p. 346. 1935 p. 449.

16. Ibid., p. 360.

17. And critics would remark that history has told us that at different times and in different places political and religious leaders have claimed they have attained this absolute truth and knowledge.

18. Abraham Edel, *Interpreting Education* (New Brunswick, N.J.: Transaction Books, 1985), p. 107.

19. Ibid., p. 108.

20. Ibid., pp. 108–110.

21. Ibid., p. 109.

22. Ibid., p. 110.

23. Stuart Hampshire, "Morality and Pessimism," in Stuart Hampshire, ed., *Public and Private Morality* (Cambridge, Eng.: Cambridge University Press, 1978), pp. 1–22.

24. Fydor Dostoevsky, "Notes from the Underground," in Fyodor Dostoevsky, *Notes from Underground and the Grand Inquisitor,* trans. Ralph E. Matlaw (New York: E. P. Dutton, 1960), p. 35.

25. Iris Murdoch, *The Sovereignty of Good* (London: Routledge & Kegan Paul, 1970).

26. Ibid., p. 90.

27. Marcel Proust, *Remembrance of Things Past,* trans. C. K. Scott Moncrieff and Terence Kilmartin, vol. I (New York: Random House, 1981), p. 229.

28. Murdoch, *Sovereignty,* p. 104.

Index